JOURNAL FOR THE STUDY OF THE NEW TESTAMENT
SUPPLEMENT SERIES
79

Executive Editor
Stanley E. Porter

JSOT Press
Sheffield

The Theme of Recompense in Matthew's Gospel

Blaine Charette

Journal for the Study of the New Testament
Supplement Series 79

Published by JSOT Press
JSOT Press is an imprint of
Sheffield Academic Press Ltd
343 Fulwood Road
Sheffield S10 3BP
England

Typeset by Sheffield Academic Press
and
Printed on acid-free paper in Great Britain
by Biddles Limited
Guildford

British Library Cataloguing in Publication Data

Charette, Blaine Burgess
    Theme of Recompense in Matthew's Gospel.
    - (JSNT Supplement Series, ISSN 0143-5108;
    No. 79)
    I. Title II. Series
    226.2

    ISBN 1-85075-385-7

CONTENTS

Preface   7
Abbreviations   9
Introduction   11

Chapter 1
'I SET BEFORE YOU A BLESSING AND A CURSE'
THE OLD TESTAMENT COVENANTAL BACKGROUND
TO THE MATTHAEAN TEACHING ON RECOMPENSE   21
    The Promise to Abraham   23
    Promise and Threat in Deuteronomy   29
    The Loss of Land in Jeremiah   38
    The Planting and Uprooting of Israel   44
    Exile as a State of Darkness   49
    The Restoration of Israel   51
    Conclusion   61

Chapter 2
'THOSE YAHWEH BLESSES SHALL INHERIT THE LAND'
THE TEACHING ON REWARD IN THE GOSPEL OF MATTHEW   63
    The Restoring of Israel   64
    Reward Texts in Matthew   83
    Conclusion   117

Chapter 3
'BUT THOSE HE CURSES SHALL BE CUT OFF'
THE TEACHING ON PUNISHMENT IN THE GOSPEL OF MATTHEW   119
    Fruitlessness and Judgment   121
    'There will be Weeping and Gnashing of Teeth'   140
    A Picture of the Last Judgment   155
    Conclusion   159

Chapter 4
CONCLUSION   162

Bibliography   169
Index of References   176
Index of Authors   183

PREFACE

In preparing this study on recompense in Matthew, a subject which encompasses both heaven and hell and which spans the epoch from Abraham to the close of the age, I was often reminded of the prudent words from the Talmud: 'Whoever reflects on four things, it were better he had never been born: that which is above, that which is below, that which is before, and that which is after'. Nonetheless, with my reflections now concluded, and feeling none the worse for the exercise, I would like to express my gratitude to some of the people who assisted me during my course of study.

My time spent at Sheffield has been most memorable. I wish to thank the staff and fellow graduate students of the Department of Biblical Studies for making it a stimulating environment in which to conduct research. In particular, I would like to express my gratitude to Dr David Hill, who initially supervised my thesis, for his continuing interest in my work after his retirement from the Department. His helpful criticisms and suggestions have been of inestimable value. I owe a very special debt to my supervisor, Dr Andrew Lincoln. He brought to the task of supervision an incisive mind and meticulous manner which have effected a better thesis than would otherwise have been the case. Those flaws which remain have not escaped his rigorous scrutiny, only my clumsy attempts at improvement.

I am obliged to the Tyndale Fellowship for the very generous research grant they awarded me during my period of study in England. My mother is also deserving of my appreciation for her timely financial assistance and, in particular, for helping me to purchase a computer which has greatly facilitated the writing up of the thesis.

My greatest praise is reserved for my family. My wife Judy is by now a veteran student wife, although I am sure that has not made the burden any easier to bear. Yet the years of marriage to a 'skint' graduate student have not changed her good nature. I am grateful for her commitment and good-humoured friendship. My two sons Blaeden and Eliot have given me much joy. Their simple ways and cheerful moods have provided a refreshing respite from the demands of research and writing.

ABBREVIATIONS

BAGD	W. Bauer, W.F. Arndt, F.W. Gingrich and F.W. Danker, *Greek–English Lexicon of the NT*
Bib	*Biblica*
BJRL	*Bulletin of the John Rylands University Library of Manchester*
BZ	*Biblische Zeitschrift*
CBQ	*Catholic Biblical Quarterly*
CollTh	*Collectanea Theologica*
EBT	J.B. Bauer (ed.), *Encyclopedia of Biblical Theology*
ExpTim	*Expository Times*
HBT	*Horizons in Biblical Theology*
HTR	*Harvard Theological Review*
IBS	*Irish Biblical Studies*
IDBSup	Supplementary Volume to G.A. Buttrick (ed.), *Interpreter's Dictionary of the Bible*
IKZ	*Internationale katholische Zeitschrift*
Int	*Interpretation*
JBL	*Journal of Biblical Literature*
JSNT	*Journal for the Study of the New Testament*
JSS	*Journal of Semitic Studies*
Neot	*Neotestamentica*
NIDNTT	C. Brown (ed.), *The New International Dictionary of New Testament Theology*
NKZ	*Neue kirchliche Zeitschrift*
NovT	*Novum Testamentum*
NTS	*New Testament Studies*
RevQ	*Revue de Qumran*
RSPT	*Revue des sciences philosophiques et théologiques*
RSR	*Recherches de science religieuse*
SBLSP	*SBL Seminar Papers*
TDNT	G. Kittel and G. Friedrich (eds.), *Theological Dictionary of the New Testament*
TDOT	G.J. Botterweck and H. Ringgren (eds.), *Theological Dictionary of the Old Testament*
ThWAT	G.J. Botterweck and H. Ringgren (eds.), *Theologisches Wörterbuch zum Alten Testament*
TS	*Theological Studies*

TZ	*Theologische Zeitschrift*
VT	*Vetus Testamentum*
ZAW	*Zeitschrift für die alttestamentliche Wissenschaft*
ZNW	*Zeitschrift für die neutestamentliche Wissenschaft*
ZST	*Zeitschrift für systematische Theologie*

INTRODUCTION

The following study is an investigation into the theme of recompense in the Gospel of Matthew. This brief description discloses two important propositions concerning the substance of the study. The first is that the present examination is interested solely in the teaching on recompense as it is presented in Matthew. Thus the question as to what the 'historical Jesus' may or may not have taught on the subject lies beyond the purview of this inquiry. The second point is that both reward (positive recompense) and punishment (negative recompense) receive proportional treatment in this investigation. A presumption which has guided the study from the beginning, and which the results bear out, is that an adequate assessment of the theme of recompense requires the analysis of both aspects of the theme. All too frequently in the past, studies have devoted attention to the particular topic of reward while virtually ignoring the corresponding and equally important topic of punishment.[1] The schema of recompense which Matthew has fashioned from the tradition he received is understood accurately only when due consideration is given to the two-sided emphasis which inheres in the subject.

All three synoptic Gospels contain references to recompense.

---

1. The following list, which is representative of previous studies on the subject, reveals that the predominant concern of scholars has been with the teaching of Jesus, on the one hand, and the concept of reward, on the other: G.W. Stewart, 'The Place of Rewards in the Teaching of Christ', *Expositor* 10 (1910), pp. 97-111, 224-41; O. Michel, 'Der Lohngedanke in der Verkündigung Jesu', *ZST* 9 (1931), pp. 47-54; W. Pesch, *Der Lohngedanke in der Lehre Jesu verglichen mit der religiösen Lohnlehre des Spätjudentums* (Munich: Karl Zink, 1955); J. Schmid, 'Der Lohngedanke im Judentum und in der Lehre Jesu', in his *Das Evangelium nach Matthäus* (Regensburg: Friedrich Pustet, 1959), pp. 287-94; G. de Ru, 'The Conception of Reward in the Teaching of Jesus', *NovT* 8 (1966), pp. 202-22; J.I.H. McDonald, 'The Concept of Reward in the Teaching of Jesus', *ExpTim* 89 (1978), pp. 269-73; S. Travis, 'Reward in the Teaching of Jesus' (*The Drew Lecture on Immortality*, 1983: unpublished lecture).

However, a review of the evidence reveals that the subject receives by far the most extensive treatment in the Gospel of Matthew. This can be demonstrated quite easily by a statistical analysis of the relevant vocabulary. A survey of the major terms for reward, namely the noun μισθός (Matthew, 10×; Mark, 1×; Luke, 3×) and the verb ἀποδίδωμι (in the sense of divine repayment) (Matthew, 5×; Mark, 0×; Luke, 1× = ἀνταποδίδωμι), reveals that they are much more typical of Matthew than of the other Gospels. With respect to punishment, a similar conclusion can be drawn when one examines the occurrences of such terms as 'Gehenna' (Matthew, 7×; Mark, 3× [all in one passage]; Luke, 1×) and 'the outer darkness' (Matthew, 3×; Mark, 0×; Luke, 0×), as well as of the phrase 'there will be weeping and gnashing of teeth' (Matthew, 6×; Mark, 0×; Luke, 1×). The disparity in the distribution of this evidence is so great that it invites the question as to whether the subject of recompense would be listed at all among the themes of Jesus' teaching, and, in consequence, become the subject of many articles and monographs, were it not for the attention it receives in Matthew. The few sayings in Mark and Luke which employ the vocabulary of recompense are such that they would undoubtedly provoke scholarly interest; nevertheless, on their own they could hardly claim to constitute a significant theme in Jesus' teaching. It is only in Matthew's Gospel that the subject of recompense comes into its own, as it were, and is developed in a manner which allows for such a claim. One would seem justified in concluding, on the basis of this evidence, that the initial stimulus for and the primary content of a description of Jesus' teaching on recompense is to be found in Matthew's presentation of that teaching.

It is of interest to note, however, that more often than not the results of scholarly investigation into the teaching of Jesus, particularly on the topic of reward, are quite different in emphasis and tone from those conclusions which might be inferred from a careful reading of Matthew's Gospel. What impresses most about this Gospel is that in it Jesus frequently promises reward to those who do the will of the Father and is not at all reluctant to use promises of reward, and especially threats of punishment, to motivate proper behaviour. It is clear from the Gospel that in the end each person will be judged on the basis of his or her character and conduct. A unique and characteristic statement which epitomizes the recompense teaching found in Matthew is the saying of 16.27, which affirms that in the future the

Son of man will repay each according to what has been done.[1] It is, perhaps, not surprising that Matthew's view has proved an obstacle for many scholars.[2] Evidence of scholarly unease is seen in the fact that discussions of Jesus' teaching on reward are frequently dominated by the issue of 'grace versus merit' and are concerned to highlight the differences between the teaching of Jesus and the teaching of early Judaism. It is affirmed, for example, that, whereas the teaching of early Judaism is characterized by *quid pro quo* reckoning based on the equating of recompense with achievement, in the teaching of Jesus any thought of reward as repayment has been removed. Accordingly, it is asserted that promises of reward and threats of punishment are never utilized by Jesus as an inducement to obedience.[3] It is one of the ironies of modern research on the theme of recompense in the Gospels that the reconstituted teaching of Jesus is so dissimilar to the teaching of Jesus as reported in Matthew, especially when one considers that Matthew is the most important source of what can be known about Jesus' teaching on this theme.

Two passages in particular are generally regarded as central to the definition of Jesus' teaching on the subject of recompense. These are the parable of the servants' duties in Lk. 17.7-10 and the parable of the workers in the vineyard in Mt. 20.1-15.[4] It is the opinion of many scholars that the Lukan parable, in which the relationship between God and the disciples is likened to that of a lord to his 'unworthy' servants, presents the key principle upon which the correct understanding of the

1. R. Mohrlang (*Matthew and Paul* [Cambridge: Cambridge University Press, 1984], p. 52) does not overstate the case when he describes the Matthaean view as 'a traditional Jewish view of judgement, based on works, as recompense for how one lives'.

2. Compare the acute comment of R.T. France (*Matthew: Evangelist and Teacher* [Exeter: Paternoster, 1989], p. 268), that 'at the level of terminology it must be recognised that Matthew does not seem to share the coyness of many modern Christians with regard to rewards'.

3. A typical remark is that made by Günther Bornkamm ('Der Lohngedanke im Neuen Testament', in *Studien zu Antike und Urchristentum. Gesammelte Aufsätze* [Munich: Kaiser, 1963], II, p. 80) 'Der Inhalt der Forderung wird also nirgends aus den Folgen—Lohn oder Strafe—begründet'.

4. Note, for example, the statement of Schmid (*Matthäus*, p. 286), when commenting on the latter parable, that 'für das Verständnis des Lohngedankens in der Lehre Jesu ist dieses Gleichnis neben dem vom Knecht (Lk. 17, 7-10) das wichtigste Dokument'.

teaching of recompense must be based.[1] According to this view, the disciple is under obligation to serve his Lord unconditionally and this fact imposes severe limitations on the idea of reward.[2] Reward loses all character of return for service. The disciple has no right to reward; whatever reward is given for the efforts of the disciple is undeserved and indeed cannot be deserved.[3] Implicit in this approach to the subject is the claim that the description of the teaching of Jesus on recompense that obtains in Matthew must be incorrect. It is not surprising, then, that Mt. 20.1-15 should frequently be interpreted without reference to its context. In Matthew the parable, sandwiched as it is between the two sayings of 19.30 and 20.16, serves to illustrate the reversal of position which will characterize the final judgment. Yet that emphasis is invariably pushed to the side, if not eliminated altogether, in the interests of interpreting the parable as one which declares the undeserved grace of God.[4] The parable is thus interpreted as a Matthaean counterpart to the parable of the prodigal son, insofar as it declares the unmerited goodness of God while at the same time vindicating the gospel of Jesus against his critics. At times this exegesis involves the acknowledgment that the Matthaean context has no claim to originality and that the true meaning of the parable is clear only when it is removed from its context. On other occasions the Matthaean perspective is simply ignored. In either case, this serves to

1. The parable prompts Travis ('Reward', p. 11) to remark that 'whereas Judaism spoke readily of rewards for obedience, Jesus' use of the slave-master image rules out in principle any such contractual understanding of man's relationship to God'.

2. It is curious that the corresponding, and yet sharply contrasting, parable of Lk. 12.35-38, in which 'vigilant' servants are 'rewarded' by a returning master, who girds himself and serves them at table, is rarely referred to and never emphasized in discussions.

3. This attempt to make passages such as Lk. 17.7-10 the 'touchstone' of Jesus' real message is challenged by P.S. Minear (*And Great Shall Be Your Reward* [New Haven: Yale University Press, 1941], p. 52), who argues that

> the absence of sanctions in such teachings, however, does not signify a contradiction of sanctions used elsewhere. Neither does the appeal to reward in other teachings make them thereby less noble. All Jesus' teachings, with or without such an appeal, center in the need for complete obedience to the will of God.

4. According to McDonald ('Concept of Reward', p. 270), the focus of the parable is 'upon the grace of God, the operation of which is not dependent upon nor in proportion to human achievement'.

illustrate, once again, that the emphasis on recompense present in Matthew is often ignored, since it is regarded as unrepresentative of, and perhaps even contradictory to, what is customarily understood to be the prevailing emphasis in the original teaching of Jesus.

It is not the intention of the present study to enter into this debate on the issue of grace and merit as it relates to recompense, although the results of the study will have a distinct bearing on this issue. Neither will this study be concerned with the matter of whether or not the Gospel of Matthew accurately reflects the teaching of Jesus on the subject of recompense. Rather, the present study undertakes to offer an adequate explanation of the function of the reward and punishment statements within the total conceptual framework of the Gospel. It represents an attempt to answer the question as to why Matthew should be so interested in this particular aspect of Jesus' teaching that he awards it substantial treatment in his account of that teaching.[1] It has already been observed that recompense terminology is a characteristic feature of his Gospel. Moreover, this terminology, which appears in both narrative and discourse material, is prevalent at many important junctures in the Gospel, as will increasingly become apparent. Consequently, it is not an overstatement to speak of recompense as a significant theme in Matthew. Yet it is a theme which has not received the attention it deserves.[2] This neglect is due in part to the theological disquiet occasioned by the subject, which has hindered the disinterested evaluation of all the evidence. Inasmuch as the present study is interested primarily in analysing the theme of recompense as it is presented in the final form of Matthew's text, and not in dogmatic questions, one can expect it to avoid those preoccupations which, in many earlier studies, effected results that are less than satisfactory.

When this investigation was first devised it was assumed that it would encompass a thorough exegetical examination of those passages

---

1. The term 'Matthew', when it appears in this study, refers to the text in its final form and its author. The identification of the author with the tax collector of 9.9 need not be inferred from this designation.

2. The chapter on 'Reward and Punishment' in the monograph by Mohrlang is quite instructive, yet justifiably brief since it forms but one section of a much larger study. The Matthaean emphasis on the judgment threatening the disobedient in Israel and the church, that is, negative recompense, receives a careful and thorough treatment in D. Marguerat, *Le jugement dans l'évangile de Matthieu* (Geneva: Labor et Fides, 1981).

in the Gospel which employ the vocabulary of recompense. As the study progressed, however, it became apparent that an adequate investigation of the theme would entail much more than the treatment of these passages alone. These texts are, of course, central to the study of recompense in Matthew, for they not only introduce and underscore the importance of the theme but, in addition, establish the framework of thought that is essential to a thorough understanding of the theme. Even so, in themselves they do not constitute sufficient material for a comprehensive investigation. A thorough analysis which contributes to a more complete assessment of the subject requires the introduction of other elements from the Gospel which are related to the same framework of thought even though they utilize different terminology. In the course of the investigation it transpired that the principal key which granted access to the full significance of the theme was located among this other material. To be more precise, the recognition that the inheritance language of the Gospel is essential to its teaching on reward, that is to say, the reward in prospect corresponds to the inheritance promised the faithful disciple, prompted an exploration into the possible relationship between Matthew and the Old Testament in respect of the concept of inheritance.[1] It is in this relationship that a cogent explanation for Matthew's interest in and application of the theme of recompense was found. Thus a study which began with Matthew gradually broadened its scope to comprehend a significant part of the Old Testament.

To the extent that the present study seeks to explain the purpose of the teaching on recompense within the total conceptual framework of the Gospel of Matthew, the critical method deemed most appropriate to realize this objective was a form of composition criticism. In composition criticism the attention of the exegete is concentrated on the final or extant form of the text. Thus the method is well suited to the

---

1. On three occasions in Matthew (5.5; 19.29; 25.34) Jesus declares that the righteous will receive an inheritance. Comparable assertions are not found in the other Gospels. In Mark and Luke the subject of inheritance is generally broached by those questioning Jesus (which is not the case in Matthew) and is never initiated or encouraged by him. The order in which the present study unfolds, from a discussion of the Old Testament background to an examination of Matthew, is appropriate; yet it should be noted that the subject was investigated in the opposite order. The exegesis of Matthew was nearly completed when the study of parallel themes in the Old Testament commenced.

task of analysing one aspect of the Evangelist's thought in terms of the Gospel as a whole. Inasmuch as composition criticism undertakes to elucidate the theology of the Evangelist, it shares much in common with redaction criticism, to which it is closely related. In fact, the method may aptly be described as a holistic variation of redaction criticism.[1] Yet the two methods are distinct from each other as regards their respective points of departure when attempting to uncover the theological perspective of the Evangelist. Whereas redaction criticism seeks to discover the distinctive emphasis of the evangelist by means of a thorough examination of his redactional activity, composition criticism begins with the finished work of the Evangelist, the final product of this editorial activity, and treats this as an intelligible whole.

Composition criticism is the product of a recent trend in redaction criticism which, admitting the limitations of earlier forms of the method, recognizes that the concerns and interests of an Evangelist are to be found not merely in the study of the changes he has made to his sources but also in the study of the completed work he has produced.[2] Compositional or final form analyses of the Gospels have been carried out at least since the 1970s.[3] According to this methodological approach, the horizontal analysis of the differences that obtain

---

1. S.D. Moore, *Literary Criticism and the Gospels* (New Haven: Yale University Press, 1989), p. 179.

2. C.M. Tuckett ('Redaction Criticism', in R.J. Coggins and J.L. Houlden [eds.], *A Dictionary of Biblical Interpretation* [London: SCM Press, 1990], p. 581) speaks of many today who

> would adopt a more 'literary' approach to the Gospels, looking at each as a literary whole in its own right and seeking to illuminate the theology of the author as much from the work as a whole. . . as from an analysis of the ways in which sources and traditions have been changed by the evangelist.

J.D. Kingsbury (*Matthew as Story* [Philadelphia: Fortress Press, 1986], p. vii), accordingly, describes composition criticism as a 'refinement of the method of redaction criticism'.

3. Within Matthaean studies one of the first exegetes to describe himself as a composition critic was W.G. Thompson. In an article published in 1974 ('An Historical Perspective in the Gospel of Matthew', *JBL* 93, pp. 243-62 [p. 244 n. 2]), he defines as his basic methodological presupposition that Matthew's editorial activity 'was so thorough-going and proceeded out of such a unique vision that it transformed all that he touched'. For that reason, Thompson is not so much interested in 'separating tradition from redaction' or 'confronting Matthew with his sources' as beginning with Matthew's 'final composition'.

between the three synoptic Gospels, which constitutes a major part of
the redaction critical method, is, to an extent, maintained but is supplemented by the vertical or linear analysis of the Gospel as a literary
whole. In the preparation of the present study horizontal analysis was
carried out and in the course of the discussion attention will be
directed to the differences between Matthew and Mark and Luke when
these differences provide special insight into the Matthaean perspective. Yet, a comprehensive redactional examination of the way in
which Matthew has modified his sources was not viewed as essential,
or indeed well-suited, to the demonstration of the thesis. Given the
nature of this particular study, in which the conceptual relationship
between Matthew and the Old Testament is of greater consequence
than the relationship that exists between it and the other synoptic
Gospels, a classical redactional approach was of limited value. The
conceptual framework present in Matthew, which is the focus of this
inquiry, is not evident in the sources Matthew utilized when compos-
ing his Gospel For that reason, the method of redaction criticism,
which would have involved a detailed investigation of the use made by
Matthew of the pre-existing materials at hand, was unable to provide
the procedure suitable to the task. Rather, a composition critical
approach, which allows one to stand back, as it were, in order to gain
a broader perspective of the Gospel, was best suited to the accomplishment of the study.

In applying composition criticism to the study of recompense in
Matthew the present study will examine in particular how the themes
of reward and punishment function in relation to other themes
featured in the Gospel. In order to appreciate fully the treatment the
topic receives in Matthew, attention will be directed to such compositional techniques as the reiteration of significant terms and phrases,
the juxtaposition of topics, and the use of *inclusio* to bind together
pericopes or even larger sections of the Gospel. Moreover, special
consideration will be given to those terms and concepts which, in
establishing a link with recompense ideas inherent in the Old
Testament, reveal the design of the Matthaean conception of recompense as it is developed in the Gospel.

Although composition criticism represents a more literary approach
to the Gospels than does redaction criticism, insofar as greater significance is attached to the examination of the final form of the text than
to the analysis of the relation between tradition and redaction, it must

be distinguished from a fully developed literary critical approach such as narrative criticism.[1] Inasmuch as narrative criticism is so attentive to the story world created in the Gospel that it disallows the topical statement of the Evangelist's theological thought apart from the narrative form in which it is cast, it stands apart from both redaction criticism and composition criticism, which seek to extract from the Gospel narrative the ideas and emphases of the author. The importance accorded to plot in narrative criticism is beneficial and necessary to a full appreciation of the nature of each Gospel, yet it is less helpful when one wishes to isolate and explore one particular theme within a Gospel as in the present inquiry. The method adopted in this study thus stands at a stage beyond classical redaction criticism; yet its interest in isolating a particular theological objective of Matthew places it closer to redaction criticism than to narrative criticism. It might be the case that composition criticism, falling as it does between these two other methods, is vulnerable to criticism from proponents of either one of these methods. Scholars committed to a rigorous redactional investigation of the Gospels may regard the method as deficient since it does not provide a thorough description of the editorial activity of the Evangelist. Scholars committed to narrative criticism may feel that greater attention to the plot and narrative world of the Gospel is needed. Yet it must be acknowledged that for certain tasks composition criticism represents the most appropriate method.

It was noted above that a convincing explanation for the importance Matthew attaches to the theme of recompense is to be found in the relationship between his Gospel and the Old Testament, especially in respect of specific conceptual links. Indeed, one objective of this study is to demonstrate that Matthew's conception of recompense can be understood fully in terms of his understanding of the Old Testament. The question as to whether (and if so, how) other writings subsequent to the Old Testament may have influenced Matthew is not of interest to the present study. For that reason, parallels to other materials (e.g. Deutero-canonical writings, Qumran texts, Rabbinic works) have not been cited. Since it is indisputable that Matthew was influenced by the Old Testament, it makes for a sound methodology to turn first to the Old Testament for insight before looking elsewhere. One need not infer from the concentration on this particular influence that Matthew,

1. For a helpful discussion of the distinction between composition criticism and narrative criticism see Moore, *Literary Criticism*, esp. pp. 6-8, 10, 18.

as a first-century Jewish Christian, was impervious to other currents
of influence. As will become evident, the advantage in highlighting
this one important source of influence is that it facilitates the objective
of the study which is to explain the purpose and function of the
recompense theme within Matthew's Gospel.

Matthew's concern with the Old Testament, especially the prophetic
corpus, is well known. Consequently, it is commonplace for interpreters of the Gospel to note allusions and significant terminological
parallels to the Old Testament. Nevertheless, it is a fair criticism that
scholars do not sufficiently exploit the more expansive conceptual
links between Matthew and this collection of writings which form the
backdrop against which it is best interpreted. The exercise of relating
an entire structure of ideas present in Matthew to a corresponding
structure in the Old Testament is rarely attempted.[1] Yet such an
exercise was essential to the accomplishment of the present study.
Matthew's interest in recompense is inevitably linked to his interest in
the redemptive purpose of God. The theme forms an indispensable
part of that sweeping story of salvation which is recounted in the
Gospel. The story related in Matthew is, of course, the resumption of
an earlier story which had its beginnings in the Old Testament. In a
similar way, the theme of recompense developed in Matthew is the
resumption of a matching theme that is crucial to the earlier story. In
order to appreciate the full significance of recompense in Matthew, it
is necessary that this earlier story be retold.

1.   One example which may be cited is the study by H. Frankemölle (*Jahwebund
und Kirche Christi* [Münster: Aschendorff, 1974]), in which the conception of Jesus
as the one who is 'with' his disciples (cf. 1.23; 18.20; 28.20) is related to the Old
Testament covenantal idea of Yahweh's bond with Israel. In some respects the present study corresponds to that of Frankemölle, insofar as the basis of a theme in
Matthew is located in the covenant teaching of the Old Testament; yet at the level of
methodological approach the two studies are dissimilar.

Chapter 1

'I SET BEFORE YOU A BLESSING AND A CURSE'
THE OLD TESTAMENT COVENANTAL BACKGROUND TO THE
MATTHAEAN TEACHING ON RECOMPENSE

One of the most notable, and indeed interesting, characteristics of the Gospel of Matthew is its careful, almost meticulous, concern with the Old Testament. Even the most superficial reading of the Gospel will not fail to produce the impression that the author has gone to considerable lengths in order to relate the life and teaching of Jesus to the Old Testament, and in particular to demonstrate that much that had been anticipated and expected in the Old Testament scriptures has been brought to fulfilment through the actions and words of Jesus. For Matthew the events of Jesus' life constitute a climactic moment in the history of God's dealings with his people. Israel's history, though marked by vicissitude and disappointment, has reached its goal and found new hope in Jesus. It is not too much to say that this interest has led Matthew to produce a Gospel which does not merely recount the story of Jesus, but which also provides the reader with a storehouse containing his reflections on the connections between the story of Jesus and the story of the Old Testament. For that reason, it is incumbent on interpreters of Matthew to be mindful of such possible connections when engaged in the task of describing and explaining certain themes and emphases within the Gospel, since these connections may in fact hold the key to a more faithful interpretation.

In the present study the theme of recompense in Matthew will be approached in this manner, for it is not unreasonable to suppose that Matthew's presentation of Jesus' teaching on recompense has been influenced, perhaps significantly, by his conception of how that teaching is associated with the expectation and fulfilment framework which had exercised such a profound influence on the construction of his Gospel. In order to test the legitimacy of this proposition it is important first to identify an Old Testament schema of recompense which, by virtue of an intrinsic link with the history of God's dealings with his people, could have provided the impetus for Matthew's treatment of the theme, and then to demonstrate that Matthew has developed his own teaching on the subject with reference to just such a schema. The present chapter will concern itself with the first matter of identifying and describing a credible Old Testament schema of recompense.

A comprehensive examination of Matthew's teaching on recompense reveals that reward is frequently presented in terms of 'inheritance' (the obedient disciple can look forward to inheriting 'the land', 'eternal life' and 'the kingdom') and 'entrance' (the outcome of faithful service is entrance into 'the kingdom', 'life', 'the marriage feast' and 'the joy of the master'), whereas punishment is often described in terms of removal (the worthless and the wicked are cast into 'the fire', 'Gehenna' and 'the outer darkness'). Matthew is not alone among the Synoptists in the use of these terms. However, he does employ such imagery more frequently than do the others. And, more importantly, it would appear that he alone has fully exploited the force of this imagery, since he is able to construct from it a meaningful conceptual framework that not only relates to his teaching on recompense but indeed lends weight to that teaching. If one is correct in the assumption that in this instance Matthew's teaching has come under the influence of his reflection on and understanding of the Old Testament, then one would be interested in noting the appearance of such imagery in the Old Testament.

The language of inheritance and entrance does play an important role in the Old Testament and is, of course, central to the Sinai covenant which Yahweh entered into with the nation of Israel at the time of the exodus. In that covenant the people of Israel become the people of Yahweh and he in turn promises them a land which they are to enter and inherit. This gift of land is not without condition, however. To remain in the land the nation must live in accordance with his commandments. Failure to do so results in the removal of the nation from the land. The appearance of this imagery in the context of the covenant and, in particular, its occurrence within a schema of recompense is certainly of interest to the present study and thus demands a more thorough examination. For that reason, the story of Israel, to the extent that it is a story of a people who receive a promised land but who lose it through disobedience, will be reviewed. No attempt will be made to furnish an exhaustive survey of this aspect of Israel's story as it is described in the Old Testament. Thus in the course of the inquiry more attention will be given to Deuteronomy and Jeremiah, the two books which are especially interested in the relationship between Israel and its land. Furthermore, no attempt will be made to provide a comprehensive exegesis of the passages under consideration. Many of the questions addressed and difficulties confronted by modern interpreters of the Old Testament would have been of little concern to Matthew. Presumably, he read these books in their canonical form and accepted the implied sequence of events in Israel's history at face value. The primary objective in conducting such a survey is that the narrative outline which is produced may confer a perspective from which one might view the Matthaean teaching on recompense to greater advantage. The examination will begin with the promise of land to Abraham since it is that promise which provides the basis for the later promise to the nation.

The Promise to Abraham

In the book of Genesis a number of promises are made to Abraham and the other patriarchs, yet the most prominent and significant is the promise of the land.[1] It is true that at the time of Abraham's call no mention is made of a gift of land. The content of the main promise given on that occasion is that God would make of Abraham a great nation (Gen. 12.2). Even so, God's command to leave Haran in order to go to 'the land that I will show you' (v. 1) introduces an element of expectation which anticipates the pledge that is made to Abraham when he arrives at Shechem, 'To your descendants I will give this land' (12.7), and which is repeated when Lot separates from him,

---

1.   The promise of land is found in Gen. 12.7; 13.15, 17; 15.7, 18; 17.8; 24.7; 26.3; 28.13; 35.12; 48.4; 50.24. R.E. Clements (*Abraham and David* [London: SCM Press, 1967], p. 57) is correct to speak of the divine promise initially made to Abraham and reiterated to the succeeding patriarchs as a threefold one (concerning the possession of the land by Abraham's descendants, their growth into a great nation, and their becoming a blessing to the nations of the earth) of which the primary element is that of possession of the land. Compare C. Westermann, *The Promises to the Fathers* (Philadelphia: Fortress Press, 1980), p. 143: 'The texts show that all the emphasis is on the promise of the land made to Abraham'; and W. Brueggemann, *Genesis* (Atlanta: John Knox, 1982), p. 109: 'The governing promise concerns the land'.

'Lift up your eyes...for all the land which you see I will give to you and to your descendants for ever' (13.14-15).[1] From that point on, the promise of land runs through the patriarchal narratives 'like a red thread'.[2]

The central narrative concerning the gift of the land is the covenant episode of ch. 15, in which the divine promise of land is confirmed by an oath. In the opening section of the chapter (vv. 1-6) there is no explicit reference to the land. The point of emphasis in these verses is the question of who will become Abraham's heir. This question is answered by God's declaration that 'your own son shall be your heir (ירשׁ; κληρονομέω)'.[3] However, the promise of land is implicit in this promise of an heir; for without an heir the promise of the land cannot be fulfilled.[4] The remaining part of the chapter is enveloped by the same promise: in v. 7 God's purpose in bringing Abraham from Ur of the Chaldees is stated, 'to give you this land to possess (ירשׁ; κληρονομέω)';[5] and in vv. 18-21 Yahweh gives solemn confirmation of that promise. The action of God on this occasion is decisive, for

---

1.   Questions concerning the authenticity and historical development of the patriarchal narratives are of no concern to the present study since they would have been of little concern to Matthew. Cf. W.D. Davies, *The Gospel and the Land* (Berkeley: University of California Press, 1974), p. 18: 'What is important is not the rediscovery of the origins of the promise to Abraham, but the recognition that that promise was so reinterpreted from age to age that it became a living power in the life of the people of Israel'.

2.   M. Ottosson, 'אֶרֶץ', *TDOT*, I (1974), p. 403.

3.   Throughout this discussion those terms which are related to the study of recompense will be frequently noted in their Hebrew and Greek (i.e. Septuagint) renderings since it is probable that Matthew was familiar with, and influenced by, the vocabulary of both versions.

4.   On the importance of the promise of land in this context see the discussion in F. Dreyfus, 'Le thème de l'héritage dans l'Ancien Testament', *RSPT* 42 (1958), pp. 3-49 (22-24). On p. 24 he remarks that 'Si Dieu promet à Abraham un héritier, c'est parce que cet héritier devra hériter de la promesse faite à Abraham, à savoir la possession future de la Terre de Canaan'. Brueggemann (*Genesis*, p. 109) observes that 'the promise of the heir is always in the service of the land promise'. Cf. Clements, *Abraham and David*, p. 19: 'The question dealt with is not simply that of the descendants of Abraham, and their growth in numbers, but with Abraham's inheritance'.

5.   C. Westermann (*Genesis 12–36* [Minneapolis: Augsburg, 1985], p. 224) draws attention to the parallel between the present passage and Lev. 25.38 (cf. Exod. 3.7-8) in which one finds the same close link between the bringing out from one land and the promise of a new land.

although he had already promised the land to Abraham he now makes the promise under oath. And it is in the enactment of this oath that the land truly becomes the possession of Abraham and his descendants. The 'I will give' of the earlier promise has now become the 'I give' of a covenant oath.

The covenant between Yahweh and Abraham is established by means of the enigmatic ceremony which is described in Gen. 15.9-17. The precise interpretation of this ceremony, which involves the cutting in two of animals and the passing between their parts, is the subject of some debate; yet it is widely regarded as an enacted curse whereby one demonstrates acceptance of the obligations of the covenant by calling upon oneself the fate of the animals should these obligations be transgressed.[1] In the present passage it would appear that God, represented by the smoking pot and flaming torch, is invoking upon himself the curse should he fail to honour his promise.[2] It is certainly the case that the Abrahamic covenant is widely interpreted as being unilateral in nature; that is, all the obligations of the covenant are assumed by Yahweh, while no reciprocal responsibilities are imposed upon Abraham.[3] The covenant is indeed preceded by an act of faith on the part of Abraham (cf. v. 6), and his loyalty and devotion to Yahweh are undoubtedly presupposed; yet at no place in the narrative is the fulfilment of God's promise made contingent upon Abraham's actions. In ch. 17 certain imperatives are placed before Abraham: he is to walk before Yahweh (v. 1), be blameless (v. 1), keep the covenant (v. 9), and practise circumcision (v. 10). Nonetheless, these imperatives are not to be regarded as preconditions for the establishment or continuation of the covenant. God has committed himself to Abraham;

---

1. According to M. Weinfeld ('בְּרִית', *TDOT*, II, p. 262), the ceremony 'makes palpable the punishment befalling the one who will violate the pact'. The present passage is frequently interpreted with reference to Jer. 34.18-20 which describes the same, or at least a similar, practice.

2. Cf. G.J. Wenham, *Genesis 1–15* (Waco, TX: Word Books, 1987), p. 332.

3. See, for example, N. Sarna, *Understanding Genesis* (New York: Schocken Books, 1966), pp. 126-27. Weinfeld, ('בְּרִית', pp. 258, 270-72), speaks of the Abrahamic and Davidic covenants as belonging to the type of the covenantal or royal grant which are distinguished by the fact that God swears an oath without imposing any obligation. D.N. Freedman ('Divine Commitment and Human Obligation', *Int* 18 [1964], pp. 419-31 [420]), describes the Abrahamic covenant as a 'covenant of divine commitment' in contradistinction to the Sinaic covenant which is a 'covenant of human obligation'.

in consequence, the covenant he has established with him is everlasting
(17.7, 13, 19) and the gift of land is to be an everlasting possession
(17.8; cf. 13.15). The unconditionality of the Abrahamic covenant
appears to be contradicted by Gen. 18.19 where the fulfilment of the
promise seems to be conditioned upon the obedience of Abraham's
children, and by Gen. 26.3-5 where the covenant oath appears to have
been made in response to Abraham's obedience and faithfulness.[1] Yet
it is perhaps unwise to make too much of such discrepancies.
Throughout the Bible, and not least in the Gospel of Matthew, the line
of demarcation separating grace from demand is, at best, ambiguous.
One must therefore be guided by the prevailing tendency in the text
under examination. In the patriarchal narratives the prevailing tendency
is that the Abrahamic covenant is unconditional. This would not
exclude the element of demand, however, for at all times God is concerned with the human response to his gracious activity. This type of
unconditional promise would naturally stimulate expectation. It will
be noted later that the irrevocability of the promise to Abraham was
to become the ground of hope for the nation. At a time when the
people were suffering on account of their transgression of God's
commands, the continuing validity of the promise to Abraham served
as a reminder that Yahweh was still committed to Israel and would
one day restore the nation.

Yahweh's declaration in Gen. 15.1 that 'your reward (שׂכר; μισθός)
shall be very great' is of interest to the study of the theme of recompense, especially in view of Matthew's allusion to this promise in the
statement which he attaches to the eighth beatitude (Mt. 5.12). There
the persecuted disciple is encouraged to rejoice, for 'your reward is
great in heaven' (ὁ μισθὸς ὑμῶν πολὺς ἐν τοῖς οὐρανοῖς; compare the
LXX of Gen. 15.1 which reads ὁ μισθός σου πολὺς ἔσται σφόδρα).
The Genesis text (like the Matthaean) does not specify what the great
reward refers to, and for that reason one must exercise caution when
interpreting this promise.[2] Nonetheless, when one considers that the

---

1. See J. Van Seters, *Abraham in History and Tradition* (New Haven: Yale
University Press, 1975), pp. 273-74.
2. One can appreciate why some exegetes wish to preserve the ambiguity of this
promise so as to allow it to encompass all the promises made to Abraham. For
example, John Ha (*Genesis 15* [Berlin: de Gruyter, 1989], p. 122) wants to speak of
an 'elasticity for inclusion' by which he means that the promise is intentionally left
unspecified to permit a wide range of possible referents.

most decisive promise given to Abraham is that of the land and that it is this promise which constitutes the central emphasis of ch. 15, it is not unreasonable to suggest that that same promise stands in the foreground here as well.[1] Moreover, the internal logic of the narrative points in the direction of the land promise. Abraham's immediate response to God's promise of the great reward concerns the question of the heir. This implies that Abraham, at least, understood the promise to refer to the gift of land.[2] If one accepts this conclusion, then this verse provides evidence that the land is regarded as a reward for Abraham and, through him, his descendants.

The promise of land, though of primary importance, is not the only significant promise made to Abraham. There are two other key promises which deserve attention. The first of these is the promise given at the time of Abraham's call that God would make of him a great nation (Gen. 12.2; cf. 17.6; 18.18). This promise is, of course, intimately related to the promise of land. In fact, the two promises of land and nation are essentially interdependent, even though it is the case that the former is predominant. The land that has been promised will never be possessed unless there is a large group of descendants to possess it and, at the same time, these descendants will never become a great nation unless they possess a land of their own.[3] It was observed above that the promise of an heir is closely linked to the promise of land, since it is principally the land which the heir inherits. A corresponding connection exists with respect to the promise of a nation, for this multitude of descendants is in truth a nation of heirs.

The other key promise, which similarly appears in the context of Abraham's call, is notable because it affirms that the calling of Abraham is to be of consequence not only for himself and his descendants but ultimately for 'all the families of the earth' (Gen. 12.3; cf. 22.18; 26.4; 28.14). Hence he is to be both the father and source of

---

1. Cf. Brueggemann, *Genesis*, p. 141.

2. Note the argument in Dreyfus, 'L'héritage', pp. 22-24.

3. J.D. Hester, *Paul's Concept of Inheritance* (Edinburgh: Oliver & Boyd, 1968), p. 23. Cf. V.P. Hamilton, *The Book of Genesis: Chapters 1–17* (Grand Rapids: Eerdmans, 1990), p. 395: 'The expansiveness of the divine promise regarding descendants is mandatory in the light of the expansiveness of the divine promise regarding the acquisition of land'. A further pointer to this close link between land and nation consists in the fact that not only are both referred to as the inheritance of Yahweh (compare, for example, Jer. 2.7 with Jer. 10.16), but it is difficult at times to determine which of the two is in view (cf. 2 Sam. 14.16).

benefit to one great nation and also a source of blessing to all nations. Connected to this promise is the declaration that God will treat others in accordance with the way they treat Abraham. Yahweh has called Abraham and is now emphasizing through this word that he is concerned with the welfare of his servant and will actively intervene on his side.[1] The talion principle comes into effect here insofar as the resulting reward or punishment corresponds directly to the initial action: those who bless are blessed and those who curse are cursed.[2] The role that has been assigned to Abraham is of such importance that salvation and judgment are determined by the attitude one adopts towards him. No distinction is made between Abraham and that work of God which is focused on him.[3] This is not to say, however, that the pronouncement applies only to Abraham. He is here being addressed as a patriarch and as such the representative of all his descendants.[4] The work that begins with Abraham is continued and ultimately will be brought to completion by his descendants. This pronouncement of blessing and curse which lends support and protection to that work will remain in effect until the work has been accomplished.

An additional feature of God's covenant relationship with Abraham and the other patriarchs concerns their fruitfulness. Repeatedly throughout the patriarchal narratives it is observed that Abraham and his descendants will become, or are to become, fruitful (note the appearance of the verb פרה in Gen. 17.6; 26.22; 35.11; 48.4). In a sense, this concept of fruitfulness brings together all the promises mentioned above. As an agricultural metaphor it is splendidly suited to a people who have received from God a particular gift of land. In addition, it serves to remind the people that they have been given the land for a purpose; namely that they might keep the covenant with all which that implies and in so doing accomplish the task which God has

---

1.   According to Westermann (*Genesis 12–36*, p. 151), this statement functions as an assurance of protection for Abraham.

2.   Wenham, *Genesis 1–15*, p. 277.

3.   Cf. G. von Rad, *Genesis* (Philadelphia: Westminster Press, 1972), p. 160. U. Cassuto (*A Commentary on the Book of Genesis. Part 2* [Jerusalem: Magnes Press, 1964], p. 315) paraphrases the negative statement in this way: 'Whoever is opposed to you is opposed to the mission that I gave you, and hence it is right that he should be punished'.

4.   G.W. Coats, 'The Curse in God's Blessing', in J. Jeremias and L. Perlitt (eds.), *Die Botschaft und die Boten* (Neukirchen–Vluyn: Neukirchener Verlag, 1981), pp. 31-41 (34 n. 11).

committed to them. In part this task is accomplished when the descendants of Abraham have settled in the land and have increased in number so that they are truly a great nation (note that the verb פרה is frequently coupled with the verb רבה 'to multiply'). Yet the task, and thus the fruit that is to be borne, is also concerned with the blessing to the nations. Clearly, the concept of fruitfulness encompasses all the good which God had intended when he called Abraham. The descendants and heirs of Abraham are fruitful when, and only when, they are faithful to Yahweh and carry forward that work which had begun with Abraham.

Yahweh calls Abraham and pledges to him and his descendants a gift of land. The promise is later confirmed by oath, through which action the land is made over to Abraham as an everlasting possession. As such it constitutes a great reward. Inhering in the promise is a work to be done that will have ramifications for the entire world. The fulfilment of the task is not made a condition of the fulfilment of the promise, but it does relate to the question of whether or not the heirs of Abraham have fulfilled the expectation of fruitfulness.

Promise and Threat in Deuteronomy

When one moves from the period of the patriarchs to the time of the exodus it is not uncommon to find reference to the promises mentioned above. When the descendants of Abraham are first described at the opening of the book of Exodus they are strong and numerous, well on their way to becoming a great nation (1.7). A few chapters later Moses is called by Yahweh to bring the people out of Egypt on account of the promise of land given to the patriarchs (3.8, 16-17; cf. 6.2-8). Later, when the people break the recently established covenant at Sinai by worshipping the golden calf, Yahweh is turned from his wrath solely because of this promise to the patriarchs (32.13-14). The episode demonstrates that God will honour his promise of land to the descendants of Abraham even though they are a 'stiff-necked people'. It is clear from the exodus narratives that of all the promises made to the patriarchs that of the land is the most prominent. Certainly in the book of Deuteronomy, the book which will be the focus of attention in this section, the promise made to Abraham and the other patriarchs is understood completely in terms of the land.[1] The land is viewed as the

1.   G. von Rad, 'The Promised Land and Yahweh's Land in the Hexateuch', in

pre-eminent gift of Yahweh and is given a decidedly important role in the theological formulation of the book.[1] Essentially, the land is made the goal of the nation.

The major concern of the book of Deuteronomy is the Sinai covenant, a covenant which is based on the promise to the patriarchs and which, to an extent, brings to fulfilment that promise.[2] When the book opens, the nation stands on the threshold of the promised land, and receives encouragement to 'go in and take possession (ירש; κληρονομέω)' of it (1.8; cf. 1.21; 1.39).[3] The covenant promise to Abraham, at least on one level, is about to be fulfilled. Yet it is soon evident that in order for the nation to have success in the land it must abide by those covenant stipulations laid upon it by Yahweh at Sinai. The correspondence between the two covenants is set forth in Deut. 4.37-40. There it is affirmed that, because of his love for the patriarchs and his choice of their descendants, Yahweh has brought the people out of Egypt to enter into the land of inheritance. This is followed, however, by the exhortation that the people should keep Yahweh's statutes and commandments so that it may go well with

his *The Problem of the Hexateuch and Other Essays* (Edinburgh: Oliver & Boyd, 1966), pp. 79-93 (80): 'Deuteronomy understands the oath to the early patriarchs only as a promise of the land'. Cf. Ottosson, 'אֶרֶץ', p. 404. Throughout the book there are eighteen references to Yahweh's promise of land to the patriarchs (1.8, 35; 6.10, 18, 23; 7.13; 8.1; 9.5; 10.11; 11.19, 21; 19.8; 26.3, 15; 28.11; 30.20; 31.7; 34.4)

1. Von Rad ('There Remains Still a Rest for the People of God: An Investigation of a Biblical Conception', in *The Problem of the Hexateuch*, pp. 94-102 [95]) does not overstate the case when he observes that according to Deuteronomy 'the land is undeniably the most important factor in the state of redemption to which Israel has been brought'. Compare his remarks in 'Promised Land', pp. 90-91: 'Deuteronomy is dominated from beginning to end by the idea of the land which is to be taken in possession. It forms the theme both of the laws and of the paraenetic discourse.' Note also the discussion in P.D. Miller, Jr., 'The Gift of God: The Deuteronomic Theology of the Land', *Int* 23 (1969), pp. 451-65 (452-54).

2. See R.E. Clements, *God's Chosen People* (London: SCM Press, 1968), p. 40. Cf. Clements, *Abraham and David*, p. 66. F.C. Fensham ('Covenant, Promise and Expectation in the Bible', *TZ* 23 [1967], pp. 305-22 [310]) observes, only this time with respect to the book of Exodus, that 'the impression is created that this promise [the patriarchal promise of land] is one of the main causes of the institution of the covenant at Sinai'.

3. The notion of possessing the land is a major theme in Deuteronomy. Accordingly, the vocabulary of inheritance (ירש and נחל) appears frequently throughout the book.

them in the land. The two covenants stand together almost as indicative to imperative: God has loved the fathers and chosen the nation, therefore the nation should do as he commands. Though rooted in the earlier covenant, it is apparent that the Sinai covenant is developed along separate lines. No longer is the emphasis placed on divine commitment as had been the case with the Abrahamic covenant. Now the emphasis is placed firmly on human obligation and great importance is attached to the human element in the maintenance of the covenant relationship.[1] God's grace does continue to operate even through this shift in emphasis, however. He has, after all, brought the nation out of captivity in Egypt, the 'iron furnace' (4.20), and is about to bring it into a rich and bountiful land. The emphasis here on demand is anchored in God's wish that his people prosper in their land; and that prosperity is unavoidably connected with their adherence to the divine guidance which is provided in the covenant stipulations.

The land may indeed be Israel's particular gift, but it ultimately remains the possession of Yahweh alone (cf. Lev. 25.23).[2] The people have no absolute claim to the land; rather it is theirs in trust. They may enjoy the blessings of possession provided that they fulfil the responsibilities of possession.[3] These responsibilities are set forth in the stipulations of the covenant. In a sense, it is through these stipulations that Yahweh continues to exercise control over his land.[4] It would be incorrect, however, to regard the commandments simply as the means by which Yahweh tests the obedience of his people. Their function, much more than that of establishing the condition for the continuing existence in the land, is to lead the people to a knowledge of the ways of Yahweh that they might be influenced by his nature and thus be able to perform the task he has committed to them. In particular, it

1. Freedman, 'Divine Commitment', p. 427. The part played by the human element within the framework of a divine gift is well expressed by Miller ('Gift of God', p. 461): 'Israel cannot justify her *original* possession of the land on the basis of her behavior; she must, however, justify or preserve her *continuing* and *future* possession on the basis of her behavior' (his italics).

2. The notion of Yahweh's ownership of the land though never made explicit in Deuteronomy may be inferred from the law of the tithe (Deut. 26.1-11).

3. Miller, 'Gift of God', p. 458: 'It is not possible to speak of the gift of the land apart from obedience to Yahweh and his law'. According to Ps. 105.44-45, Yahweh gave the people the land to the end that they might keep his statutes and laws.

4. Cf. J. Eichler, 'Inheritance', *NIDNTT*, II, p. 297.

was Yahweh's express purpose that the nation be characterized by his own righteousness: 'You shall pursue that which is just (צדק; δίκαιος), and only that, so you may live and inherit the land which Yahweh your God gives you'. (Deut. 16.20). The people will prosper and have success in the land only to the extent that they are committed to this goal of becoming a righteous and just people. It is clear from Deuteronomy that the former occupants of the land are to be expelled on account of their wickedness (9.4-5; cf. Gen. 15.16). In the language of Leviticus, these nations had not only defiled themselves but had defiled the land as well, so that in the end 'the land vomited out its inhabitants' (Lev. 18.24-25).[1] The land, as Yahweh's land, is a holy land and it will become defiled if the people of Israel act in a manner which violates the holy and righteous demands of Yahweh.[2] In order to preserve the land and maintain their place in it the nation must observe the covenant stipulations. If not, it will experience the same punishment that befell these other nations.

The enjoyment of a long and full life in the land God has given represents for Deuteronomy the ultimate blessing in store for the people of Israel. Throughout the book the promise of reward is generally expressed in terms of a good life in a good land.[3] It is assumed throughout the book that the land of promise is a most desirable land which provides the nation with everything that it could ever require or want. The goodness of the land is vividly expressed in the recurring affirmation that it is a land 'flowing with milk and honey'.[4] One feature of the good life in the good land is the experience of joy. When

1.   Israel became the instrument of God's judgment on these nations (Deut. 9.3), just as later Assyria and Babylon would become the means by which God would punish his own people.

2.   In Deuteronomy certain acts of disobedience are said to bring defilement upon the land, for example, allowing a corpse is to remain on a tree over night (21.22-23) and remarrying a divorced wife who has since remarried (24.1-4).

3.   S.R. Driver, *A Critical and Exegetical Commentary on Deuteronomy* (Edinburgh: T. & T. Clark, 1902), p. 63: 'Life, coupled with the secure possession of the Promised Land, is constantly held out in Deuteronomy as the reward for obedience to God's commandments'. Note the valuable discussion on 'Life and Good' in M. Weinfeld, *Deuteronomy and the Deuteronomic School* (Oxford: Clarendon Press, 1972), pp. 307-13. On p. 307 Weinfeld observes that '"Life" in the book of Deuteronomy. . .constitutes the framework of reward'.

4.   See 6.3; 11.9; 26.9, 15; 27.3; 31.20; compare also the descriptions of the land in 8.7-10 and 11.9-12.

the people begin to receive the benefits of life in the land they will 'rejoice in all the good' that Yahweh has given them (26.11; cf. 12.7; 16.15). Moreover, it was Yahweh's intention that the nation should know 'rest' (מנוח; κατάπαυσις) in the land. In the context of Deuteronomy, rest means the cessation of those difficulties experienced during the time of wilderness wanderings and, more importantly, a secure and unthreatened life free from the troubling interference of enemies (3.20; 12.9-10; 25.19).

This goal of blissful existence in the land is not attained, however, without faithful obedience to God's commands.[1] A typical expression of the interplay between obedience and reward is found in Deut. 5.33 where the people are instructed to 'walk in all the way' Yahweh has commanded, 'that you may live, and that it may go well with you, and that you may live long in the land which you are to possess (ירשׁ; κληρονομέω)' (cf. 4.1; 8.1). Life, with accompanying joy and rest, is the consequence of fearing Yahweh and walking in all his ways. But there is an alternative path, that of turning aside from the way which Yahweh commands (11.28; cf. 13.5; 31.29). The people are thus presented with a choice. This choice receives its classic presentation in Deut. 30.15-20. The passage opens with the declaration of an ultimatum: 'I set before you this day life (חיים; ζωή) and good, death (מות; θάνατος) and evil' (v. 15). Obedience receives as its reward the continuing enjoyment of the good life in the land. Disobedience, on the other hand, results in the the loss of everything. In 30.19 the ultimatum appears in a slightly different form, wherein life is portrayed as a blessing and death as a curse.[2] This statement echoes that found in an earlier passage where Yahweh issues the sharp pronouncement: 'Behold, I set before you this day a blessing and a curse' (11.26). There is no middle way. One either obeys and is rewarded with God's blessing, or one disobeys and is punished with his curse.[3] But in truth

---

1. P. Diepold (*Israels Land* [Stuttgart: W. Kohlhammer, 1972], p. 101) notes that 'nur wenn Israel hört und tut, was Jahwe ihm gebietet, kann es in der Wirklichkeit leben, die ihm als Volk Gottes angeboten ist, und den Segen Jahwes empfangen. Abwendung von ihm. . . verschließen Israel die Verheißungen seines Gottes'.

2. H. Ringgren, 'חָיָה', *TDOT*, IV, p. 334.

3. Concerning this recompense schema in Deuteronomy, J.G. Plöger (*Literarkritische, formgeschichtliche und stilkritische Untersuchungen zum Deuteronomium* [Bonn: Peter Hanstein, 1967], p.195) writes: 'Segen und Fluch werden zu einem Instrument göttlicher 'Vergeltung'. In der dtr Theologie stehen

there is no choice; Israel must cleave to Yahweh and follow his commandments.

In view of the fateful decision that faces the nation, it is fitting that in Deuteronomy 28 blessings and especially curses, which disclose in striking detail the result of obedience and disobedience, are utilized to encourage the nation to choose rightly.[1] It is significant that in both blessing and curse the consequences bear directly on the land of promise. Evidently such forceful encouragement is required because the continuing fulfilment of God's promises to the people depends directly on their response to his demands. The possibility exists that the people through negligence and deliberate disobedience may interrupt and even reverse God's programme of fulfilment.

In ch. 28 almost every reference to blessing has to do with the land. The people will enjoy agricultural abundance: their fields will be fruitful (vv. 3-5, 11) and their barns will be full of produce (v. 8). Yahweh will provide the rain in its season and bless the work of their hands (v. 12). Their flocks and their herds will be fertile (vv. 4, 11). The people themselves will increase in number in the land (vv. 4, 11) and will become established as a people holy to Yahweh (v. 9; cf. 7.6; 26.19). Furthermore, they will experience rest in the land with the spectacular defeat of their enemies (v. 7), who will not only come to fear them but will also acknowledge their relationship to Yahweh (v. 10). The obedient nation will thrive and advance in the direction

Segen und Fluch in innerer Korrespondenz zu Gehorsam und Ungehorsam'.

    1.   Note the remarks of D.J. McCarthy (*Treaty and Covenant* [Rome: Pontifical Biblical Institute, 1963], p. 130): 'The vivid picture of the promised good or evil, turns them [the blessings and curses] into a means of convincing, or producing in the hearer or reader the will to obey because he is moved and persuaded'; and Plöger, *Untersuchungen*, p. 217: 'Im Gesamtzusammenhang des Segen-Fluch-Abschnittes fungiert die Fluchreihe als ein Mittel der Gesetzespredigt, die Wahl des "Lebens", nicht des "Todes" zu motivieren'. At the conclusion of an article on the subject of the covenantal blessings and curses, F.C. Fensham ('Malediction and Benediction in Ancient Near Eastern Vassal-Treaties and the Old Testament', *ZAW* 74 [1962], pp. 1-9 [9]) makes the intriguing observation that these covenant forms might be the background of the entire Old Testament idea of salvation and damnation. Cf. D.R. Hillers, *Treaty-Curses and the Old Testament Prophets* (Rome: Pontifical Biblical Institute, 1964), p. 88: 'If the covenant idea is an ancient element in Israelite religion, then blessing and curse, or to use other terms, an eschatology involving salvation and doom, is equally ancient'. Although a similar list of blessings and curses appears in Lev. 26, the present discussion will be limited to the list found in Deut. 28.

of continuing prosperity.[1] As a people they will have achieved all the benefits of the promise given to Abraham.

A long list of curses follows upon these blessings. The space allotted to the covenantal curses seems excessive in comparison with the much smaller space given to the blessings. Most probably this was done in order to underscore the seriousness of covenant transgression. The nation will not simply cease to thrive if it turns from Yahweh, it will unequivocally deteriorate. Many of the curses directly correspond to the blessings and thus provide ample evidence that the good which Yahweh intended for his people can just as easily turn to ruin.[2] The land that had been so pleasant shall become the stage of a great national nightmare. Agricultural plenty shall be replaced by scarcity when the earth turns to iron and the rain to dust (vv. 23-24). Their animals shall be violently taken from them (v. 31). Their life on the land will be marked by futility: every enterprise will end in failure and every plan will meet with disappointment (vv. 20, 30-32, 38-42). They shall suffer the same diseases which afflicted Egypt, and even diseases from which the Egyptians were spared (vv. 27, 60-61). The population of the nation, which had greatly increased in accordance with God's promise, shall be diminished until only a few remain (v. 62). The people will suffer defeat at the hands of their enemies who have now become the tools of an offended God (v. 25). Their corpses will litter the ground and be food for the birds and beasts (v. 26). Those who survive are hardly to be envied. They shall be forced from the land of Israel and scattered among the nations and peoples. In exile not only will they serve their enemies under a yoke of iron (v. 48), but they will serve other gods as well (vv. 36, 64). Their end will be like their beginning inasmuch as once again they will become slaves in Egypt (v. 68). The lot of the people under the domination of hostile masters will be that of continual harassment and oppression (vv. 29, 33). Their light will have turned to darkness (v. 29). Separated from the land of their inheritance the people will languish in soul and find no rest (v. 65). In the end, far from

1. P. Craigie (*The Book of Deuteronomy* [Grand Rapids: Eerdmans, 1976], p. 338) summarizes the potential blessing for the nation with the words, 'Israel would be a prince among nations, rich in produce and harvest, strong against her enemies, glorious in the presence of God in her midst'.

2. K. Baltzer, *The Covenant Formulary* (Oxford: Basil Blackwell, 1971), p. 154: 'The curse merely threatens the reverse of the blessings'.

becoming a holy people and the praiseworthy representatives of Yahweh in the midst of other nations, they will have become a horror and a byword among those same nations (vv. 25, 37). According to the scenario sketched by these curses, the history of the people of Israel will, in effect, be annulled.[1] The promises will come to nothing. Yahweh, who had taken delight in providing the nation with many good things, will now take delight in devastating the land and destroying the nation (cf. v. 63).[2] The nation under God's curse will be as good as dead.

If reward in Deuteronomy consists in a good life in a good land, then punishment consists in death in a destroyed land and the eventual ejection of the nation from it. As early as ch. 4 the people are warned of the dreadful ramifications should they provoke Yahweh to anger: 'You will soon utterly perish (אבד; ἀπωλείᾳ ἀπολεῖσθε) from the land which you are going over the Jordan to possess; you will not live long upon it, but will be utterly destroyed' (v. 26; cf. 11.17). Later, the same warning appears in a passage which notes that the gifts of Yahweh can prove to be a mixed blessing, insofar as the people, once filled and satisfied, may lift up their hearts and forget Yahweh (8.11-20). This affront to Yahweh's goodness invites the divine pronouncement: 'You shall surely perish (אבד; ἀπωλείᾳ ἀπολεῖσθε)'. In the curse section of ch. 28 this threat of judgment receives additional expression. The nation shall perish quickly and be destroyed thoroughly when the curses come upon it (vv. 20, 45). The appalling destruction of the land, which is both the consequence of the nation's sin and, perhaps justly, the occasion of the nation's ruin, is graphically depicted in the 'Song of Moses'. In the poem, the conduct of the faithless and perverse nation, which follows foreign gods and serves worthless idols, stirs Yahweh to jealousy and provokes his wrath which like a fire 'burns to the depths of Sheol', devouring the land and its produce (32.22). However, the ultimate sign of Yahweh's judgment is the forcible removal of the nation from the land. This removal is described in terms of 'consuming' (28.21, כלה; ἐξαναλίσκω) and 'plucking' (28.63, נסח; ἐξαίρω) the people off the land. In the supplementary warnings stated in ch. 29 this judgment, now viewed from the perspective of the future, is described by means of related

---

1. J.A. Thompson, *Deuteronomy* (London: Inter-Varsity Press, 1974), p. 277.

2. Plöger, *Untersuchungen*, p. 216: 'Für das bundesbrüchige Volk wird der Gott des Heiles zum strafenden Richter'.

imagery: Yahweh in his great wrath 'uprooted (נתש; ἐξαίρω) them from their land' and 'cast (שלך; ἐκβάλλω) them into another land' (v. 28). With the loss of their land the people of Israel lose the foremost gift of Yahweh; and along with it go all of the promises and blessings associated with the land. The great nation is reduced to a few scattered and dejected survivors. The descendants of Abraham who were to enjoy Yahweh's protection and become his instrument in bringing blessing to the nations are now defeated by other nations who act as Yahweh's instruments of destruction. With Israel out of the land, Yahweh's programme of salvation has come to a halt. The promises made to Abraham are suspended.

Before concluding this section, it is valuable to note that, although Deuteronomy speaks primarily in terms of divine judgment on the covenant people as a whole, it is not unfamiliar with the notion of judgment for individual members of the covenant community.[1] In 13.1-5 the false prophet or dreamer, whose unchecked influence may cause the people to turn from the way of Yahweh to follow other gods, is to be put to death as one who has taught rebellion. In the following verses (6-11) it is emphasized that no mercy is to be shown to the one who would tempt others into idolatry, even if that person happens to be a close relative. Such people must surely be put to death. A similar declaration is found in 17.2-7, wherein the people are instructed to stone the man or woman who violates the covenant by advocating forbidden worship. Perhaps the most interesting passage of this kind is that found in 29.18-21. There the person whose heart has turned away from Yahweh to serve other gods is described as 'a root bearing (פרה; φύω) bitterness and poison'. This individual may be deluded into thinking that he or she is safe in spite of their stubbornness of heart. Yet God will not pardon. He will single out that person from all Israel for disaster. In accordance with the covenant, 'all the curses written in this book' will fall upon him or her. The appearance of פרה in v. 18 is noteworthy, especially since the verb is used to denote the relationship that exists between disposition and conduct: the stubborn and wayward heart produces as its fruit idolatrous behaviour. And not only this, for as the metaphor is developed in the next verse it becomes apparent that this evil root will have consequences for the entire plant. Presumably the phrase about the sweeping away of 'moist

1. Cf. R.E. Clements, *Prophecy and Covenant* (London: SCM Press, 1965), p. 41.

and dry alike' points to the fact that all will suffer as a result of the evil which spreads out from that single source. In view of the subsequent history of Israel one might reflect on the tragedy suggested by this verb. The nation which was to be fruitful is swept away and becomes barren because the root in its midst bearing poisonous fruit is allowed to flourish.

In Deuteronomy two alternative histories of the nation are sketched. These histories correspond to the two ways which are set before the people of Israel. When they enter the land of promise, the people may choose to walk in the way of Yahweh. If they do so, they will possess the land in the truest sense of the word, in that they will experience the fullness of God's blessing in the land. They may, however, choose to turn away from Yahweh. If this course is followed, they will soon encounter the full force of his curse. Their life in the land will become increasingly bitter until finally they are cast from it.

The Loss of Land in Jeremiah

The subsequent history of the nation answers the question as to which of these two paths Israel chose to follow. For although there were times of national faithfulness, especially when the nation benefitted from the guidance of judges and kings who were committed to Yahweh, the usual course of the nation was in a direction away from God and toward the worship of other gods. Throughout this long period of disobedience Yahweh did not permit the nation to drift unknowingly to its destruction. He continued to berate and warn his people through a series of prophets. The function of the prophets was to remind the nation of its covenant obligations and, if possible, to bring it back to the way of faithfulness. In order to achieve this end it was not uncommon for the prophets to draw attention to the many curses connected with the covenant.[1] The evidence suggests that the covenant idea formed the foundation of the prophetical preaching. The covenant tradition is especially clear in the ריב, or covenant law-

---

1.   Hillers (*Treaty-Curses*, see especially pp. 82-89) convincingly demonstrates that the prophets knew the terms of the covenant including the curses associated with it. Many scholars have abandoned the view, once championed by Wellhausen, that the prophets were the originators of the covenantal ideas which appear in the Pentateuch, and have come to favour a view which regards the prophets as fulfilling a 'policing' function with respect to the covenant.

suit, form.[1] As spokespersons for Yahweh the prophets admonished the nation which for too long had presumed upon Yahweh's goodness and patience. They forcefully pointed out those areas in which the nation had failed to carry out its covenant responsibilities, and effectively utilized the covenant threats to alert the nation that, should it not turn from its course of disobedience, it would soon run headlong into the curses of Yahweh.

A review of the relationship between the preaching of the prophets and the covenant tradition lies beyond the purview of the present discussion which is interested primarily in describing the story of Israel as that of a people who receive and then lose their inheritance of land. One prophet who stands out from the rest as especially concerned with this aspect of Israel's history is Jeremiah.[2] For that reason, and because the objective of providing a narrative outline will be facilitated by narrowing the focus of inquiry, more attention will be given to Jeremiah than to the other prophets, although by no means will they be excluded entirely from the discussion.

Jeremiah understood that there was a covenant dimension to Israel's possession of the land. The nation could continue in the land and enjoy its benefits only as long as it remained faithful to Yahweh. Furthermore, Jeremiah recognized that the nation in his day had strayed far from God and had miserably failed to keep the requirements of the covenant. Yahweh had brought the people of Israel out of the land of Egypt, that 'iron furnace' (11.4), had led them through the wilderness of 'deep darkness' (2.7), and finally had brought them into a rich land 'flowing with milk and honey' (32.22; cf. 11.5) so that they might enjoy its good things. Yet the response of the nation to this demonstration of grace and love was in no way commensurate. The people, once devoted and holy (2.2-3), now refuse to listen to Yahweh's voice or answer his call (7.13; 17.23). They have perverted their way (3.21), preferring to follow the dictates of their own evil hearts (18.12) rather than the instructions of Yahweh as set forth in his law (9.13). Furthermore, they have become an adulterous people who forsake the God who had chosen them in order to play the harlot

---

1. D.J. McCarthy, 'Covenant in the Old Testament: The Present State of Inquiry', *CBQ* 27 (1965), pp. 217-40 (232).

2. In his book *The Land* (Philadelphia: Fortress Press, 1977), W. Brueggemann describes Jeremiah as 'the poet of the land par excellence' (p. 107) and observes that 'Jeremiah tells the whole story of Israel as the story of the land' (p. 121).

with many lovers (3.1). Even though Yahweh has continually pleaded with them through his servants the prophets, they have stiffened their neck and become worse (7.25-26).[1] They are truly a people who have moved backward and not forward (7.24). This spiritual and moral decay of the nation is portrayed poetically in 2.21: 'I planted you a choice vine, wholly of trustworthy stock. How then have you turned degenerate and become a wild vine?'

It must be noted that the people had become a 'wild vine' in part because of corrupt leadership. Although this does not eliminate the guilt of the people it does help to explain their waywardness. The king was obliged to read, keep and do all the statutes of Yahweh (cf. Deut. 17.19); the prophets were to be reliable channels of Yahweh's word, speaking only what he commanded them to speak; and the priests were to maintain the holiness of the people. Yet by Jeremiah's day leadership was deficient at every level. It was observed earlier that God intended his people to be characterized by righteousness. Now, however, even the king, who was to set an example for the people, stands in need of the reminder that he is to 'do justice and righteousness' (22.3). The case of Jehoiakim, which is related in ch. 22, is highly instructive. His father Josiah had done justice and righteousness (v. 15), yet his own reign is characterized more by unrighteousness and injustice (v. 13, 17). As a consequence, Jehoiakim shall be 'cast forth' (v. 19, שלך; cf. 36.30) outside the gates of Jerusalem. Moreover, his son Jehoiachin with his children will be hurled and 'cast out' (v. 28, שלך; ἐκβάλλω) into a foreign land so that in the end there shall be left none of his line to sit on the throne of David. The prophets of Israel have been no better. In truth, they could be described more accurately as the prophets of Baal (2.8) rather than prophets of Yahweh. Though they claim to speak for God, they are lying, for they prophesy only the delusions of their own hearts (23.26; cf. 14.14; 27.15). Because of their deceit Yahweh will feed the prophets on 'bitterness and poison' (23.15). And because the people have listened to these false prophets and dreamers, and by their influence have forsaken the law to go after the Baals, they too will be made to eat 'bitterness and poison' (9.13-15). The people had failed to follow the advice of Deuteronomy concerning the need to nip in the

---

1. In 25.5 (cf. 35.15) the message of the prophets is recounted: 'Turn from evil so that you might remain in the land that Yahweh gave to you and your fathers for ever'.

bud such evil influences. They permitted the root to bear its fruit and must now suffer the consequences. The prophets prophesy falsely and the priests rule at their direction (5.31). Both groups lack knowledge (14.18), both are godless (23.11), and both practice deceit (6.13; 8.10). The shepherds of the people have failed in their responsibilities and have brought misfortune upon themselves and upon those in their charge. They will not escape the judgment of God: 'Woe to the shepherds who destroy and scatter the sheep of my pasture!' (23.1). Neither will the people who gladly followed their lead escape judgment. The people, the prophets and the priests will all be 'cast off' (23.33, נטש). Everyone, from the king down, will be destroyed (13.13-14).

The sin of the people had consequences for the land as well. Virtually from the moment the people entered the land they defiled it, making a desecration of Yahweh's inheritance (2.7, נחלה; κληρονομία). The religious prostitution of the nation, especially with the god Baal, was a particular source of pollution in the land (3.2). And not only the land, but even the very temple of Yahweh had been defiled by their abominations (7.30; 32.34). Perhaps the worst offence of all, however, and definitely the most shocking indication of the moral and spiritual depths to which the nation had sunk, was the sacrifice of children at the high place of Topheth, in the valley of the son of Hinnom (7.31; 19.4-5; 32.35), a place defiled by the blood of innocents. Certainly there could be no question that the people of Israel had broken the covenant which Yahweh had made with their fathers (11.10; cf. 22.9). Therefore, as a people who had not heeded the words of the covenant, they are cursed (cf. 11.3). Accordingly, 'all the words of this covenant' are being brought down upon them (11.8). Their fruitful land is to become a desert and they themselves are to be removed from it. Because they had refused to honour the covenant, the people of Israel will now lose their inheritance.[1] The state of the nation in the land is epitomized by the words of Isa. 24.5-6: 'The land is defiled by its people; for they have transgressed the laws, violated the statutes, and broken the everlasting covenant. Therefore a curse consumes the land.'

The curses come upon the land of Israel in accordance with the

---

1. Diepold, *Israels Land*, p. 163: 'Jahwes Volk hat die Nachalah verspielt, hat die Bedingungen für einen dauernden Besitz des Landes nicht erfüllt. Darum wird das Land verwüstet, muß das Volk ins Exil.'

deuteronomic pattern. Because the people have turned aside and gone after Baal, Yahweh will withhold rain from the land (3.3; 5.24-25). The resulting drought (12.4; 14.1) is the beginning of the devastation of the pleasant land. The ruin which commences with this natural disaster is significantly intensified when a foreign army invades the land. Yahweh brings disaster from the north (4.6-7) in the form of the Babylonians who lay waste the countryside and cities, and massacre the inhabitants of the land.[1] The bodies of the slain of the people become food for the birds and the beasts (16.4; 19.7). The destruction of the nation is total. In 25.9 the verb חרם is used; the same verb appears in Numbers and Deuteronomy with reference to the complete destruction of the former occupants of the land. The people will have truly become an object of horror and scorn (15.4; 25.9). Yahweh allows this to happen because he has rejected his people (6.30), forsaken his house, and abandoned his נחלה (12.7). Moreover, he himself actively fights against the people with 'outstretched hand and a mighty arm' (21.5). It is ironic that a similar phrase is used in 32.21 to describe Yahweh's act of bringing the nation out of Egypt. His energies are now employed in taking the people back into captivity. His wrath is poured out on the land like an unquenchable fire (7.20). Indeed, his anger kindles a fire which will burn forever (17.4; cf. Deut. 32.22). In his wrath Yahweh has set loose on the land a merciless enemy; and their invasion of the land reaches its climax in the deportation of the people.

The people, through disobedience, had chosen the curse and not the blessing. Yet even now Yahweh mercifully offers them a new choice, similar to that offered at an earlier time: 'Behold, I set before you the way of life and the way of death' (21.8). The difference is that the way of life now lies in captivity. Life in the land is no longer an option available to the nation. It must go into exile. Yahweh shall cast (שלך) the people out of his sight (7.15; 52.3; cf. 15.1) and hurl them from the land (10.18, קלע; 16.13, טול). The forsaken nation will be scattered like chaff driven by the wind (13.24).[2] The people have lost

1. W.L. Holladay ('The Covenant with the Patriarchs Overturned: Jeremiah's Intention in "Terror on Every Side" (Jer. 20.1-6)', *JBL* 91 [1972], pp. 305-20 [317]) makes the striking observation that God summons a גוי גדול from the north (cf. 6.22) against Israel which is no longer a גוי גדול.

2. Cf. Zech. 7.14: 'With a storm I scattered them among all the nations which they had not known. The land was left desolate behind them so that no one could

their hold on the inheritance Yahweh gave them (17.4). The nation which had refused to serve under Yahweh's yoke (2.20) will now know the yoke of foreign domination (28.14).[1] In a land they do not know they shall serve their enemies and foreign gods.

As a consequence of the destruction of the land and their exile from it, the people of Israel lose those blessings associated with life in the land. The sounds of joy and gladness, together with the voices of the bride and bridegroom, come to an end (7.34; 16.9; 25.10). The promised rest which they should have realized is now denied to the people because they had refused to walk in the good way leading to it (6.16). A great reversal has taken place. It would appear that in Jeremiah's time Yahweh's covenant with the patriarchs has been overturned.[2] The land of promise is no longer the possession of Israel. The descendants of Abraham had presumed upon the land and as a consequence are now expelled from it.[3] The nation itself is neither great nor fruitful. The promise made to Abraham that his descendants would be as numerous as the sand on the seashore (Gen. 22.17; cf. 32.12) receives a sinister rejoinder in the words of Jer. 15.8: 'I have made their widows more numerous than the sand of the sea'. Furthermore, it is noted in Jer. 4.2 that if only Israel would return to Yahweh, the nations would be blessed.[4] Israel would not return; hence the

---

come or go. Thus the pleasant land was made desolate.'

1.   Jeremiah effectively employs the same image for the nation's servitude to Yahweh as for its servitude to foreign powers. In his discussion of Jer. 2.20, Holladay (*Jeremiah 1* [Philadelphia: Fortress Press, 1986], p. 97) notes: 'The question then is not the presence or absence of a yoke, but which yoke is to be present'.

2.   On this matter of the reversal of Yahweh's covenant with the patriarchs, see the article by Holladay on Jer. 20.1-6 (see p. 42 n. 1). On p. 319 Holladay comments that 'Jeremiah saw a total reversal of *Heilsgeschichte*'. Similarly, M. DeRoche ('Contra Creation, Covenant and Conquest [Jer. 8.13]', *VT* 30 [1980], pp. 280-90) argues that Jer. 8.13 concerns, among other things, the reversal of the patriarchal covenant; that is, many things are 'passing away' from Israel.

3.   Brueggemann (*The Land*, pp. 15-16) speaks of 'presuming upon the land' as the negative paradigm in the land theology delineated in the Bible. A clear example of this sort of presumption is found in Ezek. 33.24 where the people boast that if Abraham who was only one man could possess the land, how much more could they, who are many, possess the land. They had forgotten that land possession depends upon faithfulness to the covenant. With reference to this passage Davies (*Gospel and Land*, p. 106) comments: 'The covenant with Abraham provides no reassurance against failure to keep the commandments'.

4.   These reflections of the patriarchal tradition are noted by Holladay ('Jer.

fulfilment of this patriarchal promise, like all the others, meets with delay. The heirs of Abraham had not fulfilled the expectation of fruit-fulness. Yahweh wanted the people of Israel to prosper in the land and fulfil the role he assigned to them, but their obduracy had made this impossible. In the end, with his patience finally exhausted, Yahweh turned against his people and brought upon them the curses of the broken covenant. The disinherited and unfruitful nation is cast into captivity.

The Planting and Uprooting of Israel

Throughout this discussion occasional reference has been made to the subject of fruitfulness. It was suggested in an earlier section that the notion of the nation's fruitfulness denotes more than just its numerical growth. The term, rather, encompasses all the good which Yahweh intended for and through the descendants of Abraham. In addition, it was noted above that by the time of the exile it was obvious that the nation was deficient in this regard. It had not fulfilled the promise of becoming the holy and righteous nation that would be the means of extending blessing to all the peoples of the earth. On the contrary, the nation which had strayed far from Yahweh was found to be without fruit, and thus very deserving of judgment. At this point in the review of Israel's story the theme of Israel as an unfruitful nation will be examined. In particular, this matter will be examined with reference to the Old Testament imagery of the planting and uprooting of the nation.

In a number of passages the establishment of the people of Israel in Canaan is described in terms of Yahweh 'planting' the nation in the land.[1] For example, according to Exod. 15.17 Yahweh will bring the people in and plant (נטע; καταφυτεύω) them on the mountain of his inheritance. In Ps. 44.3 [2] the conquest is depicted as Yahweh's act of

---

20.1-6', p. 320 n. 57a). According to R.P. Carroll (*Jeremiah* [London: SCM Press, 1986], p. 156), in Jer. 4.2 'the well-being of the nations is made dependent upon Israel's turning'.

    1.   R. Bach ('Bauen und Pflanzen', in R. Rendtorff and K. Koch [eds.], *Studien zur Theologie der alttestamentlichen Überlieferungen* [Neukirchen–Vluyn: Neukirchener Verlag, 1961], pp. 7-32 [14]) remarks that in certain cases the verb 'to plant' is used as 'ein bildlicher Ausdruck für das heilsgeschichtliche Thema der Hineinführung in das verheißene Land'.

driving out the other nations and planting (נטע; καταφυτεύω) the
Israelites. Similarly, in Ps. 80.9-10 [8-9] the chosen nation is described
as a vine planted by Yahweh: 'You brought a vine (גפן; ἄμπελος) out
of Egypt; you drove out the nations and planted (נטע; καταφυτεύω)
it. You cleared the ground for it; it took root and filled the land'.[1] On
its own the verb נטע is not a term rich in theological significance. In
contexts such as these, however, the term has come to possess a
definite theological quality.[2] In the examples just noted the verb is
employed not only to emphasize that Israel's entrance into the land
was Yahweh's own deed, but also to place stress on the particular concern and love with which Yahweh established his people in the land.[3]
This is especially clear in Psalm 80 where Yahweh is portrayed as
diligently preparing the ground so that the vine might have the best
opportunity for growth and development. This idea of Yahweh's
providential care for his planting is especially highlighted in the 'Song
of the Vineyard' in Isaiah 5. In the allegory Yahweh is presented as a
landowner who does everything that is necessary to ensure that his
vineyard has every advantage. He sets the vineyard (כרם; ἀμπελών)
on a fertile hillside, and for its protection provides it with a hedge.
Before he plants (נטע; φυτεύω) it with choice vines he clears away the
stones and ploughs the ground.[4] He even builds a watchtower for his
vineyard. All of these preparations prompt the landowner to ask what
more could be done for his vineyard.[5] Clearly Yahweh had not

---

1. On the use of the vine to represent Israel, compare the statement of
A.A. Anderson (*The Book of Psalms* [Grand Rapids: Eerdmans, 1972], II,
p. 584), that since the vine was one of the most valued plants, 'it provided a fitting
metaphor for the people of God, the most privileged nation of the nations'.

2. Cf. J. Reindl, 'נטע', *ThWAT*, V, col. 423.

3. With respect to this aspect of the verb נטע, I.F.M. Brayley (' "Yahweh is the
Guardian of His Plantation" A Note on Isa. 60, 21', *Bib* 41 [1960], pp. 275-86
[284]) observes that the choice of this word indicates that Yahweh's relation to his
people was more readily conceived 'under the image of the painstaking and separate
setting out of shoots rather than under that of the regardless broadcast sowing of seed'.

4. Both here and in Jer. 2.21 the original condition of the nation is expressed by
the figure of a 'choice vine' (שׂרק).

5. It may be inferred from the judgment pronouncement in 5.6 that the
landowner also pruned, cultivated and provided rain for his vineyard. In the related
passage found in Isa. 27.2-6 Yahweh's care for his vineyard is illustrated by his
faithfulness in watering it frequently, guarding it night and day, and ridding it of
thorns and briers.

merely brought the people of Israel into the land of promise but had made certain that it was a land appropriate to their needs and a land in which they could fulfil the promise of their calling.

The imagery of planting also gives rise to the whole idea of expectation.[1] When a vine is planted, it is in the anticipation and hope that one day it will produce fruit. This idea is certainly present in the allegory of Isaiah 5, for the landowner who had carefully nurtured the vineyard begins to look for a yield of fine grapes (v. 2). When in v. 7 the allegory gives way to the explanation, it becomes clear that Yahweh too had expected a return from Israel, his vineyard and pleasant planting. He looks to the house of Israel for justice (מִשְׁפָּט; κρίσις) and righteousness (צֶדֶק; δικαιοσύνη), but regrettably he finds only bloodshed (מִשְׂפָּח; ἀνομία) and crying (צְעָקָה; κραυγή). Israel should have produced good fruit, but instead yielded only bitter fruit. The allegory in Jer. 2.21 describes an identical situation. The choice vine of trustworthy (אֱמֶת; ἀληθινός) stock had degenerated into a corrupt (סוֹרִי; πικρία) wild vine. Yahweh's intention when he planted his people in the land was that they should be faithful and true; yet they turned from him and corrupted themselves.

The failure of the nation to produce good fruit is also expressed through the imagery of Jer. 8.13. Yahweh comes to the nation expecting to gather grapes and figs but is unable to find anything of value. The nation is barren; even its leaves are withered.[2] Hosea also recounts the decline of the nation under the figure of a plant which had turned bad. According to Hos. 9.10, when Yahweh first took Israel to himself the people were a delight to his eyes. It was to him like finding grapes in the wilderness or seeing the first fruit on the fig tree. However, once the nation was planted in the land as a luxuriant vine (10.1) decay began to set in. As it became more prosperous the nation also became more idolatrous. Yahweh's kindness in planting his people in a pleasant place had met with unfaithfulness and deceit. Israel the plant had become rotten and its fruit, to the extent that it produced any, was inedible.

In Jer. 17.7-8 a blessing is pronounced upon the person who trusts

1. The theological use of the verb נטע pertains also to the effects of planting. Cf. Reindl, 'נָטַע', col. 419: 'נָטַע ist in dieser Bedeutung ein affektiver Begriff; mit dem Pflanzen verbindet sich eine bestimmte Erwartung'.

2. When commenting on Jer. 8.13, Carroll (*Jeremiah*, p. 232) remarks that as a vineyard the nation is a miserable failure.

in Yahweh. Such a person is likened to a tree planted by the water which sends out its roots and never fails to bear fruit.[1] Following upon this idyllic picture is the stern warning of v. 10, in which Yahweh is portrayed as searching the mind and examining the heart so as to give to everyone according to his or her way (דרך; ὁδός) and according to his or her fruit (פרי; καρπός).[2] When such language is applied to the nation as a whole, one can note that Israel has refused to walk in the way of Yahweh and as a consequence has produced the kind of fruit which is abhorrent to him. The heart of the nation has been revealed to be full of deceit and corruption. As a consequence, the nation must receive the recompense owing to it.

In the discussion of the covenant curses in Deuteronomy it was noted that the ultimate punishment facing the nation, that of its removal from the land, is described by means of the imagery of 'plucking' (28.63) and 'uprooting' (29.28). This imagery corresponds directly to the metaphor of Israel as the planting of Yahweh. The figure of Yahweh uprooting his people is found in a variety of contexts. In 2 Chron 7.19-20 Solomon is warned by Yahweh that should the people turn away, forsake his commands and serve other gods, then he will 'uproot' (נתש; ἐξαίρω) the people of Israel from the land he had given them.[3] According to the pronouncement of judgment in 1 Kgs 14.15, because the nation had provoked Yahweh to anger he is determined to 'uproot (נתש; ἐκτίλλω) Israel from this good land which he gave to their fathers and scatter (זרה; λικμάω) them beyond the river'. In the lament of Ezekiel 19 (vv. 10-14) the story of Israel is recounted as that of a once fruitful vine which had been uprooted (נתש; κατακλάω) in fury and thrown down to the ground and which is now planted in a dry and thirsty wilderness. It is in Jeremiah, however, that this motif of Israel being rooted out of its land appears most

1. In Jer. 12.2 the wicked are similarly depicted as being planted by Yahweh, taking root, flourishing, and bearing fruit. Yet the type of fruit borne is suggested by the observation that 'you are near in their mouth but far from their heart'.

2. Compare the parallel statement in Jer. 32.19 where Yahweh, whose eyes are open to the ways of everyone, rewards each person according to his or her ways and according to the fruit of his or her deeds. The Septuagint (39.19) lacks the phrase 'and according to the fruit of his or her deeds'. Possibly the phrase was dropped in order to preserve the symmetry created by the double mention of 'ways'.

3. In 1 Kgs 9.6-7 the warning is virtually the same except that Yahweh threatens to cut off (כרת; ἐξαίρω) Israel from the land.

frequently.[1] At the time of his call, Jeremiah is told that his task will be both destructive and constructive. He has been set over nations and kingdoms 'to uproot (נתשׁ; ἐκριζόω) and tear down, to destroy and overthrow, to build and to plant' (1.10; cf. Sir. 49.7). With regard to the negative side of his mission, Jeremiah is to announce to the nation that the time has arrived for Yahweh's judgment on his useless plant: 'Yahweh Sebaoth, who planted you, has pronounced evil against you' (11.17) and 'Behold, what I have built I overthrow, and what I have planted I uproot (נתשׁ; ἐκτίλλω), that is, the entire land' (45.4).[2] The vineyard which had yielded such offensive fruit is rejected by Yahweh and will be completely destroyed.[3] The land of Israel, like the vineyard of Isaiah 5, is to become a waste. And the people of Israel, like an uprooted and discarded vine, are to be sent into exile far away from their land.[4] Yahweh's care in establishing his people in the land had been to no avail. The return he expected from the covenant nation had not materialized.

---

1.   The verb נתשׁ appears 19 times in the Old Testament, of which 11 appearances are in the book of Jeremiah (1.10; 12.14, 15, 17; 18.7; 24.6; 31.28, 40; 42.10; 45.4). It is notable that in the Septuagint 14 different Greek verbs are used to translate this one Hebrew verb.

2.   Compare also 6.19: 'Hear, O Land; behold, I am bringing evil on this people, the fruit (פרי; καρπός) of their schemes', which is of particular interest since it employs 'fruit' in the metaphorical sense of indicating the relationship between action and result, and 18.9-10: 'And if at any time I declare concerning a nation or kingdom that I will build or plant it, and if it does evil in my sight and does not listen to my voice, then I will reconsider the good which I intended to do to it'.

3.   Concerning this matter of Yahweh's rejection of Israel, compare the remarks of Holladay (*Jeremiah 1*, p. 186) on Jer. 5.10:

> The last colon of v. 10 is literally 'For they are not to Yahweh'. It is the reverse of the situation in the first colon of 2.3, which is literally 'Israel is holiness to Yahweh'. In the honeymoon time Israel was loyal to Yahweh and was his possession, but that time is past.

Bach ('Bauen und Pflanzen', p. 28) notes that the term 'to uproot' refers not to a general crisis for the people, 'sondern das Ende der Heilsgeschichte'. He also avers that the concepts 'to plant' and 'to uproot' correspond closely to the concepts 'to choose' and 'to reject'.

4.   J. Hausmann ('נתשׁ', *ThWAT*, V, col. 730) suggests that the utilization of the image of an uprooted plant as an analogy for exile underscores the significance of the land for the people.

Exile as a State of Darkness

Israel experienced one of the greatest reversals that could ever befall a nation. In the beginning Yahweh had liberated the nation from bondage in Egypt. He had brought the people into a special covenant relationship with himself, and had graciously showered them with every good gift. But now, having broken the covenant, they have lost possession of all those good things, not least of which is the land. Moreover, they have been rejected by God and find themselves, perhaps appropriately, once again in captivity. The story of the nation, in effect, has been that of rags to riches and back to rags again. The national catastrophe which had come upon them would have certainly impressed itself upon the people as a movement from day to night, or from light into darkness. It is not surprising, then, to discover that frequently the ordeal of exile and captivity is likened to a period of darkness.

Among the covenant curses listed in Deuteronomy 28 is that of darkness. In v. 29 the people are warned that when disaster comes upon them they 'shall grope about at noon, just as the blind do in the dark'. This 'blindness' that will afflict the people is to be understood metaphorically. The people will not actually be blind, but their condition will be just as wretched.[1] They will, in a manner of speaking, be living in the dark. The light which gave meaning and purpose to their lives will have been extinguished. It is clear from other parts of the Old Testament, especially the book of Isaiah, that the image of darkness corresponds well to the circumstance of captivity. One passage which specifically recalls the deuteronomic curse is Isa. 59.9-10. In these verses the exiles describe their gloomy predicament: 'We look for light, and behold, darkness; for brightness, but we walk in the dark. We grope along the wall like the blind, we grope like those without eyes. We stumble at noon as in the twilight.'[2] Similar language is used to illustrate the plight of the exiles in Lam. 4.14: 'They

---

1. Reference to physical blindness can be found in the previous curse of v. 28. Yahweh will smite the people with madness, blindness, and confusion of mind.

2. The verbal similarities between the two passages are quite striking. Compare Deut. 28.29: 'You shall grope (מֹשֵׁשׁ; ψηλαφάω) about at noon (צהרים; μεσημβρία), just as the blind (עור; τυφλός) do in the dark (אפלה; σκότος)' with Isa. 59.9-10: 'We walk in the dark (אפלה; ἀωρία). We grope (שׁשׁ; ψηλαφάω) along the wall like the blind (עור; τυφλός)... We stumble at noon (צהרים; μεσημβρία) as in the twilight'.

wander through the streets like blind men'.[1] It would appear that by
turning from Yahweh and his instructions, the source of their light,
the people have been cast not only from their land but also into darkness. In Isa. 8.22 the punishment in store for those who reject
Yahweh's word is announced: 'they will be thrust into thick darkness'.[2] As a consequence, the people now 'walk in darkness' and 'live
in a land of utter darkness' (Isa. 9.1 [2]).[3] The close association
between darkness and captivity is clearly stated in Ps. 107.10-11. In
this passage the miserable lot of the people under foreign domination
is compared to that of a prisoner in a dungeon: 'Some sat in darkness,
utter darkness, prisoners in affliction and irons, for they had rebelled
against the words of God'.[4] Rebellion against Yahweh had brought the
nation into the bleakest state imaginable.

This strong imagery could very easily lead one to assume that the
fate of the nation was sealed. Yet, according to Isaiah, Yahweh did not
intend that Israel should remain in this state of darkness. He has
ordained that one day a light will shine on those who dwell in gloom
(9.1). Furthermore, he will send his servant who shall open blind eyes
and free the prisoners who sit in dark dungeons (42.7).[5] This servant
will say to the captives, 'Come forth!', and to those who are in darkness, 'Appear!' (49.9).[6] A fresh offer of redemption is to be tendered

---

1.   Cf. Zeph. 1.17: 'I will bring distress on the people and they will walk like the
blind, because they sinned against Yahweh'.
2.   Cf. Jer. 13.16: 'Give glory to Yahweh your God before he brings darkness'
and Lam 3.2: 'He has driven me away and forced me to walk in darkness'.
3.   In his study of the word צלמות, D.W. Thomas ('צַלְמָוֶת in the Old Testament',
JSS 7 [1962], pp. 191-200) argues that it denotes darkness in a superlative degree.
His conclusion on p. 200 is that it may be 'the strongest word that Hebrew
possessed for darkness'.
4.   H. Ringgren, 'חָשַׁךְ', *ThWAT*, III, col. 271: 'Die Dunkelheit des
Gefängnisses macht Finsternis als Bild für Gefangenschaft geeignet'.
5.   Blindness, like imprisonment, is a symbol of the exiles' condition. Cf.
C.R. North, *The Second Isaiah* (Oxford: Oxford University Press, 1964), p. 112
and J. Lust, '"Gathering and Return" in Jeremiah and Ezekiel', in P.-M. Bogaert
(ed.), *Le livre de Jérémie* (Leuven: Leuven University Press, 1981), pp. 119-42 (132).
6.   Babylon is to receive the same fate which it had inflicted on Israel: 'Go into
the darkness!' (47.5). Compare the oracle of Jer. 30.16: 'All who devour you shall
be devoured, all your enemies shall go into exile; those who plunder you shall be
plundered, and all who prey on you I will make a prey'. Those who had cursed
Israel now find themselves cursed.

to Israel. A new day will dawn for the people in which they can enjoy once again the benefits of Yahweh's grace.

The Restoration of Israel

It is intimated already in the book of Deuteronomy that the destruction of the land and the exile of the nation is not the end of Israel's story.[1] Whereas it is true that disobedience brought upon the nation the full weight of God's wrath, this did not mean that disobedience brought the covenant relationship to an irrevocable end. Israel continued to be the people of Yahweh, despite the fact that as an unfaithful people they had experienced his judgment and the curses of the violated covenant. Yahweh was not finished with the descendants of Abraham, for there was yet a task to be accomplished. He intended to restore the fortunes of the people so that the programme implicit in the promises of the covenant with the patriarchs might be brought to completion.

The broken covenant of Sinai provided little hope for the continuing existence of the nation. Hope could be grounded only on the mercy and compassion of Yahweh, and, in particular, on the promises given in the everlasting covenant he had established with Abraham. It was to these promises, which remained in force even when the people turned away from Yahweh, that the prophets looked when they contemplated the return of the people from exile and their restoration as the people of God. At the conclusion to the book of Micah (7.18-20) appears the reminder that Yahweh will always be true to the covenant promise he gave to Abraham. He is a God who forgives sin and who does not stay angry for ever. Therefore, he will again have compassion on the people of Israel. In Isaiah the call of Abraham, the progenitor of the nation, or to use the prophet's metaphor, the rock

---

1. In the book of Deuteronomy as it now stands and in the books of the prophets as they now stand promises of restoration appear alongside prophecies of judgment. The question as to whether these promises are original to the books or are later additions lies beyond the concern of the present study since one can be reasonably certain that Matthew would have read these books in their totality as they are found in the scriptures. With reference to the oracles of the prophets, Davies (*Gospel and Land*, p. 48) notes: 'The dissection that might compel us to de-emphasize the prophecies of restoration is irrelevant to the effective role played by the totality of the prophetic texts in moulding the thought of Judaism'.

from which it was hewn, holds significance for the destiny of the nation as a whole. As Yahweh redeemed Abraham (29.22), he will also redeem the repentant nation. The call of Abraham from a distant land is to be repeated in the call of his descendants from the farthest corners of the earth (41.8-10). In addition, the blessing and promise of great offspring granted at the time of Abraham's call becomes a symbol of hope for restoration (51.1-2).[1] The Sinai covenant had been broken beyond repair, yet the Abrahamic covenant, which preceded it, ensures a future for the descendants of Abraham.

The third major covenant of the Old Testament is that established between Yahweh and David. Like the earlier covenant with Abraham, but unlike the Sinai covenant, it is promissory in nature, that is, God makes a gracious promise to David which is not subject to condition.[2] The two covenants may be characterized as 'gracious covenants'. When Yahweh avows in 2 Samuel 7 that he will establish the house and kingdom of David for ever, he promises that his 'steadfast love (חסד)' will never be taken away from him. The same term is used in Deut. 7.12 in connection with the Abrahamic covenant which is concerned with the gracious gift of land.[3] Hence these two covenants ensure that the two promises of land and kingdom will be brought to fulfilment regardless of the many obstacles introduced by Israel's turbulent history.

The judgment of Yahweh which had fallen hard upon Israel did not leave the house of David untouched. It was observed earlier that as a consequence of the unrighteousness of the Davidic kings the line is threatened with extinction. According to Jer. 22.28-30, Jehoiachin is to be cast aside along with his children so that none will sit on the throne of David ever again. And yet in the very next chapter (23.5) Yahweh announces that in the future he will raise up for David 'a righteous Branch' who will reign wisely and practice justice and righteousness. At the restoration the yoke of foreign domination will be lifted from the people and they shall serve Yahweh and David their king (Jer. 30.8-9). The coming of this Davidic king is seen in

1.   Cf. Van Seters, *Abraham*, p. 276.
2.   M. Weinfeld, 'Davidic Covenant', *IDBSup*, p. 189.
3.   The Davidic covenant shares other similarities with the Abrahamic covenant: David is promised that his name will be made great (2 Sam. 7.9; cf. Gen. 12.2); moreover, it is stated in Ps. 72.12, concerning a son of David, that all nations will be blessed through him.

Jer. 33.14-26 as the fulfilment of the promise Yahweh made to Israel and as evidence that the covenant with David had not been broken.[1] It is clear from Jeremiah and other prophetical books that the throne of David will be occupied by one of his descendants when Yahweh restores the nation of Israel.

A succinct overview of the prospective restoration of Israel is given in Deut. 30.1-10.[2] In these verses it is envisaged that the people in exile will recall the reason for their national misfortune and will be moved to return to their obligations of loyalty. When the people do return in sincerity to Yahweh, by obeying his voice with heart and soul, he will respond and 'restore their fortunes'.[3] He will gather the people he had once scattered and will bring them back into the land their fathers possessed that they might inherit (ירשׁ; κληρονομέω) it. Moreover, he will make them become more prosperous and numerous then their fathers had ever been. Whereas Yahweh, in the time of his anger, had taken delight in devastating the land and destroying the nation (Deut. 28.63), his original intention will be renewed and he will once again take delight in making the people prosper. The circumstance of the nation will change one more time.[4] Israel, which had known the pitiful transition from chosen nation to rejected nation, will experience again the call and blessing of Yahweh. The original relationship of Israel to Yahweh will be restored.

Many prophetical books deal with this theme of Israel's restoration,

---

1.   References to a future Davidic ruler in the time of restoration can be found throughout the prophetical corpus. Compare Isa. 9.1-6; 11.1; 16.5; Ezek. 34.23-24; 37.24-26; Hos. 3.5; Amos 9.11; Mic. 5.[1]2.

2.   The entire sequence of disobedience–judgment–return is presented very briefly in Deut. 4.25-31.

3.   The Hebrew phrase שׁוב שׁבות appears numerous times in passages which announce the restoration of Israel. It literally reads 'turn the turning' and denotes a return to an original state of well-being. The most comprehensive discussion of the phrase is that of E.L. Dietrich, שׁוב שׁבות: *Die endzeitliche Wiederherstellung bei den Propheten* (Giessen: Töpelmann, 1925) which can be supplemented by J.M. Bracke, 'shûb sheḇût: A Reappraisal', *ZAW* 97 (1985), pp. 233-44. In the Septuagint there is no single corresponding phrase. The Hebrew term is rendered in a variety of ways; for example, Deut. 30.3 is translated καὶ ἰάσεται κύριος τὰς ἁμαρτίας σου.

4.   Clements (*Prophecy and Covenant*, p. 118) describes the changed circumstance as a 'new beginning when Israel would be reborn, and would become once again the people of the covenant'.

yet it receives a most thorough and systematic treatment in Jeremiah
30–33. In fact, the Hebrew phrase שׁוב שׁבות ('restore the fortunes')
may be said to provide a thematic summary for this section of
Jeremiah.[1] The phrase occurs in the declaration that opens the section
(30.3) and functions, more or less, as the heading for the entire discourse. In addition, it appears in the concluding statement of 33.26.
Jeremiah's discussion of the future restoration of the nation is thus
enveloped by this phrase which signifies the end of the time of judgment and the return of the nation to a state of prosperity and well-
being. In the introductory announcement of 30.3 the theme of restoration is connected with the two promises of return from exile and the
're-inheritance' of the land: 'I will restore the fortunes of my people,
Israel and Judah, says Yahweh, and I will return them to the land
which I gave their fathers, and they will inherit it'. The latter promise
of land inheritance is certainly of greater importance to the present
study. Nonetheless, the matter of the nation's return from captivity is
not without significance, especially since this return constitutes the
precondition for the eventual repossession of the land. For this reason,
the theme of the returning exiles will be examined first.

The return of Israel from captivity constitutes a major emphasis in
the restoration chapters of the book of Jeremiah. Yahweh, who had
subjected the rebellious people to foreign domination, will break the
yoke of servitude from off their necks and snap their bonds in two
(30.8). He shall redeem the nation from the hand of a stronger nation
(31.11). Indeed, all those who had ravaged Israel shall themselves be
punished (30.11, 16, 20). He will save his people from a distant place
(30.10); he will save the remnant of Israel, bringing them from the
land of the north and gathering them from the most remote parts of
the earth (31.7-8). The cry of Rachel weeping for her exiled children
will be heard no more, for her children shall return from the land of
the enemy (31.15-17). This return of the people to their land will be,
in effect, a new exodus. An oracle of hope which appears earlier in
Jeremiah (16.14-15; 23.7-8) compares this new act of Yahweh with
the one he had performed during the first days of the nation's history.
People will no longer swear by Yahweh who brought Israel out of
Egypt, but by Yahweh who brought Israel out of the countries of

---

1.   See Bracke, 'shûb shᵉbût', p. 236. The phrase שׁוב שׁבות appears 27 times in
the Old Testament; 11 of these are in Jeremiah of which 7 are in chs. 30–33.

exile.[1] The motif of the new exodus appears elsewhere in the prophets. The first hint of the possibility of a new exodus is found in Hosea 11. In that chapter the threat of a return to Egypt (v. 5), the land of slavery from which the 'child' Israel was called, is followed by the promise in v. 11 that the people will return to their homes.[2] The imagery of the exodus is also present in the book of Ezekiel (cf. 20.34-42). It is in the book of Isaiah, however, that the new exodus theme is most fully developed. The people are reminded that once again Yahweh will choose Israel (14.1). One more time he will dry up the Red Sea; he will also dry up the Euphrates river. There will be a highway for the remnant just as there was for the Israelites when they came up from Egypt (11.15-16; cf. 43.19; 57.14; 62.10). Furthermore, as the redeemed journey along the highway, the wilderness will blossom (35.1-10; 43.19). The spectacle of the second exodus will thoroughly outshine that of the first. It is of little wonder that the people are told to forget the former things (43.18). Yahweh will indeed do a new and surpassing thing.

The action of Yahweh in gathering the people from the places to which they were scattered is frequently likened to a shepherd gathering his flock. It has already been observed that in Jeremiah the leaders of the nation are condemned because they 'destroy and scatter the sheep of my pasture' (23.1). As a consequence of such ill treatment the people have become 'lost sheep' (50.6, צאן אבדות; LXX [27.6], πρόβατα ἀπολωλότα).[3] In the future restoration of Israel, however, Yahweh will gather his people and be to them as a shepherd who watches over his flock (31.10). Micah also refers to the gathered remnant of Israel under the image of assembled sheep.[4] They will be brought together like sheep in a fold (2.12), and cared for by a shepherd out of Bethlehem (5.2-4). A detailed summary of this motif is found in Ezekiel 34. The people are scattered over the face of the

1. According to Holladay (*Jeremiah 1*, p. 623), the implication of this oracle is that the new exodus 'will have to overshadow the old'.

2. D.E. Gowan, *Eschatology in the Old Testament* (Edinburgh: T. & T. Clark, 1986), p. 26.

3. Compare Jer. 10.21: 'The shepherds are stupid. . . and all their flock is scattered' and Zech. 10.2: 'Therefore the people wander as sheep oppressed for want of a shepherd'.

4. Note also Isa. 49.9 where it is said of the returning exiles that they will feed beside the way and find pasture on the barren hills. In Isa. 40.11 Yahweh is portrayed as a shepherd tending his flock.

earth because the shepherds of Israel had been negligent in their duty. Therefore, Yahweh himself will seek out his lost sheep and deliver them from harm. He will set over them one shepherd, his servant David, who will provide for them.[1] In the end, they shall know that Yahweh is with them and that they are his people.

This remnant of gathered sheep is made up of those who have turned back to Yahweh. In Jer. 29.13 the restoration of the people is made contingent on their repentance. He will listen to those who call upon him and be found by those who seek him. Presumably, these are the only ones he will bring back from captivity.[2] The people acknowledge in 31.18-20 that even though they had turned away they were now repentant, having learned from Yahweh's harsh discipline.[3] The terrible experience of exile had taught Israel what it had been unwilling to learn from generations of prophets, namely, the futility of straying from Yahweh and his commands. Listed among that remnant who will return from exile are the blind and the lame, pregnant women and those in labour. Yahweh will lead these ones along a level path where they will not stumble (31.8-9). An interesting parallel to this image is found in Mic. 4.6-7 where Yahweh declares, 'I will gather the lame and I will assemble the scattered ones and those whom I have injured; I will make the lame a remnant and those cast off a strong nation'. In Ezek. 34.16 it is noted that Yahweh will bind up the sheep which are crippled and strengthen the weak, but will destroy the fat and the strong. Similarly, it is announced in Zeph. 3.11-13, another passage which refers to the gathered flock, that Yahweh will remove from their midst those people who are proud and haughty and leave a people meek and humble who seek refuge in him.[4] All of these

1.   Compare Ezek. 37.24: 'My servant David shall be king over them, and they shall all have one shepherd'. In Jer. 23.4 it is *shepherds* which Yahweh will set over the people to care for them, although the following verse speaks of the Davidic king who will be raised up.

2.   Diepold (*Israels Land*, p. 139) observes that 'Umkehr und Rückkehr gehören zusammen; Umkehr ist die Bedingung für die Rückkehr'.

3.   The Septuagint renders 31.19 (LXX 38.19): ὕστερον αἰχμαλωσίας μου μετενόησα.

4.   A.S. Kapelrud (*The Message of the Prophet Zephaniah* [Oslo: Universitetsforlaget, 1975], p. 33) remarks that 'in Zeph. 3.11f. the dominating view is clearly that the poor and humble people were the truly righteous, while the proud and haughty were considered as enemies of Yahweh'. On this matter of the 'humility' of the remnant, compare Isa. 14.32; 29.19; 49.13; 61.1-3; Hos. 2.17 [15].

passages suggest that the remnant is comprised of those who are truly dependent upon Yahweh. Their weakness and vulnerability leaves little room for pride and self-sufficiency. They are the ones who have learned humility from the hardship of adversity and who are now willing to return in obedience to the ways of Yahweh. The new exodus means the return to the land of a new people of God.

The new exodus also means that Yahweh will establish a new covenant with his people. The principal passage in which this new covenant is introduced is Jer. 31.31-34, where it is emphasized that the new covenant will be different from the earlier covenant of the first exodus.[1] The problem with the Sinai covenant is that, because it was written outwardly on tables of stone, it engendered insincere obedience and even outright disobedience. Under the old covenant the people had rebelled against the law of Yahweh and in the end had come to forsake him. The result was the reversal of the relationship between Yahweh and Israel. In the new covenant the law will be internalized; Yahweh will write it upon the hearts of the people. Thus the law will become part of the total will of the people.[2] They will obey the commands of Yahweh because they want to and not from any sense of obligation. The law itself will not be changed; it remains a true expression of the will of Yahweh. Rather what is changed are the hearts of those who are required to obey the law: 'I will put the fear of me in their hearts, that they may not turn from me' (32.40). This conception of a new condition of the human heart corresponds to the image of the 'circumcised heart' which appears in Deuteronomy and Jeremiah.[3] In the exhortation of Deut. 10.16 this image, which denotes a radical change of heart, appears in contrast to the stubborn heart. The implication is that this operation is essential to remedy the chronic obduracy of the human heart. It is emphasised in Deut. 30.6 that when Yahweh restores the people he will perform the operation

---

1.   This is the only passage in the Hebrew Bible where ברית is qualified by 'new' (חדשה).

2.   W.L. Holladay, 'The New Covenant', *IDBSup*, p. 624.

3.   In Deut. 10.16 and Jer. 4.4 the people are urged to circumcise their hearts; in Deut. 30.6 it is Yahweh who will perform the operation. Concerning this matter of a new condition of the heart, one might compare those passages in Ezekiel which speak of Yahweh giving the people a new heart and a new spirit so that they might keep his commands (11.19-20; 18.31; 36.26-27). Note also that in Zeph. 3.13 it is said of the remnant that they will neither do wrong nor speak with deceit.

himself. Clearly the people had been unable to effect the necessary change; it required the direct action of Yahweh. Yet once he brings about this transformation in the people they will be able to walk according to his ways. When the new covenant is concluded, Yahweh's people shall all know him. He in turn will forgive their wrongdoing and remember their sin no more.

At that time Yahweh will plant in the land the remnant of Israel, the people of the new covenant, just as earlier he had planted the nation of the first exodus. The time of judgment, with its destruction and uprooting, has ended; Yahweh is now committed to 'watch over them to build and to plant' (Jer. 31.28; cf. 24.6-7). As Yahweh plants them in the land, 'with all my heart and soul', he will rejoice in doing them good (32.41). Once again there will be heard the sounds of joy and gladness, together with the voices of the bride and bridegroom and those bringing thank offerings to the house of Yahweh (33.10-11). All of those things which the people had lost during the time of judgment will be returned in abundance as the people will dwell in the land in peace and security.[1] This picture of Yahweh replanting the returned exiles also appears at the end of Amos (9.14-15) in a context describing Yahweh's promise to 'restore the fortunes' of Israel. In the concluding statement of the book Yahweh affirms that Israel will be planted in the land, 'and they will never again be uprooted from the land I have given them'. An even more magnificent portrayal of Israel's renewal is found in Isa. 60.19-22. The dark night of exile will give way to a bright and glorious day. The sun will never again set for Israel, for Yahweh will be its everlasting light. In the passage the remnant is characterized as the shoot of Yahweh's planting, the work of his hands to display his glory. Similar language is used in Isa. 61.3 where the people are called oaks of righteousness,[2] the planting of Yahweh. Yahweh's earlier attempt to nurture a plant that would produce good fruit had ended in failure. He will attempt the project again

---

1.   It is observed in Jer. 31.25 that Yahweh will refresh and satisfy every languishing soul, which stands in marked contrast with the curse of Deut. 28.65. Note also that Yahweh promises David in 2 Sam. 7.10-11 that he will appoint a place (מָקוֹם; cf. Jer. 32.37) for his people Israel, will plant (נָטַע; καταφυτεύω) them, and will give them and David rest (נוּחַ; ἀναπαύω) from their enemies. There is considerable debate as to whether the verbs in vv. 9-11 should be rendered in the past or future tense. Usually they are given a future translation as in the Septuagint.

2.   The Septuagint at this point reads κληθήσονται γενεαὶ δικαιοσύνης.

and this time it will succeed. Part of the reason for the success is that all the people will be righteous. The intention of Yahweh when he first called the people of Israel, that they would become a righteous people, will have now been realized. His other objective, that this righteous people possess the land, will also be achieved: 'they shall inherit (ירשׁ; κληρονομέω) the land for ever' (60.21).

It was noted above that the remnant which returns to inherit the land is comprised of those who are meek and humble, that is, those who have learned to seek refuge in Yahweh and who are willing to submit to his will. The proud and arrogant, on the other hand, are dispatched. A similar emphasis is evident in Psalm 36 [37]. A major concern of the psalm is to provide an answer to the question of who will inherit the land. The wicked appear to enjoy prosperity despite the fact that their ways are evil. Yet they are not to be envied, since they shall be 'cut off' (כרת, vv. 9, 22, 28, 34, 38). They will perish (v. 20) and be destroyed (v. 38); like the grass they will wither (v. 2). The righteous, however, will 'inherit (ירשׁ; κληρονομέω) the land' and dwell in it forever (v. 29). Throughout the psalm the attributes of the righteous ones who inherit the land are catalogued. They are those who hope in Yahweh (v. 9),[1] who are meek (v. 11) and blameless (v. 18).[2] Hence the people who follow a course of patient trust in Yahweh, who acknowledge their dependence upon him and who keep his way will receive from him the land of promise. Such meek ones he will exalt to possess the land (v. 34). A précis of the teaching of the psalm is furnished in v. 22: 'Those Yahweh blesses shall inherit the land, but those he curses shall be cut off'.[3] This declaration would function just as well as a summary of the entire story of Israel as it has been outlined in the present discussion. Those who are unfaithful to Yahweh stand under his curse and in the end are cut off. The

1. Cf. Isa. 57.13: 'The one who takes refuge in me will inherit the land'.
2. Of the meek it is further said that they will take delight in great peace and of the blameless that their inheritance (נחלה; κληρονομία) will last for ever.
3. The psalm's associations with the covenant tradition, especially at v. 22, are frequently noted by commentators; cf. A. Weiser, *The Psalms* (Philadelphia: Westminster Press, 1962), p. 322: 'The psalmist reverts to the ideas associated with the tradition of the Covenant, that is to say, to the promise of the land, to judgment and salvation, and to blessing and curse'; and P.C. Craigie, *Psalms 1–50* (Waco, TX: Word Books, 1983), p. 298: 'The language of the proverb recalls the blessing and curse section of the Hebrew covenant'.

faithful, however, receive his blessing and become the recipients of the promise made to Abraham.

The disobedience of Israel, which resulted in the exile of the nation, had meant the deferral of Yahweh's promises to the patriarchs. But now the presence of a righteous remnant who are able and prepared to fulfil Yahweh's purpose, and who for that reason may be considered the true descendants of Abraham, makes the realization of those promises a certainty. At various places in the prophetic restoration oracles references to the patriarchal promises occur. On some occasions the allusion is quite subtle as in Zeph. 3.20 where it is stated that, when Yahweh 'restores the fortunes' of the people, he will give them a name and make them to be praised among all the peoples of the earth. This reflects the promise given to Abraham in Gen. 12.2-3 (cf. Deut. 26.19). On other occasions the promises impose themselves more forcefully as in Isaiah 60. The theme of inheriting the land (v. 21), which is the central promise given to Abraham, has already been noted. The promise that the descendants of Abraham would become a great nation (Gen. 12.2; 17.6) clearly resonates in the affirmation of v. 22 that 'the least will become a thousand, and the smallest a mighty nation'. And finally, the promise that all nations would benefit from the calling of Abraham (Gen. 12.3; 22.18) meets its fulfilment in the first part of the chapter which portrays the coming of the Gentiles to the glorious city of Yahweh. In Jer. 12.14-17 this theme is treated under the familiar imagery of planting/building and uprooting/destroying. The nations which learn the ways of Yahweh's people will be 'built up in the midst of my people'; but those who do not listen will be uprooted and destroyed. It would seem that in much the same way that Israel endures as a 'purged' remnant, so also these other nations survive God's judgment in the form of a remnant which does the will of Yahweh.[1] When Israel is restored, the purpose of Yahweh for the descendants of Abraham and for all the families of the earth will near its completion. In fulfilment of the everlasting covenants made with Abraham and David, Yahweh will plant the descendants of Abraham securely in the land where they shall be ruled over by a son of David. Yahweh will be their God for ever, and, as his pleasant planting, they will flourish in the land and bear fruit for his glory.

---

1.   It is noteworthy that in Jeremiah the phrase שׁוב שׁבות is also employed with reference to other nations (Moab, 48.47; Ammon, 49.6; Elam, 49.39).

Conclusion

The objective of this chapter was to identify and describe a credible
Old Testament schema of recompense which could have provided the
background against which Matthew developed his own teaching on the
theme. A very convincing schema, and indeed the fundamental recompense schema of the Old Testament, is that which is centred on the
land. The promised land along with the blessings associated with it
became, in effect, the reward for the people of Israel. Conversely, the
loss of the land became for the nation the ultimate punishment. The
immense importance attached to the land becomes clear when it is
considered that the three major covenants in the Old Testament are all
intimately connected with it. The gift of the land forms the heart of
the Abrahamic covenant. Similarly, the Sinai covenant is concerned
with setting forth the essential requirements for entrance and success
in the land. The land is also implicit in the Davidic covenant, which
refers to a continuing Davidic dynasty, since without the land there is
neither realm nor rule. The two covenants made with Abraham and
David guarantee that there will always be land and kingdom for the
people of God.

The system of recompense which is of relevance to the present
study inheres, however, in the Sinai covenant. Yahweh gave to his
people laws and commandments to the end that they might become a
holy and righteous people. At the same time, the laws established the
condition for their continuing existence in the land. Presumed in the
law of Yahweh is the possibility of blessing and curse, blessing if the
people are obedient and curse if they are not, and both of these are
understood to be connected with the land. Obedience means that the
nation will enjoy a good and peaceful life in the land. Disobedience
inevitably brings the devastation of the land, the death of its inhabitants and ultimately the ejection of the nation from the land.
Lamentably, the nation chose the latter course leading from disobedience to destruction. Hence the curse of the spurned God consumed the
land and the people of Israel suffered greatly under the full weight of
his wrath. In the end those who survived were uprooted from their
once pleasant land and were cast into the darkness of exile. This
recompense schema which undergirds the story of Israel in the land is
epitomized in the words of Psalm 36 [37].22: 'Those Yahweh blesses
shall inherit the land, but those he curses shall be cut off'.

The prophets discerned that the story of God's dealings with his people was not to end in such ignominy. They understood that the promises made to Abraham and David were yet to be honoured and that these promises provided hope for the people of Israel. Yahweh would restore a righteous remnant of the people to the land of promise where they would dwell in joy and peace under a Davidic king. When the Old Testament story of Israel is concluded, the fulfilment of these promises still lies in the future. It is at this point that the story is taken up and continued by Matthew.

Chapter 2

'THOSE YAHWEH BLESSES SHALL INHERIT THE LAND'
THE TEACHING ON REWARD IN THE GOSPEL OF MATTHEW

In the previous chapter a recompense schema was outlined which
commends itself as a very credible background to the Matthaean treatment of the subject. The task now remains to demonstrate that
Matthew has indeed formulated his own teaching on the topic with
reference to this schema. In the present chapter the positive side of the
Matthaean teaching on recompense, that is, the teaching on reward,
will be examined. The next chapter will treat the subject of punishment, that is to say, negative recompense. It is important to note at the
outset, however, that in the Gospel of Matthew the two themes of
reward and punishment do not receive such individual and separate
treatment. In many contexts they appear together side by side, thus
creating a fearful symmetry of promise and threat. Nonetheless, it is
often the case that the weight of emphasis falls more slightly on the
one side than on the other. For this reason, it is possible to consider
some passages under the rubric of reward and others under the rubric
of punishment. It is, of course, unavoidable that certain passages must
be considered in both chapters, albeit from different perspectives.
This presents no problem, however, and since the examination of the
two themes is greatly facilitated when they are dealt with separately,
such an approach would appear to be justified.

It is clear from Chapter 1 that the system of recompense described
there is closely connected with the history of God's dealings with the
people of Israel. The gift of the land, which, according to this schema,
becomes the locus of the people's reward, is central to the three great
covenants which give meaning and impetus to the story of God's
people. That story had its beginnings in the covenant promise of the
land given to Abraham the patriarch at the time of his call. Centuries
later this promise received partial fulfilment in the nation's possession

of the land at the time of the conquest. Not long before the conquest Yahweh had entered into a covenant relationship with the descendants of Abraham at Sinai; and it is the stipulations contained in this covenant which were to govern Israel's life in the land. Later still, at the high point of the monarchy, a covenant is made with David the king, promising him an everlasting dynasty. Yet in spite of these many gifts and blessings, the nation plunged into a spiritual decline which witnessed the breaking of the Sinai covenant, the cutting off of the Davidic line and the eventual ejection of the people from the land. This did not mean, however, the conclusion of Israel's story nor the termination of God's promises. Israel's prophets looked forward to a renewal of the promises of land and kingdom when Yahweh would once again restore the fortunes of his people.

It is evident that Matthew is interested in the history of God's dealings with the people of Israel, and, in particular, in presenting the life of Jesus as the culmination of that story and as the point at which the ancient promises converge. Thus, before examining Matthew's teaching on reward, it would be beneficial to draw attention to certain noticeable features of his Gospel which relate it to the Old Testament story of God's dealings with his people and which provide insight into how Matthew envisages the continuation of that story from the climactic moment of Jesus' appearance in Israel. Such an exercise is of value since this story is very much of a piece with Matthew's teaching on recompense.

The Restoring of Israel

Matthew's keen interest in the history of God's people is reflected in the fact that he has chosen to begin his Gospel in a rather distinctive way by means of a genealogical list which traces the lineage of Jesus from Abraham. This opening feature of the Gospel makes it unique among the writings of the New Testament and of early Christian literature.[1] Presumably, Matthew took great care in the construction

---

1. H.C. Waetjen, 'The Genealogy as the Key to the Gospel according to Matthew', *JBL* 95 (1976), pp. 205-30 (205). The additional comments which appear alongside some of the names in the list prompt R.T. Hood ('The Genealogies of Jesus', in A. Wikgren [ed.], *Early Christian Origins* [Chicago: Quadrangle Books, 1961], pp. 1-15 [10]) to describe it as 'a brief history written in the genealogical manner'.

of this introduction to his account so that it might announce to his readers certain themes and emphases which will recur throughout the Gospel.[1] It is of particular significance for the present study that Matthew begins his narrative with the statement that Jesus Christ is 'the son of David, the son of Abraham' (υἱοῦ Δαυὶδ υἱοῦ 'Αβραάμ). Implicit in this statement is the notion that the promises which were given to these two prominent historical figures, with whom Yahweh established everlasting covenants, find their fulfilment in Jesus. He is the descendant of Abraham and David *par excellence*, inasmuch as the blessings and hopes which were identified with the father of the nation and with its greatest king will be realized definitively in him.[2] Matthew's intention of presenting the life of Jesus as the acme of Israel's history is thus evident at the very outset of his Gospel.

The structure of the genealogy is also worthy of note. Matthew, in a highly artificial manner, divides the history of Israel into three separate periods, each comprising fourteen generations.[3] The first period extends from Abraham to David, the second from David to the exile (ἡ μετοικεσία Βαβυλῶνος), and the third from the exile to Jesus. It is interesting that the catastrophic event of foreign captivity and not a person should mark the end of the second period and the beginning of the third. One may suggest from this schematized overview of Israel's history that the two gifts of land (Abraham) and kingdom (David) which were lost at the time of the exile are about to be restored with the coming of Jesus.[4] Jesus, therefore, would stand at that point in time which marks the end of the era of exile and the beginning of the

1. Note the comment of J. Gnilka (*Das Matthäusevangelium* [Freiburg: Herder, 1988], I, p. 6): 'Antike Autoren haben die Anfänge und die Schlüsse ihrer literarischen Werke mit besonderer Sorgfalt gestaltet'.

2. W.D. Davies and D.C. Allison, Jr (*The Gospel according to Saint Matthew* [Edinburgh: T. & T. Clark, 1988], I, p. 187) observe that the genealogy portrays Jesus as the '*telos* of salvation-history, in whom the promises to Abraham and David find their yes'.

3. It is generally accepted that the contrived pattern of the genealogy was suggested by the name of David, which in Hebrew has three consonants whose numerical value is fourteen.

4. Davies and Allison (*Matthew*, I, p. 180) note that the second major break in the genealogy provides a clue to Matthew's eschatological orientation, that is, the kingdom that was established with David and lost at the exile will be restored. However, they fail to notice that the coextensive concept of restoration to the land is also in view.

period of restoration. Regardless of how one interprets the phrase βίβλος γενέσεως which appears at the very beginning of the Gospel,[1] it is clear that according to Matthew the appearance of Jesus signifies the beginning of a new era for the people of God.[2] The day of redemption, regathering and blessing to which the prophetic salvation oracles had pointed has now dawned for the people of Israel.

The affirmation that Jesus is the son of Abraham signifies much more than that he is a true Israelite.[3] As it has already been observed, the statement infers that the promises given to Abraham find their fulfilment in him. Most often this connection between Jesus and Abraham is associated with the specific promise that Abraham would become a source of blessing to all nations. This view is generally supported with reference to the universalistic emphasis which is implicit in the genealogy and quite evident elsewhere in the Gospel, especially in the mission charge with which the narrative is concluded.[4] Thus, in

---

1.   Davies and Allison (*Matthew*, I, pp. 149-54) believe that there is a strong case for reading Mt. 1.1 as a general title: 'Book of the New Genesis wrought by Jesus Christ, son of David, son of Abraham'. Note also the discussion in W.D. Davies, *The Setting of the Sermon on the Mount* (Cambridge: Cambridge University Press, 1964), pp. 67-73, in which he argues that the implication of the first verse of the Gospel is that the coming of Jesus 'inaugurates a new era, and, indeed, a new creation'. Gnilka (*Matthäusevangelium*, I, pp. 6-8), on the other hand, prefers to understand the phrase as referring to the genealogy alone. Even so, he acknowledges that Mt. 1.1 has 'übergreifende Bedeutung' and perhaps should be read as 'eine Art Resümee der matthäischen Theologie'.

2.   Waetjen ('Genealogy', p. 212) remarks that Matthew's design is to present Jesus as the culmination of Israel's history and, at the same time, as the beginning of the history that is yet to be written.

3.   Matthew's characterization of Jesus as not only the 'son of David' but also the 'son of Abraham' has created difficulties for some scholars. Concerning the latter title, M.D. Johnson (*The Purpose of the Biblical Genealogies* [Cambridge: Cambridge University Press, 1969], p. 219) avers: 'It is clear that this title does not have the importance of "Son of David" in Matthew'. Similarly, U. Luz (*Matthew 1–7* [Minneapolis: Augsburg, 1989], p. 104) remarks that the title does not appear to make a special statement about Jesus. The same author affirms (p. 109) that the genealogy would be easier to understand if it began with David rather than with Abraham. Whereas it is true that the title 'son of David' resonates clearly throughout the subsequent narrative, one should not conclude from this that the title 'son of Abraham' is any less important. It too is resonant in the Gospel, though, admittedly, in a more subtle manner.

4.   With respect to the genealogy, E. Schweizer (*The Good News according to Matthew* [Atlanta: John Knox, 1975], p. 25), for example, notes that the four non-

Jesus, the true seed of Abraham, the promise is fulfilled and salvation is brought to the Gentiles. This would appear to be a valid explanation of the evidence. At the same time, however, one is justified in asking whether that is the only Abrahamic promise to which Matthew is referring. Certainly it is possible, and indeed probable, that the new era for the people of God which is introduced by the coming of Jesus includes as part of its dimension the restoration of the people to the land in accordance with the covenant promise given to Abraham. An examination of the references to Abraham in the Gospel suggests that this indeed is the case

Apart from the genealogy Abraham is not mentioned very often in the Gospel. Nevertheless, two of the three passages in which his name does appear are of considerable interest to the theme of the restoration of Israel, since they address the question as to which people compose the true descendants of Abraham and thus become the heirs to the promise.[1] The first such reference to Abraham is found in the preaching of John the Baptist. Within the context of the Gospel the description of John's ministry immediately follows upon the first two chapters of the Gospel which treat Jesus' birth and infancy. In those introductory chapters Matthew is careful to note that the events there described are a fulfilment of prophecy. In a similar way, John's appearance in the wilderness is depicted as the fulfilment of prophecy. It is noteworthy that in Mt. 3.3 the work of John is described with reference to Isa. 40.3, a text which encourages the exiles with the anticipation of an imminent return to the land with Yahweh. One might infer from this connection that the second exodus is about to begin.[2] In Mt. 3.7-10 John the Baptist is shown attacking the presumption of the Pharisees and Sadducees, who mistakenly believe that physical descent from Abraham confers on them a status which is

Jewish women listed there (Tamar, Rahab, Ruth and Bathsheba) are meant to prefigure the work of God in Jesus that will embrace Gentiles as well as Jews.

1.   In the third passage, at 22.32, Abraham's name appears as a component of the formulaic expression qualifying God which occurs frequently in the Bible (see p. 69 n. 3). The formula is utilized there to support the argument that God is the God of the living, thus implying that Abraham, along with Isaac and Jacob, will share in the resurrection.

2.   Note also that the return of the infant Jesus from Egypt is described in Mt. 2.15 with reference to Hos. 11.1. This appears to portend the new exodus that will take place.

proof against the coming wrath.[1] In language very reminiscent of the Old Testament prophets he warns them that unless their repentance is genuine they will be destroyed in God's judgment like so many worthless trees. Physical descent from Abraham possesses no advantage unless it is accompanied by the faith, humility and gratitude which should characterize those who look to Abraham as a forebear.[2] In essence, those Jews whose conduct provides no support to back up their claim of ancestry will receive no better treatment at the judgment than unbelieving Gentiles.

The pride and self-assurance of the Pharisees and Sadducees is further undermined by the pronouncement that God is able to raise up children to Abraham from the stones of the ground. This curious image probably is to be understood as an allusion to Isa. 51.1-2, in which Abraham is represented as the rock from which his descendants were hewn. Just as God formerly caused children to come forth from the rock Abraham, so he can now raise up from the stones new children.[3] The implication of John's observation is that those Jews who assume that genetic membership in the covenant nation is sufficient for redemption will receive a tragic surprise when the verdict goes against them and their place in the redeemed community is taken by others. It was noted in the previous chapter that Isa. 51.1-2 is one of the passages that extended the hope of restoration to the exiled nation by reminding the people of the promises given to Abraham. If John's words are in fact an allusion to this text, then it is possible that the point of his remark is that, even though God will honour his promises to Abraham by restoring his descendants, some of those descendants, represented by these Pharisees and Sadducees, will be

---

1. The implicit claim of the Pharisees and Sadducees, which John so vigorously denounces, is defined succinctly by Davies and Allison (*Matthew*, I, p. 307): 'Abrahamic descent was not only a necessary condition for salvation but a sufficient condition'.

2. Compare the comment of P. Gaechter (*Das Matthäus Evangelium* [Innsbruck: Tyrolia, 1963], p. 93): 'Nur wer den Sinn Abrahams hatte, brauchte sich vor dem Strafzorn Gottes nicht zu fürchten'.

3. J. Jeremias ('λίθος', *TDNT*, IV, p. 271) interprets John's words with reference to Isa. 51.1-2; but, in addition, he notes that stones are mentioned because they are lifeless, thus corresponding to the miraculous birth of Isaac from the 'lifeless rock' Abraham. This interpretation is possible; however, the word-play that is frequently noted between the Hebrew words 'sons' (בנים) and 'stones' (אבנים) offers a more direct explanation.

excluded from God's redeeming activity because of their refusal to repent (cf. Mt. 21.31b-32). In the prophets, repentance is often depicted as the condition of restoration.[1] Thus, those Jews for whom reliance on a physical link with Abraham precludes a return to God in true repentance will become disinherited children of Abraham. They will have no claim to the blessings, but will receive instead the penalty which is in store for the unrepentant. On the other hand, those Jews who do repent, along with the believing Gentiles who make up the 'new children' of Abraham, constitute the true heirs of Abraham who shall receive the promised blessings.

A similar emphasis is found in Mt. 8.10-12. In chs. 8–9 Matthew recounts a series of miraculous deeds performed by Jesus which, on the one hand, complement the authoritative teaching presented in chs. 5–7 and, on the other hand, highlight the faith and unbelief which Jesus encountered in the course of his ministry. An impressive example of faith is provided in the anecdote of the centurion who had come to Jesus to find healing for his servant. Jesus, amazed at the vigour of the man's faith,[2] is prompted to remark that, although many will come from 'east and west' to share with the patriarchs the joys of the kingdom, the 'sons of the kingdom' will themselves be excluded. This passage includes the first mention in Matthew of the word πίστις, which, according to 23.23, is one of the 'weightier matters' of the law. Yet the faith that is present in this Gentile centurion is sadly lacking among the people of Israel. For this reason, many in Israel will not take their place alongside Abraham, Isaac and Jacob in the future inheritance.[3] They may be 'sons of the kingdom', that is, one might expect that as descendants of the patriarchs they should inherit

1. Isa. 55.6-7; Jer. 29.13; 31.18-20; Hos. 5.15–6.3; 14.2-4 [1-3]; Joel 2.12-14; Mal. 3.7; cf. Deut. 30.2.

2. It is noteworthy that the verb θαυμάζω is used of Jesus only at Mt. 8.10 (= Lk. 7.9), where he marvels at the faith of a Gentile, and at Mk 6.6, where he marvels at the lack of faith among his Jewish neighbours.

3. It is interesting to note that throughout the Old Testament whenever the three patriarchs are named together it is either with reference to Yahweh, that is, he is the God of Abraham, Isaac and Jacob (e.g. Exod. 4.5; 1 Kgs 18.36; 1 Chron. 29.18; cf. Mt. 22.32), or with reference to the land of promise (e.g. Gen. 50.24; Exod. 33.1; Lev. 26.42; Deut. 34.4; 2 Kgs 13.23; Ps. 105.8-11). It is possible that the land of promise is concealed in this mention of the patriarchs, especially when one considers the close conceptual link between land and kingdom. Moreover, the eschatological banquet will be enjoyed by those who are restored to the land (see Isa. 25–27).

the promises; nevertheless, because of their unbelief any privilege they might lay claim to has been revoked.[1] The place of these unbelieving Jews, and, in a sense, the claim to the title 'sons of the kingdom' (cf. 13.38), is taken by the many from east and west who will come to feast with the patriarchs at the future consummation of the kingdom.

This picture of a multitude which will come from 'east and west' is regularly interpreted with reference to the prophetic motif of the eschatological pilgrimage of the nations to Mount Zion (e.g. Isa. 2.2-4).[2] According to this view, the centurion is representative of the many Gentiles who will come to believe in the God of Israel and who will, as a consequence, receive a share in the future kingdom. It is doubtful, however, whether this interpretation provides the best assessment of the evidence.[3] The fact that the 'many' stand in contrast with the 'sons of the kingdom' does suggest that Gentiles are in view. However, it need not follow that the 'many' who will partake of the eschatological meal are comprised exclusively of Gentiles, any more than it follows that all Jews, that is, 'sons of the kingdom', will be excluded from the meal. It is important to realize that the two directions, east and west, frequently appear in texts which speak of the return of the Jewish exiles to their land.[4] Furthermore, the theme of the returning exiles is linked to the motif of the eschatological feast

---

1.   G.R. Beasley-Murray (*Jesus and the Kingdom of God* [Grand Rapids: Eerdmans, 1986], p. 172) observes that the scandal of this saying is difficult to imagine, since it was axiomatic for Jesus' Jewish contemporaries that the kingdom belonged to them. Cf. Marguerat, *Jugement*, pp. 253-54: 'Le jugement prononcé sur Israël est par excellence *un acte de dépossession*, dans lequel Dieu retirera à ceux qui étaient les siens les promesses sacrées du passé' (his italics).

2.   The most influential presentation of this interpretation of Mt. 8.11-12 is found in J. Jeremias, *Jesus' Promise to the Nations* (Philadelphia: Fortress Press, 1982), pp. 55-63.

3.   Note the valuable discussion of the present passage and critique of Jeremias's position in D.C. Allison, Jr, 'Who will Come from East and West? Observations on Mt. 8.11-12–Lk. 13.28-29', *IBS* 11 (1989), pp. 158-70.

4.   Note, for example, Isa. 43.5 and Zech. 8.7 (cf. Deut. 30.4). Allison ('Observations', p. 162) observes that in the biblical tradition 'east' often denotes Assyria or Babylon, while Egypt can function as the equivalent of 'west'. He notes a number of passages which speak of the exiles returning not from east and west but from Assyria and Egypt (cf. Isa. 27.13; Hos. 11.11; Zech. 10.10). Additionally, Allison is able to affirm that not once is 'east and west' associated with the eschatological journey of the Gentiles.

(cf. Isa. 25–27). Thus, it must be acknowledged that these verses are as suggestive of the return of Jewish exiles as they are of the ingathering of Gentiles. In fact, it would appear that an interesting blend of concepts is reflected in these verses.[1] The centurion and other believing Gentiles are numbered among the 'many', but so also are those faithful Jews whom the prophets envisaged returning to the land.

An important implication of this passage is that the remnant which will be restored to the land is comprised of faithful Jews and Gentiles. It is important to bear in mind that although Jesus does praise the faith of the centurion in a way which reflects poorly on the Jewish nation (compare also his commendation of the great faith of the Canaanite woman in 15.28), it is clear from Matthew that there are some in Israel who do possess faith (cf. 9.2, 22, 29). It is significant, however, that these are people who are afflicted in one way or another. One is struck by the correspondence with those passages such as Jer. 31.8-9 and Mic. 4.6-7 which describe the remnant as comprised of those who are weak and injured.[2] God will raise up new children to Abraham, as demonstrated in the centurion, and these new children will be joined together with the existing faithful children to make up the remnant that will inherit the promises.[3] The Pharisees and Sadducees along with

1. Compare the comment of R.T. France ('Exegesis in Practice: Two Examples', in I.H. Marshall [ed.], *New Testament Interpretation* [Grand Rapids: Eerdmans, 1977], p. 261), that 'Jesus, in predicting the coming of the Gentiles (itself an Old Testament idea), deliberately does so in words recalling Old Testament hopes of the regathering of *Israel*' (his italics).

2. Allison ('Observations', pp. 166-67) wishes to identify the 'many' as the Jews of the diaspora and the 'sons of the kingdom' as those Jews who derive confidence from dwelling in the land of Israel. Yet geographical considerations play no role in the text. The 'east and west' whence the many come is but part of a metaphorical expression denoting the faithful who return. Jews, wherever they might live, are assigned to the categories of 'many' or 'sons of the kingdom' on the basis of their faith, or lack of faith.

3. The term 'remnant' is used here in the sense of a small part of the people, chosen on the basis of faith and holiness, which by the mercy of God survives punishment in order to become the new bearers of the promises. All the promises of the chosen people are transferred to this group. See H. Gross, 'Remnant', *EBT*, II, pp. 741-43. The designation 'remnant' is not used in the Gospels for the new community of God. Nonetheless, there are sufficient conceptual and verbal links between the Gospels, especially Matthew, and the Old Testament remnant theme to justify the use of the term. Cf. B.F. Meyer, 'Jesus and the Remnant of Israel', *JBL* 84 (1965), pp. 123-30.

all other 'sons of the kingdom' who presume upon their membership in the covenant community will, like the proud and arrogant of Zeph. 3.11-13, be removed from that community and have no share in the inheritance promised to Abraham.

The title son of David occurs frequently in Matthew's Gospel, and identifies Jesus as the righteous Davidic king of prophetic expectation who will be set over the people when the kingdom is restored. With respect to the restoration of Israel, Matthew is particularly interested in portraying Jesus as the eschatological shepherd king who will gather the scattered flock. Like David, he is born in Bethlehem, thus fulfilling the prophecy of Mic. 5.1-3 [2-4] that out of Bethlehem shall come a ruler who will shepherd (Mt. 2.6, ποιμαίνω) the people of Israel.[1] The necessity for gathering the people is made apparent by the spectacle of the weary and harrassed multitudes which are likened to sheep without a shepherd (9.36). The same image is employed in a number of Old Testament passages (Num. 27.17; 1 Kgs 22.17; cf. Jer. 23.1-2; Ezek 34.5; Zech. 10.2) in which the emphasis is on the absence of sound leadership. The care and guidance which the people are now receiving is no better than it had been during the bleakest days of their history.[2] Moved with compassion on account of their plight, Jesus sends out his twelve disciples to bring the good news of the kingdom to the 'lost sheep of the house of Israel' (10.6; cf. Jer. 50.6), the very group to whom he himself was sent (15.24).[3] In his

1.   Cf. A.S. Geyser, 'Some Salient New Testament Passages on the Restoration of the Twelve Tribes of Israel', in J. Lambrecht (ed.), *L'Apocalypse johannique et l'apocalyptique dans le Nouveau Testament* (Leuven: Leuven University Press, 1980), pp. 305-10 (308): 'The meaning is clear: With the birth of Jesus the ingathering of the tribes of Israel has started'.

2.   The implicit criticism of the Jewish leadership contained in Mt. 9.36 becomes quite explicit later on in the Gospel (cf. 15.13-14; and especially ch. 23).

3.   Geyser ('Restoration', p. 308) observes that Mt. 15.24 discloses that the regathering of the lost sheep of Israel was Jesus' own task; hence, when he appoints and commissions the twelve to it, he is delegating his personal task and authority to them. The number of Jesus' disciples is, of course, suggestive of the restoration of the twelve tribes. E.P. Sanders (*Jesus and Judaism* [Philadelphia: Fortress Press, 1985], p. 98) remarks that 'the expectation of the reassembly of Israel was so widespread, and the memory of the twelve tribes remained so acute, that *"twelve" would necessarily mean "restoration"* ' (his italics). The point is taken further by the observation of D.C. Allison, Jr. ('Jesus and the Covenant: A Response to E.P. Sanders', *JSNT* 29 [1987], pp. 57-78 [67]) that since Jesus himself stands outside

role as the messianic shepherd, Jesus regathers and cares for the lost and weary exiles. Those who follow him in discipleship are charged with the same task and opposition to his ministry is tantamount to scattering.[1] The great regathering which the Old Testament prophets had foreseen has now begun to take place in the ministry of Jesus. As a consequence of his work, the exiles are being restored to the land. It is the conviction of Matthew that the birth of Jesus, son of Abraham and of David, has been of decisive consequence both for the people of Israel and for the Gentile world. The true children of Abraham are being identified; the lost sheep of Israel are being regathered. Around him assemble the repentant and faithful remnant and in him, the consummate heir, their fortunes are restored.

Another Matthaean text that impressively links the ministry of Jesus with the restoration of Israel is 4.12-17. In this passage, which marks the transition from John's public ministry to that of Jesus, the commencement of Jesus' work in Galilee is presented as the fulfilment of the salvation oracle of Isa. 8.23–9.1 [9.1-2], which concerns the bright light that will break in upon the people who live in darkness. It has already been noted that in the Isaiah passage darkness is symbolic of exile. Thus, the prophet had envisioned a new morning for the people which would mark the end of their long period of captivity. Accordingly, the decision by Jesus to take up residence in Capernaum, in the region of Zebulun and Naphtali, signifies for Matthew that the new day of restoration has arrived. It is fitting that the restoration should have its beginnings in the region of Zebulun and Naphtali,

---

the symbolic group, it is 'hard to avoid the inference that he conceived of himself as some sort of king, the leader-to-be of the restored people of God'.

1.   This is the implication of Jesus' words in 12.30b: 'The one who does not gather (συνάγω) with me scatters (σκορπίζω)'. Both words are technical terms among shepherds. Cf. J. Jeremias, 'ποιμήν', *TDNT*, VI, p. 492 n. 72. It is the view of Gnilka (*Matthäusevangelium*, I, p. 459) that the shepherd image does not fit the context of the saying. Yet it is not surprising that Matthew should wish to associate Jesus' work of gathering the lost sheep with his work of exorcism (note that when he sends his disciples to the 'lost sheep', listed among the works they are to do is exorcism). At the time of the exile 'scattered' Israel had been subjugated to foreign political powers. From Matthew's perspective the people of Israel remain in 'captivity', except that now the spiritual powers to which the people are subject are of greater concern than political domination. It is the opinion of B.F. Meyer (*The Aims of Jesus* [London: SCM Press, 1979], p. 173) that the exorcisms of Jesus 'effected the restoration they signified', a view which Matthew appears to share.

since they were among the first tribes taken into exile.[1] There is no reason to contend that Matthew is interpreting the Isaiah passage without reference to its original meaning. On the contrary, in the light of the many links that have already been noted between his Gospel and the restoration passages of the Old Testament, it is more than likely that Matthew is both conscious of and interested in the content of the Isaiah prophecy.[2] The people of Israel, who will be described later in the Gospel as lost sheep, are here described as the people who 'sit in darkness'. The important thing to note is that both descriptions are prophetic designations for the condition of exile.

It has been argued that since darkness as a symbol of moral and spiritual bankruptcy is common in New Testament literature, this provides the best guide as to what Matthew thought by Galilee sitting in darkness.[3] While agreeing that Matthew is referring to the spiritual condition of the Jewish people, one would recommend that the denotation of darkness already present in the Isaiah quotation provides a more precise guide to what Matthew thought. What is significant is that Matthew has appropriated the imagery of the exile in order to describe the spiritual 'exile' in which the people now find themselves. The appearance of Jesus in Galilee, which follows his baptism by John and his temptation in the wilderness, is a signal that the light, symbolic of return, has begun to shine. It is perhaps significant that immediately after the quotation Matthew observes that from that moment Jesus

---

1.   Geyser, 'Restoration', p. 307: 'The restoration of the Kingdom must accordingly start where the exile began its dissolution: in Galilee in the land of Zebulon and Naphtali'. Cf. Davies and Allison, *Matthew*, I, p. 382. The phrase 'Galilee of the Gentiles' may intimate that the mission which is now underway will eventually extend to the Gentiles; nonetheless, the focus is primarily on the people of Israel.

2.   It is plausible that Matthew has in mind the whole of the oracle, which relates the future restoration to the appearance of the ideal Davidic king. Cf. F.W. Beare, *The Gospel according to Matthew* (San Francisco: Harper & Row, 1981), p. 116. It is noted in the same oracle that at that time the yoke of domination will be broken. I have argued elsewhere (see, '"To Proclaim Liberty to the Captives": Matthew 11.28-30 in the Light of OT Prophetic Expectation', *NTS* 38 [1992], pp. 290-97) that at Mt. 11.28-30 Jesus, standing in the position of the messianic figure in whom the restoration of the nation is realized, announces to the people of Israel that the time has come for the release from exile, foreign domination often being depicted as a yoke, and for the return to the yoke of Yahweh (cf. Jer. 2.20), wherein they will find the eschatological rest prepared for them.

3.   Cf. Davies and Allison, *Matthew*, I, p. 385.

began to preach repentance as he announced the imminence of the kingdom. Like John before him, Jesus is making the people of Israel ready for the restoration that is to take place.

The above discussion has touched on a problem which is of concern to every interpreter of the Gospel; namely, that when Matthew refers to an Old Testament text it is often difficult to discern just how much of its context and meaning he expects his readers to bring with them in order to fathom his own application of the text. In view of the nature of his quotations, it is not unreasonable to expect that in his quoting of the Old Testament certain things are left unstated which would be apparent only to the careful reader of the Gospel.[1] One must certainly exercise caution in attempting to understand Matthew's intention when quoting or alluding to a particular text. Nevertheless, there is some justification for speculating on possible exegetical undercurrents, since it appears that in Matthew's use of the Old Testament there is often more present than meets the eye. With respect to the theme of the returning exiles and its relation to the topic of reward, two quotations in Matthew are of special interest. When he refers to Herod's murder of the children of Bethlehem in 2.16-18, Matthew quotes Jer. 31.15 [LXX 38.15]. This verse, which concerns the exile of 'Rachel's children', appears in a context that is marked by optimism and hope for the future. For example, in the following verse Yahweh speaks to Rachel words of comfort: she is to refrain from weeping because there is a reward (שכר; μισθός) for her work; the children she has lost will be returned to their own land. It has occasionally been noted that Matthew may have intended his readers to take the full context into consideration when interpreting the quotation and thus recognize in it a paradigm of exile and return.[2] What has not been

---

1. Compare the study of R.T. France ('The Formula-Quotations of Matthew 2 and the Problem of Communication', *NTS* 27 [1981], pp. 233-51) which refers to the 'potential exegetical bonuses' that await the careful student of the Gospel who looks beneath the surface meaning. This approach, in encouraging the reader to be appreciative of Matthew's subtlety and art, is much more helpful than that approach (cf. S.L. Edgar, 'Respect for Context in Quotations from the Old Testament', *NTS* 9 [1962], pp. 55-62) which dismisses Matthew as a writer who has little regard for the original context of the verses he cites.

2. For example, R.T. France (*Matthew* [Grand Rapids: Eerdmans, 1985], p. 87) writes: 'Perhaps Matthew intends us to see also in Bethlehem's mourning a temporary sorrow, out of which God will bring joy and deliverance through Bethlehem's Messiah, returning from a foreign land'.

noted is that the return of the exiled children is portrayed in terms of reward.

A similar connection can be observed much later in the Gospel when Matthew presents the 'royal' entry of Jesus into Jerusalem as the fulfilment of prophecy. The quotation of 21.5 is actually composed from two Old Testament texts; that is, a single clause from Isa. 62.11, 'Say to the daughter of Zion', is used to introduce the main part of the quotation which is taken from Zech. 9.9. Why Matthew should do this is not clear. It is certainly true that there is no pressing reason why Matthew should incorporate this single line from Isa. 62.11, since the first words of Zech. 9.9 would convey almost the same meaning. This would suggest that the reference to Isa. 62.11 is deliberate; and if that is the case, then once again the question as to whether Matthew intended something more to be read into his quotation is justified. The words of Isa. 62.10-12 serve as a summary of the restoration hopes expressed throughout chs. 60–62: the highway of return is being prepared; the redemption of the people is taking place. In v. 11 the announcement, 'Say to the daughter of Zion', is followed by the words, 'Behold, your saviour comes. Behold, his reward (שכר; μισθός) is with him, and his recompense is before him.' Within its context the word 'reward', as well as the parallel term 'recompense', has no specific reference, but it is probably best understood in the sense of a reward for the people of Israel.[1] Thus the conception of reward is, once again, brought into association with the return of the people to their land.[2] And once more the possibility must be considered that Matthew intends his readers to draw from the quotation the additional ideas of return and reward.

The legitimacy of attaching importance to these connections is bolstered when it is recognized that the two texts mentioned above, along with Isa. 40.11, represent the only times in the Old Testament

---

1.   See C. Westermann, *Isaiah 40–66* (London: SCM Press, 1969), p. 379. It must be acknowledged, however, that there is no consensus of opinion as to how one should interpret either this verse or the related text of Isa. 40.11-12, in which the picture of Yahweh coming with his reward is brought into connection with that of his gathering together the flock. Some scholars prefer to understand the reward as that which is given to the returning exiles; others wish to see the reward as consisting in the people themselves, that is, they are God's recompense.

2.   It makes little difference that in Isaiah it is the people who receive the reward whereas in Jeremiah the recipient of the reward is Rachel, since as a matriarch she is representative of the people.

that the Hebrew שכר and the Greek μισθός are used in the transferred sense of an eschatological reward; a distinction which brings them into close conceptual proximity to the Matthaean usage of μισθός. It would appear, then, that at two important junctures in the Gospel narrative Matthew draws on the selected quotations in order to intimate the restoration of Israel: near the beginning of the story, when destruction marks the forced exile from Israel of the one born king of the Jews, and much later, when that same king enters the city of Jerusalem. Furthermore, implicit in these quotations is the suggestion that this restoration is, in fact, the eschatological reward in store for those who look to this Jesus for their redemption. It remains to be seen whether this emphasis is in agreement with the more conspicuous teaching on reward contained in the Gospel.

The prophets had looked to the restoration as a time when Yahweh would establish a new covenant relationship with his people. At Sinai, when the 'blood of the covenant' was sprinkled upon the people of Israel (Exod. 24.8), the descendants of Abraham truly became the community of God. Yet the breaking of the Sinai covenant necessitated the establishment of a new covenant that would provide the new basis of membership in the community of God. Matthew's reference to the institution of this new covenant is found in 26.28, within the context of the last supper discourse.[1] In giving the cup to his disciples, Jesus speaks of 'my blood of the covenant' which is 'poured out for many' for 'the forgiveness of sins'. The language of this verse is resonant with Old Testament allusion. The phrase 'my blood of the covenant' clearly echoes Exod. 24.8 and may also allude to Zech. 9.11, where Yahweh announces that he will free the captives from the waterless pit because of the blood of his covenant.[2] The expression that his blood is 'poured out for many' recalls the servant of Isaiah 53 (v. 12) who 'poured out' his soul to death and bore the sin of many.[3]

1. Matthew does not have Jesus speak of 'the new covenant' (ἡ καινὴ διαθήκη) as do Luke (22.20) and Paul (1 Cor. 11.25); nonetheless, that notion is implicit in Matthew.

2. J.P. Meier, *Matthew* (Wilmington, DE: Michael Glazier, 1980), p. 319. The connection in Zech. 9.11 between the blood of the covenant and the liberation of the exiles is quite suggestive, especially when one considers, following the logic of the argument advanced in this study, that it is those 'exiles' redeemed by the blood of Jesus who will be restored.

3. It is noteworthy that whereas Mark (14.24) uses the preposition ὑπέρ in the phrase 'poured out for many', Matthew uses the preposition περί; this reflects

Finally, Jer. 31.31-34 is clearly implied in the final phrase, 'for the forgiveness of sins'.[1] Jesus, who was so named because 'he will save his people from their sins' (1.21), redeems his people which, for Matthew, now includes Gentiles as well as Jews. Moreover, his death concludes a new covenant. Jesus has become the new ground of membership in the people of God.[2] The new relationship between God and his people is centred in him.

A saying which highlights the centrality of Jesus in the new order that has been introduced with his coming is 10.32-33, which functions within the mission discourse to place special emphasis on the absolute necessity of a positive and faithful response to Jesus. The confession or denial of Jesus before others in the present time leads to the confession or denial by Jesus before the Father in the future.[3] Thus a positive relationship with Jesus, defined as one in which he is acknowledged, is made the condition of a favourable verdict at the last judgment.[4] What the activity of 'confessing me before others' consists in is

sacrificial terminology in the LXX and provides an additional link with the sacrificial language of Isa. 53 (see vv. 4, 10). Cf. R.H. Gundry, *Matthew: A Commentary on his Literary and Theological Art* (Grand Rapids: Eerdmans, 1982), p. 528.

1. D. Hill, *The Gospel of Matthew* (Grand Rapids: Eerdmans, 1972), p. 339: 'That that passage is in Matthew's mind is suggested by the addition of "for the forgiveness of sins", cf. Jer. 31.34'. In Mark (1.4) and Luke (3.3) the phrase appears in the description of John's baptism. By not using the phrase in that context and inserting it only here, Matthew appears to strengthen the association between the forgiveness of sins and Jesus' sacrificial death.

2. In Isa. 42.6 and 49.8, it is said of the servant that he is given as a 'covenant to the people'. Needless to say the interpretation of these verses is the subject of considerable debate. What is most unexpected, however, is that this idea of the servant being the one through whom a covenant is mediated is not once exploited by the authors of the New Testament. For example, Matthew, at 12.17-21 (cf. 11.5), clearly identifies Jesus as the servant of Isa. 42; yet he makes nothing of this connection, even though it would serve his purposes. Perhaps this should be regarded as a further example of Matthew pointing his readers in the right direction and then leaving them to draw their own conclusions. It is noteworthy that in both passages the servant is charged with the task of liberating the exiles.

3. Allison ('Jesus and the Covenant', p. 66) describes Mt. 10.32-33 (= Lk. 12.8-9) as the 'most important' text associating salvation with the person of Jesus. It is the opinion of Pesch (*Lohngedanke*, pp. 138-39) that in such texts one finds the most significant feature of Jesus' teaching on recompense.

4. H.D. Betz ('An Episode in the Last Judgement [Mt. 7.21-23]', in his *Essays on the Sermon on the Mount* [Philadelphia: Fortress Press, 1985], pp. 125-57 [142-

not made explicit in the saying.[1] Viewed in terms of the context of ch. 10, it would no doubt include such actions as bearing witness before courts (vv. 17-20), and proclaiming from the housetops those things spoken by Jesus (v. 27). However, it is perhaps best not to restrict the interpretation of the phrase to the immediate context. The appearance of the words ἔμπροσθεν τῶν ἀνθρώπων in 5.16 (cf. 6.1) suggests that confessing Jesus before others occurs whenever one is involved in doing those things which Jesus requires of his followers.[2] Jesus is, therefore, much more than a herald of restoration. He is the one in whom the restoration takes place. Only those who recognize his position and accept his authority will be numbered among the restored community.

Before concluding this discussion of the Matthaean perspective on the restoration of Israel, it is interesting to observe that in Matthew one finds the theme of the two ways. Near the end of the Sermon on the Mount Jesus confronts his listeners with an ultimatum. They can choose either to follow the easy way that leads to destruction or the difficult way that leads to life (7.13-14). The language and form of expression that are used here clearly reflect the earlier challenges found in Deut. 30.15 and Jer. 21.8.[3] The saying, which opens with the

43]) is correct in relating this saying to the judgment scene described in 7.21-23 where Jesus disowns false disciples. On that occasion, as he points out, Jesus' ὁμολογέω (7.23) amounts to the ἀρνέομαι of 10.33. The οὖν of v. 32 connects this saying with the warning of v. 28. The point is that the acknowledgment of Jesus puts one in a propitious position before 'the one who is able to destroy both soul and body in Gehenna'. Gundry (*Matthew*, p. 198) seems to have missed this point when he regards the particle as connecting the saying with vv. 29-31, thus making the Father's concern for the disciple a reason for confessing and not denying. Verses 29-31 are parenthetical; the logical association is with v. 28.

1. The construction ὁμολογήσει ἐν ἐμοί probably reflects an Aramaic idiom. Otto Michel ('ὁμολογέω', *TDNT*, V, p. 208) defines the verb in this context as denoting an act of proclamation in which the relationship between the disciple and Jesus is expressed in binding and valid form.

2. The commentary on this saying in *2 Clem.* 3.4 is instructive: 'But in what way do we confess him? In doing the things he says, and not disobeying his commands; in honouring him not with lips alone, but with the whole heart and mind.' It is interesting to note that for the author of *2 Clement* (cf. 3.2-3) Jesus' confession before his Father is 'our reward (μισθός)'.

3. Deut. 30.15: 'I set before you this day life and good, death and evil'; Jer. 21.8: 'Behold, I set before you the way of life and the way of death'. G. Strecker (*The Sermon on the Mount* [Edinburgh: T. & T. Clark, 1988], p. 156)

charge 'Enter (εἰσέλθατε) through the narrow gate!', belongs with the other 'entrance' sayings of the Gospel. Frequently in Matthew, the object of the verb εἰσέρχομαι is 'the kingdom of heaven' (5.20; 7.21; 18.3; 19.23; 23.13).[1] Here, as in 18.8-9 and 19.17, it is 'life' that is presented as the goal to be attained. The two terms, 'kingdom' and 'life', are effectively synonymous; they both denote a final state of blessedness.[2] Yet one would wish to make a conceptual distinction between the two terms to the extent that whereas 'kingdom' can frequently connote the sphere of this final state, 'life' describes something of its quality. In this sense, 'life' along with 'joy' (25.21, 23) and 'the marriage feast' (25.10; cf. 22.12), the two other eschatological terms which are associated with the verb εἰσέρχομαι, fulfil a similar function in that they illustrate the character of the future kingdom. Thus, in the kingdom of heaven one experiences life in the fullest sense typified by joy and festivity. There is here a parallel to the Old Testament picture of the land as the place in which one enjoys the good life. Such a depiction, for example, is provided in Deut. 16.15 and 26.11; and it can be noted, in particular, that, according to Jer. 33.10-11, the time when Yahweh restores the fortunes of the land will be marked by sounds of joy and the voices of the bride and bridegroom. To be more precise, then, the land, which is promised to the faithful disciple in 5.5, and the kingdom are complementary categories sharing overlapping connotations.[3] The other terms are all descriptive of the existence enjoyed there.

Though introduced by a challenge to choose rightly, the main emphasis of the saying in Mt. 7.13-14 is found in the contrast between the many (πολλοί) on the way to destruction and the few (ὀλίγοι) on the way to life.[4] Those who are committed to the task of seeking and

observes that present in this saying is the Old Testament teaching of the two ways, the roots of which 'reach back to the Old Testament blessing-curse concept'.

1. G. Schwarz ('Matthäus vii 13a. Ein Alarmruf angesichts höchster Gefahr', *NovT* 12 [1970], pp. 229-32 [230]) rightly describes εἰσέρχομαι as a technical term for entrance into the kingdom.

2. R.A. Guelich (*The Sermon on the Mount* [Waco, TX: Word Books, 1982], p. 389) remarks that 'life itself represents but another expression for the Kingdom'.

3. The relationship between the land and the kingdom will be treated below in the discussion of Mt. 5.5, 12.

4. Note the observation of W. Grundmann (*Das Evangelium nach Matthäus* [Berlin: Evangelische Verlagsanstalt, 1968], p. 231): 'Der entscheidende paränetische Ton liegt aber auf der Entgegensetzung von vielen und wenigen'.

continuing in the way of righteousness, in spite of the sacrifices and troubles involved, will be a minority.[1] Yet it is they alone who find (εὑρίσκω) what is truly worthwhile.[2] Within the context of the Sermon on the Mount the warning implicit in these words is addressed both to Israel and to disciples; for numbered among the 'many' are all those who fail to hear and do the words of Jesus (cf. 7.26), whether they be the scribes and Pharisees of 5.20 or the false disciples of 7.21-23.[3] In view of the close correspondence between this warning and those found earlier in Deuteronomy and Jeremiah, the saying takes on a special significance for the people of Israel. The words of Jesus are very reminiscent of Yahweh's counsel in Jer. 6.16 that the people should ask after the good way and walk in it and thus find rest for their souls. At that time the people had refused to walk in the good way and the consequence was national destruction. Once again the people of Israel are instructed to walk in the good way, which is now defined by the teaching of Jesus.[4] Failure to listen this time will result in eschatological destruction.

An interesting development can be noted when the three biblical texts which treat the theme of the two ways are examined in sequence. In Deut. 30.15 the people of Israel, regarded as already in the land, are threatened with the loss of the land should they fail to hear and do what Yahweh had commanded. Later, after the threat had become a reality, the people are given a new choice, according to which the way to life is to be discovered in exile (Jer. 21.8). Now, in these words of Jesus, the people, who are still in a state of spiritual captivity, are once again presented with a choice. If they respond in obedience to the teaching of Jesus, they will be returned to the land and once again enjoy life in it, in the sense that, because they now experience renewed

1.   Marguerat (*Jugement*, p.178) characterizes the popular way as one that is clear and easy to spot, whereas the other way is discovered only after much searching and effort.

2.   Compare 10.39 and 16.25 where it is said that the person who loses his or her life (ψυχή) for the sake of Jesus will find it. At 11.29 those who take upon themselves Jesus' yoke are promised that they will find rest (ἀνάπαυσις) for their souls.

3.   Gnilka, *Matthäusevangelium*, I, p. 270: 'Mt sieht sich dem Problem des und der Bösen in der Gemeinde konfrontiert, knüpft aber grundsätzlich am Geschick Israels an'.

4.   Cf. Davies and Allison, *Matthew*, I, p. 698: 'The way to life is no longer the (pre-messianic) Torah but instead the words of Jesus'.

fellowship with God, they will ultimately attain the magnificent bounty he has prepared for them. If not, then their spiritual exile will be eternal. To enter through the narrow gate can be said to be a movement towards restoration.[1] It marks the beginning of this metaphorical return to the land. The notion that few will follow this path complements the prophetic emphasis that those who return represent a mere remnant of the people.

It is the belief of Matthew that God, through Jesus, has begun to fulfil the promise that he would restore the fortunes of his people. When the work of Jesus is initiated the people of Israel are still in a condition of 'exile'; they sit in darkness and are as lost sheep. Yet in his coming the light is introduced; and in his performance of the task given him the regathering of the people begins. Like John before him, Jesus calls upon the people to return to God. But, unlike John, he is more than a harbinger of restoration. He is the focus of the new covenant relationship between God and his people and, as a consequence, the one in whom the restoration takes place. There will be a 'return' to the land and kingdom which Israel had lost at the time of the exile, but not for all the people. Only the repentant and faithful who acknowledge him, along with their Gentile counterparts, will be counted among the remnant which returns. All others seem destined to an 'everlasting exile'. It is this paradigm of exile and restoration which provides the context for understanding the reward and punishment schema developed in Matthew.

---

1.   The relationship between the gate and the way is an interpretative crux. The gate can be regarded as standing at the entrance to the way; or as standing at the end of the way; or possibly, as some scholars suggest, the gate and way are simply synonymous metaphors, that is, one does not lead to the other. The command to enter the gate, with which the saying is introduced, appears to lend support to the first alternative, that is, the way which leads to life is entered upon through the initial action of going through the gate. One would thus agree with A. Sand (*Das Evangelium nach Matthäus* [Regensburg: Pustet, 1986], pp. 150-51) that 'der Zugang ist. . .das Tor, durch das eine Straße zum Zielort führt'. The use of these two terms in the saying may have been suggested by those Old Testament restoration texts in which the return is described with reference to gates and ways. For example, in Isa. 62.10 the call is issued to pass through the gates (שער; πύλη) and build up the highway (מסלה; ὁδός). In addition, Mic. 2.12-13 announces that when Yahweh gathers together the remnant of Israel, they will break through the gate (שער; πύλη) and go out, following their king who goes before them. These passages suggest that going through the gate is the first stage in the new exodus.

Reward Texts in Matthew

When undertaking an investigation of the Matthaean teaching on reward, it is essential that attention be directed not only to those passages which employ the vocabulary of reward (e.g. μισθός; ἀποδίδωμι), but also to those passages which utilize the language of entrance and inheritance; for those passages that are concerned with the final destination to which obedient discipleship leads are as important to a complete picture of reward as those passages that are concerned with the dividend which the obedient disciple receives in the end. Indeed, it is very probable that the payment awaiting the faithful disciple coincides with the sphere which the disciple enters or inherits. It was observed near the end of the last chapter that the Old Testament system of recompense which is of particular relevance to the present study is that inherent in the Sinai covenant, since the covenant stipulations set forth the conditions attached to the entrance into and the effective inheritance of the land. A similar emphasis certainly prevails in the Matthaean teaching on recompense, when one considers that specific conditions, stated either explicitly or implicitly, are attached to the entrance into and inheritance of the final state of blessedness. Thus, stipulations adhere to the new covenant just as they had done to the old covenant.

The conditions upon which entrance and inheritance depend will be a recurring theme throughout the present discussion of reward and punishment in Matthew. It would be valuable, however, at the beginning of this discussion to provide a brief overview of certain explicit demands that appear in the entrance sayings of the Gospel. The benefit of such a survey is that it would acquaint one from the outset with the key stipulations, expressed in an almost apodictic manner, which, according to Matthew, determine the eschatological redemption of an individual. The first of these is found in 5.20, where Jesus admonishes his disciples that they will in no way enter into the kingdom of heaven unless their righteousness surpasses (περισσεύω. . .πλεῖον) that of the scribes and Pharisees. The disciples are to be characterized by a 'better righteousness'; which is to say that, not only must they keep the commandments of the law which Jesus came to fulfil (cf. 5.17-19), but they must also perform the law in accordance with the requirements of Jesus.[1] It is this last element which makes their righteous conduct exceed that of the righteous Jews. Related to this is the response given by Jesus in 19.17 to the query of the young man concerning the attainment of eternal life: 'If you wish to enter into life, keep the commandments'. The law remains a true expression of the will of God and as such must be observed. Yet, as the subsequent words of Jesus reveal, the inheritance of eternal life depends also on faithful obedience to the demands of Jesus.

The expression 'to do the will of the Father' might be regarded as a convenient summary of what it means to keep the commandments of God in accordance with the requirements of Jesus.[2] In 7.21 Jesus declares that only the one who 'does the will of my Father who is in heaven' shall enter into the kingdom of heaven. Activity done merely in the name of Jesus is insufficient and serves as no substitute for activity done in accordance with the divine will. As will become increasingly clear in the following discussion, the will of God insists that the disciple eschew the self-seeking values that all too often lie at the root of human activity. One final entrance saying in which this emphasis is conspicuous is 18.3, where it is affirmed that turning (στρέφω) and becoming as a child is a precondition of entrance into the kingdom of heaven. The disciple must be willing to accept the status of the lowest. The essence of discipleship is found in this dramatic change in which all other sources of security are cast aside so that complete faith can be placed in the Father who is in heaven. One might summarise the results of this overview by observing that basic to these Matthaean entrance sayings is a concern for obedience to God, which is expressed in fidelity to Jesus' demands and rooted in a condition of utter dependence. The promise of reward is extended to the disciple whose character and conduct is distinguished by this obedience.

Matthew 5.5, 12
It is in the Beatitudes, which stand at the beginning of the first great discourse section of the Gospel, that the first occurrences of both

---

1.   Compare the remark of Meyer (*Aims*, p. 221), yet with respect to the historical Jesus: 'His teaching was Torah appropriate to restored Israel and requisite to perfect restoration'.

2.   Note that at 12.50 the one who does the will of the Father is described as the brother, sister and mother of Jesus. Compare also the appearance of the expression in the question which concludes the parable of the two sons (21.31).

2. 'Those Yahweh Blesses Shall Inherit the Land'   85

inheritance and reward terminology are found. In the third Beatitude of v. 5 the meek receive the assurance that they shall inherit the land, and in v. 12 those persecuted for the sake of Jesus are promised a great reward.[1] The idea of reward is, of course, implicit throughout vv. 3-10, since each Beatitude contains a promise of blessing which often indicates that a reversal of fortune will take place in the future.[2] Nevertheless, it is in these two promises that the centre of the Matthaean teaching on reward is to be found.

The Beatitude concerning the meek is one of those which are distinctly Matthaean. The concept of humility, understood as the opposite of self-exaltation and arrogance, plays an important role in Matthew. The term πραΰς, which in this verse describes an attribute essential to discipleship, is used elsewhere in the Gospel to describe Jesus.[3] In 11.29 he speaks of himself as 'meek and lowly (ταπεινός) in heart'; and in 21.5 his entrance into Jerusalem is portrayed as that of the humble king of Zech. 9.9. It is clear from the Gospel that meekness and humility should distinguish the disciple just as they do the master. Jesus declares in 11.25 that the Father reveals to infants (νήπιος)

---

1.   Although the blessed ones appear under various designations (e.g. 'the poor in spirit', 'the merciful', 'the peacemakers'), the beatitudes are all addressed to the same group of people, that is, those who are committed to the person and teaching of Jesus, his disciples. For this reason, G.W. Buchanan ('Matthean Beatitudes and Traditional Promises', in W.R. Farmer [ed.], *New Synoptic Studies* [Macon, GA: Mercer University Press, 1983], pp. 161-84 [170]) is correct to state that 'those who receive one of these blessings will receive them all'.

2.   When commenting on how in some beatitudes the reason for the blessing lies in the complete change of fate, W. Zimmerli ('Die Seligpreisungen der Bergpredigt und das Alte Testament', in E. Bammel, C.K. Barrett and W.D. Davies [eds.], *Donum Gentilicium* [Oxford: Clarendon Press, 1978], pp. 8-26 [17]) remarks: 'Vom Alten Testament her legt es sich zunächst nahe, an die Formulierung שוב שבות zu denken'.

3.   Concerning the question of whether the beatitudes are simply straightforward blessings or implicit demands, see the helpful discussion in Davies and Allison, *Matthew*, I, pp. 439-40. The imperative which is implicit in this beatitude is not to be ignored. The author of the Didache (3.7) apparently read Mt. 5.5 as a demand: 'Be meek, seeing that the meek shall inherit the land'. One cannot agree with Schweizer (*Matthew*, pp. 89-90; followed by Davies and Allison, *Matthew*, I, p. 449) that πραΰς in this verse has more to do with a condition of being powerless than with an attitude of humility. The blessing is directed not necessarily to those who are powerless, but rather to those who honestly acknowledge their dependence on God. The Capernaum centurion exemplifies the person who is not powerless in the eyes of the world and yet who evinces a genuine humility (cf. 8.8).

things he has hidden from the wise and understanding.[1] This idea corresponds with the theme which is present throughout the Gospel that the 'poor in spirit', 'meek', 'little ones' and 'childlike' are the very people whom God favours. They are favoured by him because their confidence is placed in him. Experience has taught them that they are not self-sufficient but must look to God for help and assistance. Like the remnant of Zeph. 3.12, which is described as 'meek and humble (עני ודל; πραϋν καὶ ταπεινόν)', they seek refuge in the name of their Lord.

The meek and humble are frequently the very ones who receive little in the present age where the dominant values tend to be pride and self-assertion. Yet the meek are blessed because the end of this age will be marked by a great reversal, at which time their meekness shall be vindicated and they shall inherit the land (κληρονομήσουσιν τὴν γῆν). The wording of the Beatitude follows closely that of Ps. 36 [37].11, in which meekness is listed as one of the characteristics of those who will dwell in the land for ever.[2] At this point in the discussion there is little need to comment on the associations that this Beatitude would have evoked in the mind of a Jewish reader.[3] It is sufficient to remark that the meek are considered here as the heirs of the promised land given to Abraham.[4] At the same time, it is clear that the literal land of Canaan is no longer in view. The land that is to

1. If the conjunction ὅτι in 11.29 is understood as epexegetical, which seems the best explanation, then it is precisely Jesus' meekness and humility which the hearer is being encouraged to learn. Cf. G. Strecker, *Der Weg der Gerechtigkeit* (Göttingen: Vandenhoeck & Ruprecht, 1966), p. 174.

2. According to the psalm, Yahweh will exalt (רום; ὑψόω) such meek ones to inherit the land (v. 34; cf. Mt. 23.12). Considering that Isa. 61 provides the backdrop to many of the beatitudes, it is possible that this beatitude also alludes to Isa. 61.7. In a context descriptive of the restoration, in which the 'anointed one' brings good news to the poor and proclaims liberty to the captives, the exiles are told that for a second time they will inherit the land (LXX: ἐκ δευτέρας κληρονομήσουσιν τὴν γῆν).

3. Gnilka (*Matthäusevangelium*, I, p. 123) aptly describes the inheritance of the land as 'die Sehnsucht des Volkes' as they wandered through the wilderness. The concept would have given rise to similar feelings among Jews in the time of Jesus and Matthew.

4. Cf. Dreyfus, 'L'héritage', p. 4: 'Il [Jesus] rattache ainsi clairement la Béatitude qu'il promet aux siens à l'antique promesse qui est formulée dans le premier livre de la Bible, le serment fait à Abraham de donner à sa descendance la Terre de Canaan'.

be inherited transcends its original, one might say embryonic, geographical referent and is to be understood in a spiritualized sense.[1] Already in the prophetic corpus, especially in Isaiah 60–66, it is observed that the ultimate fulfilment of the promise given to Abraham awaits the new age when, through an act of divine intervention in history, the world is transformed and restored to its original purpose in God's creation. Matthew gives testimony to his belief in such a cosmic renewal at 19.28 when he speaks of the παλιγγενεσία as a time which will witness the exaltation and vindication of Jesus' disciples. This Beatitude expresses that in the future God will intervene on behalf of the meek and humble and honour them as blessed heirs of the renewed creation.[2] The ancient promise concerning the inheritance of the land has thus been transformed. The land promised to Abraham is now understood in a sense which embraces the renewed creation that will occur at the end of the present age.

One might observe that, just as the beneficiaries of the promise are no longer the physical descendants of Abraham, so also the object of the promise is no longer the physical land of Israel. In the purpose of God the promise has outgrown its original categories. This is consistent with the pattern of fulfilment as it is described elsewhere in Matthew. The one in whom the restoration takes place is the son of David, in accordance with prophetic expectation. Yet for Matthew he is much more than the son of David. He is, in fact, the son of God (3.17; 16.16). The dark exile from which Jesus rescues his own is spiritual rather than physical. He has come to save his people from their sins (1.21). Moreover, the return from exile is itself undertaken at a spiritual level. It is through repentance and obedience to the way prescribed by Jesus that the righteous reach the inheritance prepared for them. For the accomplishment of the promised return of the people of God, the physical and terrestrial give way to the spiritual and transcendent.

It is frequently observed that this Beatitude concerning the meek and the earlier one concerning the poor in spirit are virtually synonymous.[3] One can infer from this parallelism that the land which the meek inherit corresponds to the kingdom which the poor in spirit

1. See the discussion in Davies, *Gospel and Land*, pp. 361-62.

2. J. Dupont (*Les Béatitudes* [Paris: Gabalda, 1973], III, p. 477) remarks that it is 'la félicité de la terre régénérée qui est promise aux doux'.

3. Note, for example, that in the Septuagint the Hebrew ענו is sometimes translated by πραΰς, as at Ps. 36 [37].11, and other times by πτωχός.

possess.[1] The coming kingdom in which the blessed have a share is
represented here under the image of a new possession of the land.[2] At
the time of the renewed creation the kingdom will have come in its
completion and the inheritance long promised will be fully realized.
Yet, at the same time, it is very important that the *heilsgeschichtlich*
significance of this promise is not obscured.[3] Furthermore, it is
important that the image of land not simply be absorbed into that of
kingdom. The two conceptions should be regarded as complementary
and yet distinctive: eschatologically they share the same referent; but
historically they are rooted in two different stories and two different
covenants which are associated with two different men, Abraham and
David.

The notion of inheriting the land is also present, albeit in a quite
subtle fashion, at v. 12, in the expansion of the eighth Beatitude concerning persecution.[4] The reward (μισθός) of this verse is promised
to those who are persecuted for the sake of Jesus, that is to say, his
disciples.[5] It is clear from 5.10-12, as well as from other texts in the
Gospel (cf. 10.23; 23.34), that persecution is the certain lot of the
disciple. If the teacher/master is reviled, the disciple/servant can expect
no better treatment (10.24-25). The abuse which they receive places
the disciples in succession to the prophets, God's servants of an earlier

1. The present tense (ἐστιν) in v. 3 is generally interpreted as a proleptic
present.

2. Hill (*Matthew*, p. 112) speaks of the blessed ones as 'entering the new land
of God's Kingdom'.

3. Brueggemann (*The Land*, pp. 170-71) offers a sound corrective of Davies's
position in noting that the concept of land in Mt. 5.5 is never so spiritualized that it is
'robbed of its original, historical referent'. He further observes that explications of
the concept of kingdom should not deny its 'elemental nuances'.

4. It is frequently observed that the first and eighth beatitudes form an *inclusio*
since the promise in both is identical, that is, 'theirs is the kingdom of heaven'. Karl
Kertelge ('"Selig, die verfolgt werden um der Gerechtigkeit willen" [Mt. 5,10]',
IKZ 16 [1987], pp. 97-106 [104]) notes, in addition, that the 'poor in spirit' and the
'persecuted' are bound together by their fundamental trust in the saving intervention
of God who will radically change their situation. Verse 10 functions both as a conclusion to the formally similar beatitudes and as an introduction to the enlarged beatitude of vv. 11-12. Verses 11-12 serve, to a certain extent, as a commentary on the
beatitudes, especially the eighth one. Cf. Buchanan, 'Matthean Beatitudes', p. 168.

5. The persecution mentioned in v. 10 is described more fully in v. 11 by
being linked to the phrases ὀνειδίσωσιν ὑμᾶς and εἴπωσιν πᾶν πονηρὸν καθ'
ὑμῶν ψευδόμενοι.

time, who were similarly persecuted.[1] Like the prophets, the disciples have a mission to fulfil, and as with all genuine prophets the fulfilment of that mission gives rise to opposition and adversity.[2] The phrase 'for my sake' makes it clear that the promise in view does not apply to just any persecution but only to that which is suffered because of the disciples' association with and confession of Jesus.[3] It is of interest to note that in Matthew the phrase ἕνεκεν ἐμοῦ (or the related phrase ἕνεκεν τοῦ ὀνόματός μου) is regularly found in statements concerning the cost of discipleship which are closely followed by promises of reward (5.11; 10.39; 16.25; 19.29). This juxtaposition of the demands of discipleship with recompense suggests that Matthew understands reward, at least in part, as compensation for the perils and privations of discipleship.[4] In the future those who have acknowledged Jesus in the midst of persecution will receive a marvellous return (cf. 10.32).

The nature of the reward is not specified, only that it is great (πολύς) and in heaven (ἐν τοῖς οὐρανοῖς).[5] This is the only place in

1. Beasley-Murray (*Jesus and Kingdom*, p. 168) comments that the phrase 'who were before you' implies that the disciples are persecuted as the successors of the prophets. Note that at 23.34 Jesus directly refers to his disciples as prophets who will be killed, abused and persecuted. On this matter of the disciples of Jesus standing in succession to the prophets see A. Sand, *Das Gesetz und die Propheten* (Regensburg: Pustet, 1974), pp. 171-73 and P.S. Minear, 'False Prophecy and Hypocrisy in the Gospel of Matthew', in J. Gnilka (ed.), *Neues Testament und Kirche* (Freiburg: Herder, 1974), pp. 76-93 (76-78).

2. Grundmann (*Matthäus*, p. 134) remarks incisively that 'Prophetenauftrag und Prophetenlos sind ihnen gegeben'.

3. The phrase also underscores the central position which is now taken by Jesus. ἕνεκεν ἐμοῦ recalls the earlier ἕνεκεν δικαιοσύνης of v. 10. Luz (*Matthew 1-7*, p. 242) observes that persecution 'for righteousness sake' and persecution 'for my sake' interpret one another since 'Christian practice and confession of Jesus belong to righteousness' and 'the confession of Christ manifests itself in deeds'.

4. Compare the statement of Strecker, *Der Weg*, p. 164: 'Der Lohn meint zunächts den Ausgleich, der den in der Gegenwart Verfolgten in Aussicht gestellt wird (5,12 par.)'. Similarly, Dupont (*Les Béatitudes* [Paris: Gabalda et Cie, 1969], II, p. 350) affirms that the verse encourages the persecuted disciples by assuring them 'que leurs souffrances ne sont pas perdues, que Dieu les compensera avec magnificence'.

5. According to M. Smith (*Tannaitic Parallels to the Gospels* [Philadelphia: SBL, 1961], pp. 56-57), the reward promised here is good repute or glory since those persecuted suffer from slander. However, this is to limit unduly the nature of

Matthew in which the reward in store for the disciple is described as great (cf. Lk. 6.23, 35). Mention has already been made of the close similarity between the present pledge to the disciples and Yahweh's declaration to Abraham in Gen. 15.1 that his reward shall be very great.[1] It was observed that the most convincing interpretation of this promise given to Abraham is that it refers to the land of Canaan. The subsequent history of Abraham's descendants confirms that the land is indeed the locus of reward. When Matthew's wording on this occasion is seen in conjunction with his interest in the restoration of the descendants of Abraham and, in particular, with his recent affirmation that the disciples of Jesus shall inherit the land, it is difficult to avoid the conclusion that he is deliberately alluding to Gen. 15.1 and that a similar connotation is in view here as well.[2] The comment that the reward is 'in heaven' emphasizes its transcendent and future nature. The reward is a blessing which is realized only when the kingdom of heaven has come to fruition.[3] It is a feature of Matthew's Gospel that reward is always eschatological. It is noteworthy that at 19.29 Matthew mentions only a future recompense for the disciples, whereas Mark (10.30) and Luke (18.30) speak also of a reward 'in this time'. In addition, it is perhaps significant that Matthew (10.10) has Jesus say 'the worker is worthy of his food (τροφή)', whereas in Luke (10.7) he says 'the worker is worthy of his reward (μισθός)'. It would appear that Matthew wants μισθός to denote only a future, spiritual reward. And in this case it would appear to refer to the inheritance of the spiritualized land of the renewed creation.

The promise of reward in v. 12 is looked upon as the basis for the joy that is to characterize the disciples in the present.[4] As they reflect

the reward.

1. The phrase in Matthew is ὁ μισθὸς ὑμῶν πολύς; Gen. 15.1 [LXX] reads ὁ μισθός σου πολὺς ἔσται σφόδρα.

2. The tradition history of Mt. 5.12 and the question as to how Luke understood the great reward are of no concern to the present discussion, which is only interested in what the verse means within the context of Matthew's Gospel as a finished whole.

3. Gaechter, *Matthäus*, p. 153: '"im Himmel" ist gleich "im Himmelreich", gesehen in seiner Vollendung'. Compare M. Pamment, 'The Kingdom of Heaven according to the First Gospel', *NTS* 27 (1981), pp. 211-32 (214). There is little evidence to support the assertion of Heinz Giesen (*Christliches Handeln* [Frankfurt: Peter Lang, 1982], p. 158) that the reward referred to here is already present.

4. Schweizer (*Matthew*, p. 96) notes that the two imperatives χαίρετε and ἀγαλλιᾶσθε describe more precisely what is implied in the blessing formula in the

on the change in circumstance which the future will bring, their perspective on the present situation is transformed. Suffering is now seen as something to rejoice in. The persecuted disciples receive, then, in vv. 10-12 the parallel promises of kingdom and land.[1] Both promises will be fulfilled at the future consummation; an event which will witness a great reversal of fortune and which will mark the final restoration of the people of God.

Matthew 5. 43-48

The next mention of reward in the Gospel is found in the sixth and final antithesis, which concerns the love of one's enemies. The theme of persecution also reappears in this text, since the enemies referred to in v. 44 are described further in the parallel statement as 'those who persecute you'. Thus, once again, mention of reward occurs in a context dealing with the behaviour of disciples in a situation of persecution. Even so, the connection between reward and persecution is treated in a different manner: in 5.12 the pledge of reward provides the motive for the joy of the disciple in the midst of persecution, whereas in the present passage the assurance of reward supplies the motive for loving the persecuting enemy.

The promise of reward to those who love their enemies is not stated directly in this passage.[2] Rather, the term μισθός appears within the rhetorical questions which are designed to move the disciples toward a position where their conduct more closely reflects that of their 'heavenly Father'. God acts in a loving and gracious manner to all and makes no distinction between the evil and the good or the just and the unjust. The disciples are to become like him to the extent that their behaviour towards others is not conditioned by prior attachment or affinity. They are to move beyond a strict reciprocal relationship to

ἀγαλλιᾶσθε describe more precisely what is implied in the blessing formula in the earlier beatitudes.

1. Guelich (*Sermon*, p. 96) is close to the mark when he asserts that the promised reward of v. 12 is 'ultimately the Kingdom of Heaven (cf. 5.3-10) which is given to those for whom it is promised'. However, in view of what was said earlier one would wish to distinguish between the kingdom and the land, both of which are inherited by the faithful (5.5; 25.34), since the distinction appears to be rooted in the Matthaean perspective on history. Accordingly, 5.10 promises the disciples the kingdom, whereas in 5.12 they are promised the land.

2. Note that in the parallel of Lk. 6.35 the connection between reward and the love of enemy is explicit: 'love your enemies. . . and your reward will be great'.

others, that is, a relationship based on the principle that one loves the other because one is loved by the other. The person whose love is determined by such a self-serving rule is worthy of no reward.[1] Even those who do not acknowledge God are capable of love on such terms.[2] The disciples are directed to cultivate a love which goes beyond the usual limits of human practice. Implicit in Matthew's questions is the much deeper question of whether the way of God or the way of others will determine one's own behaviour. The implicit promise of reward contained in these verses is directed to those who seek the divine way which is demonstrated in loving the enemy.

It is noteworthy that the question 'what reward have you?' is paralleled by the question 'what more (περισσός) are you doing?'[3] The latter question echoes the warning of 5.20, where the verbal form περισσεύω appears.[4] In view of this connection, vv. 46-47 may be said to contain both a veiled promise and a veiled threat: if one loves as God loves, one will be rewarded; however, if one fails to love as God loves, one has failed in that better righteousness which God demands and consequently is excluded from the kingdom of heaven. It would be too much to claim that the reward of v. 46 consists in the 'promise' of 5.20 that those whose righteousness exceeds that of the scribes and Pharisees will enter the kingdom.[5] Nevertheless, it is

1.   The three rhetorical questions of Lk. 6.32-34 serve the same purpose. The word μισθός is not used in these questions but rather the word χάρις, which means here 'favour' or 'approval'. Nonetheless, χάρις in Lk. 6.32-34 has the overtone of 'reward' as is shown by the use of μισθός in Lk. 6.35. Cf. J.A. Fitzmyer, *The Gospel According to Luke (I–IX)* (Garden City: Doubleday, 1981), p. 640. It is certainly fallacious to argue as Smith (*Tannaitic Parallels*, p. 57) does, on the basis of Luke's use of χάρις, that the reward in Mt. 5.46 probably refers to the grace by which the recipient becomes a son of God.

2.   For Matthew, tax collectors and Gentiles, when coupled and used negatively, stand for those who stand apart from God because of their behaviour (cf. 18.17).

3.   The expression 'to have a reward (ἔχειν μισθόν)' occurs only here and at Mt. 6.1. The present tense is used in the sense of a reward already laid up with God, though not yet actually possessed. M. Zerwick, *Biblical Greek Illustrated by Examples* (Rome: Biblical Institute Press, 1963), p. 94.

4.   This verbal connection is noted by many scholars. For example, Gundry (*Matthew*, p. 99) observes that by recalling v. 20 it 'reemphasizes the need for a surpassing righteousness'. According to Davies and Allison (*Matthew*, I, p. 557), vv. 46-47 illustrate the theme of the greater righteousness.

5.   This is the argument of Luz (*Matthew 1–7*, p. 345), which is flawed inasmuch as it overlooks that 5.20 does not contain a promise at all but only a threat.

probable that the reward implicit in this verse is related to the idea of entrance into the kingdom.

The Matthaean context indicates that, at least in part, the reward for those who love as God loves is to be the sons of God. The construction ὅπως γένησθε, with which v. 45 opens, is ambiguous and allows for two possible interpretations: either the disciples are to love their enemies so that they might show themselves to be that which they are already; or they are to love their enemies so that they might become that which they are not yet. In support of the first interpretation it may be noted that already in the Gospel (cf. 5.16) Jesus has used the phrase 'your Father' when addressing the disciples. Yet, the second interpretation finds support in the seventh Beatitude, concerning the peacemakers, wherein divine sonship is regarded as an eschatological state. Perhaps it is best to consider divine sonship as something dynamic: God has already accepted the disciples as sons, yet so long as they live in this world they are, in a sense, on probation. Not until the end will they irrevocably be sons.[1] Indeed, it must be emphasized that obedience to the commandment to love the enemy is a condition of divine sonship.[2] Thus, whereas vv. 46-47 states negatively that if one ignores the command to love as God loves, one can expect no reward and, in fact, invites divine disapproval, vv. 44-45 states positively that obedience to the command brings with it the assurance that ultimately one will become a son of God.

The notion that the obedient disciples are regarded as sons of God is of particular relevance to the matter of inheritance. It is sometimes argued that the utilization of the term 'sons' in this passage has to do with the reflection of the divine nature in the lives of the disciples.[3]

While it may be correct to say that failure to love as God loves will lead to exclusion from the kingdom of heaven, it does not follow that the reward for loving as God loves is entrance into the kingdom of heaven.

1. Gnilka, *Matthäusevangelium*, I, pp. 193-94. Luz (*Matthew 1-7*, p. 343) remarks that 'only the judgment will reveal the children of God'.

2. In respect of this point, J. Piper (*'Love Your Enemies'* [Cambridge: Cambridge University Press, 1979], p. 76) remarks that 'the condition of anything is that without which it does not occur or exist'. Note also the comment of P. Bonnard (*L'évangile selon saint Matthieu* [Neuchatel: Delachaux et Niestlé, 1970], p. 429): 'Remarquons cependent que, ici, l'accent ne porte pas sur la possibilité de cette filialité, mais sur sa nécessité; tout le contexte est à l'impératif'.

3. It is the view of T.W. Manson (*The Sayings of Jesus* [Grand Rapids: Eerdmans, 1957], p. 54), for example, that God will 'recognise them as His sons,

Without challenging the accuracy of this statement, one would also like to relate the term to the Old Testament idea of the 'sonship' of the nation of Israel. At the time of the exodus Yahweh refers to Israel as his 'firstborn son' (Exod. 4.22; cf. Hos. 11.1). The thought of inheritance, implicit in this designation, is clearly brought out in Jer. 3.19, where Yahweh expresses his wish that the faithless people would return so that he might treat them as a son by giving them a pleasant inheritance. In the main restoration oracle of Jeremiah, Yahweh reaffirms that he is Israel's father and that Israel is his firstborn (31.9, 20). That is the reason why he will bring the exiles back to their land. Thus, there is a suggestion in this passage that the obedient disciples now stand in the position of Israel. As the faithful 'sons' of God they will receive the pleasant inheritance prepared for them.

Matthew concludes the sixth antithesis with the command to be perfect in v. 48. The particle οὖν connects this command with the preceding argument: if loving like the Father makes one a son and if not loving like the Father makes one as the tax collectors and Gentiles, then the only reasonable course of action is to be like the Father, to be perfect.[1] At the same time, the command to be perfect serves as a summary of the instructions and demands of all the antitheses. The word 'perfect' (τέλειος), as it is used by Matthew, denotes wholeness and completeness with regard to the obedient fulfilment of the demands of God and Jesus. This command is the ultimate development of the 'more' which is necessary to enter the kingdom of heaven.[2] In the parallel charge of Lk. 6.36 the disciples are ordered to be merciful (οἰκτίρμων). However, the Matthaean version, as is commonly noted, recalls the command given to Israel in Deut. 18.13 where they are enjoined not to be like the nations which are driven out before them but to be 'blameless' (תמים; τέλειος) before Yahweh their God.[3] It is

for something of His own nature will be reflected in them'. Note that, according to Deuteronomy, it was Yahweh's intention that the people of Israel be influenced by his own nature.

1. Cf. J. Lach, 'Die Pflicht zur Versöhnung und Liebe (Mt. 5,43-48)', *CollTh* 57 (1987), pp. 57-69 (61): 'Die Bezeichnung *teleios* in bezug auf Gottvater in Vers 48 ist nämlich eine Entsprechung und Quintessenz der Charakteristik des himmlischen Vaters'.

2. France, *Matthew*, p. 129.

3. W. Trilling (*Das wahre Israel* [Munich: Kösel, 1964], p. 194), for example, comments that 'Mt. 5,48 berührt sich im Wortlaut und Gedanken eng mit Deut. 18,13, einer der wenigen Stellen, die auch die Septuaginta mit τέλειος

of interest that in both Matthew and Deuteronomy the conduct of God's people is contrasted with that of the Gentiles. It is of even greater interest that the Hebrew term תמים is frequently associated with the inheritance of and the continuance in the land. In Ps. 36 [37].18 it is said of the blameless that their inheritance will last forever (cf. Ps. 101.6). Similarly, Prov. 28.10 promises that the blameless will receive a good inheritance. Another text which demonstrates the essential connection between such integrity and land possession is Prov. 2.20-21, where the encouragement to walk in the way of the good and righteous is founded on the promise that the upright will live in the land and the blameless will remain in it.[1] It is, of course, understood in Deut. 18.13 that complete obedience to Yahweh's instructions is obligatory to land possession. It is difficult to say whether or not Matthew had these associations in mind when he composed his conclusion to the antitheses. If he did, then his choice of wording would corroborate what has been said above that the faithful disciple is an heir to the promised inheritance.

Matthew 6.1-6, 16-18
The antitheses, which are brought to a conclusion with the summary statement of 5.48, had illustrated one aspect of the better righteousness demanded of the disciple, that of the new radical approach to the commandments of God. In the introduction to the next section of the Sermon, found in the warning of 6.1, the focus is placed on another aspect of this better righteousness, namely the manner in which the disciple is to fulfil those commands.[2] This indicates that the righteousness which is necessary to enter the kingdom is characterized not only by a radical obedience to the legal and ethical demands of God, but also by an inner integrity, that is, by an intention which is focused solely on doing the will of the Father so as to bring glory to him. This second aspect of righteousness, which gives further clarification of the term 'perfection', is emphasized in order to address the danger inherent in fulfilling the requirements of God. It is possible that one

---

wiedergegeben hat'. Note that the work of Yahweh is described as 'blameless' (תמים; ἀληθινός) in Deut. 32.4.

1. It is perhaps significant that in Gen. 17.1 Abraham is instructed to be blameless.

2. Luz (*Matthew 1–7*, p. 363) notes that in ch. 6 Matthew is concerned about 'the inwardness of the same righteousness of which he spoke in the Antitheses'.

might come to forget the real reason why God demands obedience, that is, so that he may be glorified and others may be served, and substitute for that a perverted kind of obedience which serves one's own interests and brings glory only to oneself. Obviously, those who practice such 'obedience' will receive no reward from God.

The warning of 6.1 states the general principle that one must guard against practising righteousness before others in order to be seen by them.[1] This principle, which is bolstered by the sanction that such ostentatious practice brings no reward from God, is then illustrated in the following verses by three examples contrasting reward gaining and reward losing activity. The three good works which are selected as examples are the three basic duties of Jewish piety: almsgiving, prayer and fasting.[2] Yet what is said of these three is applicable to all religious actions. In each illustration two kinds of activity are described, that of the hypocrite and that of the disciple.[3] The use of the term 'hypocrite' in these verses illustrates well the ambiguity inherent in the word. On the one hand, there is the suggestion of playing a role and in that sense the term denotes the misrepresentation of one's true nature; that is, one gives the impression of being righteous without actually being righteous.[4] On the other hand, the term denotes the true nature which underlies and, in effect, necessitates the pretence.[5] The term is employed in this latter sense in the Septuagint to describe the

1.   The present imperative προσέχετε suggests that the danger in view demands constant vigilance.

2.   Commentators frequently refer to the mention of these three activities in Tob. 12.8: 'Prayer is good when accompanied by fasting, almsgiving, and righteousness'.

3.   Note that the positive examples are introduced with an emphatic 'but you' in vv. 3, 6, 17, thus setting the practice of the disciple over against that of the hypocrite. In these verses the Pharisees are not mentioned by name; however, it is evident that they are in view. Compare, for example, the statements of 6.1, 2, 5, 16 with the description in 23.5. In 15.1-9, as in 23.1-33, the scribes and Pharisees are accused of hypocrisy; in 22.15-22 the disciples of the Pharisees along with the Herodians receive the same rebuke.

4.   It is the view of Gundry (*Matthew*, p. 102) that it makes no difference whether or not these individuals have an awareness of their motives. Yet it is best to affirm with Schweizer (*Matthew*, p. 143) that conscious deception is probably meant here, especially when one considers the lengths that these individuals are willing to go in order to make an impression on others.

5.   This idea of hypocrisy denoting one's essence comes to the fore in 23.28 where the scribes and Pharisees are said to be 'full of hypocrisy'; that is, hypocrisy characterizes their true nature.

godless person who is estranged from God.[1] When discussing the term in Matthew it is best not to promote one meaning at the expense of the other, but rather to see the two meanings as interconnected. The hypocrite is one whose essence is characterized by hypocrisy, and who at the same time conceals that reality by means of hypocritical expression.[2] The lack of integrity which is suggested by ὑπόκρισις makes it a suitable contrast to τέλειος which signifies wholeness.

The hypocrites of ch. 6 appear to be people who are motivated not by the desire to gain God's approval through the obedient fulfilment of his will, but rather by the desire to gain the recognition of onlookers through the fulfilment of a religious action.[3] It is fair to say that these hypocrites perform religious duties without much reflection on the true reason why such duties should be done. What thought is given to the matter centres chiefly on how the duty can be made to serve a self-seeking end.[4] Apparently, all that concerns them is the visible world of poor people, public prayers, fast days and potential spectators, and the present moment in which praise can be solicited and enjoyed. Little thought is directed to the God 'who is in secret' and who one day 'will repay'. These hypocrites have chosen to 'ignore' God in the pursuit of temporal gratification, as is shown in their placing a higher value on human recognition than on that of God.[5] For that reason, they will in the end be rejected by God. The

1.   For a detailed discussion, see U. Wilckens, 'ὑποκρίνομαι', *TDNT*, VIII, pp. 563-64. Cf. also the discussion in P. Joüon, ''ΥΠΟΚΡΙΤΗΣ dans l'évangile et hébreu *HANEF*', *RSR* 20 (1930), pp. 312-16.

2.   See the helpful discussion of hypocrisy in Matthew in D.O. Via, Jr, *Self-Deception and Wholeness in Paul and Matthew* (Philadelphia: Fortress Press, 1990), pp. 92-98.

3.   S. Van Tilborg (*The Jewish Leaders in Matthew* [Leiden: Brill, 1972], p. 11) refers to the hypocrite of this passage as a person who 'bypasses the divine forum and patterns his life after the forum of man'. According to Wilckens ('ὑποκρίνομαι', p. 568), their hypocrisy consists in the fact that 'they are concerned about their status with men rather than their standing before God'.

4.   Giesen, *Christliches Handeln*, p. 155: 'In allen drei Beispielen sind die ὑποκριταί solche, die Gott, dem himmlischen Vater, fernstehen, die nicht die Ehre des Vaters, sondern ihre eigene suchen'.

5.   P.S. Minear (*Commands of Christ* [Nashville: Abingdon Press, 1972], p. 51) defines hypocrisy in this context as 'any intentional action which simultaneously seeks God's approval and man's praise'. However, there is no evidence in the passage that the hypocrite is at all interested in God's approval. God is far from the thoughts of the hypocrite who operates with little reference to God. Note that at 15.6

hypocrite receives (ἀπέχω) the very reward that is sought, namely the praise and recognition of others, and, having received that, has been paid in full (vv. 2, 5, 16). The use of this commercial technical term, which was used frequently in receipts to indicate a settled account, is appropriate to the hypocrite who is not giving service to God or others but merely purchasing social prestige by means of religious activity. Even so, the solemn declaration ἀμὴν λέγω ὑμῖν which introduces these statements concerning the reward of the hypocrites strikes a note of foreboding and suggests that this is not the end of the matter. On one level these hypocrites do play a role in life; and on a much deeper level they live as though God himself played no role. Such people only appear to be obedient to the commandments of God. Ultimately, they fail to do God's will because their activity stems from pride and not from the humility which pleases him.

The obedience of the disciples is to be very different from that of the hypocrites. On the surface the actions of both groups are similar, for the disciples will also give alms, pray and fast. The decisive difference is found in the underlying motivation behind their activity. An uncompromised devotion to God is to distinguish every endeavour of the disciple; and especially when others are involved, as in the case of almsgiving, the activity is to be conducted in such a way as to deflect attention to God (5.16). What sets the two groups apart is that the disciple possesses a humility before God which overrides any self-seeking desire for human praise. The disciple has no ambition for human recognition. If the disciple can be said to have any ambition at all, it is merely to serve God and to seek the reward that he alone can give. For that reason, the activity of the disciple is characterized by secrecy (vv. 3-4, 6, 17-18). The good works of the disciple will and, in a sense, should be seen by others (cf. 5.16); however, this occurs in spite of and not because of the efforts of the disciple. This is how it should be, since only unassuming behaviour can deflect glory to God.

Jesus rebukes the Pharisees and scribes with the charge 'You hypocrites!' and portrays them, by means of Isa. 29.13, as people whose relationship to God is that of the 'lip' but not of the 'heart'. The use of δοξάζω in v. 2 provides an additional insight into the nature of hypocrisy, since elsewhere the verb is used only of God. It might be inferred that the hypocrites are putting themselves in God's place. Cf. Davies and Allison, *Matthew*, I, p. 581. In his third temptation (4.8) Jesus had turned down the offer of the δόξα of this world. The hypocrites, on the other hand, seek such glory.

The disciple who does the will of God which consists in such hidden service will be rewarded (ἀποδίδωμι) in the end. This promise of reward signifies that God recognizes both the implicit sacrifice made by the disciple, that is, the willingness to forgo any visible acknowledgment that what has been done is important and praiseworthy, as well as the conviction which gives rise to such sacrifice, namely that God is always present and that his recognition is all that matters. Such character and conduct is repaid by God.[1] He will not permit any human deed that is directed to him to go unanswered but will respond in a reciprocal manner.[2] There is a tendency in much that has been written on this text to weaken or even to subvert the notion of reward, since the emphasis on reward is regarded as inconsistent with the general tone of Jesus' teaching.[3] Yet it is impossible to deny that the passage is intent on teaching that a certain mode of behaviour earns God's approval while its opposite earns his disdain. It is clear that for Matthew, at least, the promise of reward has validity as a motivation to proper conduct, otherwise he would not have employed words denoting reward seven times in the passage. At the same time, the relationship between reward and conduct in this passage is not a simple quid pro quo. References to God as the disciple's Father occur almost as frequently as references to reward. The inference that can be drawn from this relationship between the disciple and God is that reward is removed from the realm of legal obligation and rights. The Father responds to the action of the disciple with a kind of recompense which

1. Bonnard (*Matthieu*, p. 430) stresses that the verb ἀποδίδωμι may not simply be assimilated to the simple verb δίδωμι. Similarly, Strecker (*Sermon*, p. 101) notes that Matthew is not familiar with the concept of unearned compensation.

2. Grundmann (*Matthäus*, pp. 191-92) affirms this and yet insists on referring to the reward as a 'gift' (*Geschenk*) which the Father makes to his sons.

3. Compare J. Jeremias, *New Testament Theology* (New York: Charles Scribner's Sons, 1971), p. 216: 'Here it is clear that while Jesus takes up the word "reward", he in fact presupposes that his disciples have completely detached themselves from striving for a reward; they are to forget the good deeds they have done'; and H. Braun, *Spätjudisch-häretischer und frühchristlicher Radikalismus* (Tübingen: Mohr, 1969), II, p. 56: 'Nur muß man sehen. . . daß also der Gerichtsgedanke hier sich in einer naiven Lohnerwartung ausspricht, welche vom Zentrum der Predigt Jesu de facto, wenn auch nicht expressis verbis, überwunden ist'. Such statements do not treat seriously the question of why Jesus used reward language to motivate proper behaviour. They merely represent attempts to remove an element of Jesus' teaching which is found to be awkward and annoying.

is beyond recompense according to a strict legal measure.[1] Consequently, the disciple is not earning reward in the sense that it can be demanded of God. The language of reward merely indicates that God takes his children seriously and responds to their actions. He has prepared a reward for them but its attainment depends on their faithful and blameless obedience. For that reason, the disciple is not to pretend that reward from God does not matter.[2] On the contrary, by marking the goal of faithful service it provides the inducement to faithful service. Far from denying or condemning the human need for reward the present passage assumes such a need and utilizes it.[3] According to the ethic of the passage, God does not demand that the disciple relinquish recognition and reward, merely that such recognition and reward be deferred until they can be received directly from God.

Matthew 6.19-24

A characteristic feature of the passages examined thus far is that the promise of future reward is employed to motivate a type of behaviour which corresponds to the righteousness and perfection required of the disciple. In the collection of sayings which directly follows the instructions about fasting the teaching on reward is continued and augmented, inasmuch as the disciple is now commanded to store up treasures in heaven. Parallels to the sayings of Mt. 6.19-24 are found in Luke (12.33-34; 11.34-36; 16.13). Presumably, Matthew has deliberately linked these sayings together and placed them in the present context. Within the context of the Sermon on the Mount the sayings function as a bridge connecting 6.1-18 with 6.25-34 and thus may be said to combine a dual referent. On the one hand, they point forward to the discussion in the next section regarding concern over material needs, and on the other hand, they serve as reflections on the contrast between hypocritical and righteous behaviour which had dominated the preceding discussion. Although these sayings extend the teaching on reward, a slight shift in emphasis can be observed. No longer is it

---

1. Gaechter, *Matthäus*, p. 202.
2. The observation of Beare (*Matthew*, p. 166) is worth noting: 'To do our duty without any thought of reward is a noble thought, it may be; but does it rest upon a notion of individual moral autonomy which is incompatible with the nature of a servant of God?'
3. Gaechter (*Matthäus*, p. 203) remarks that 'diesen strukturellen Drang des Menschenherzens setzt Jesus überall voraus und seinetwegen spricht er vom Lohn'.

simply a matter of declaring that the good practice of the disciple is rewarded. Now the disciple is instructed to actively lay up treasure in heaven, or, to put it another way, to seek reward.[1] It will become clear that the reason for this prescription to seek reward is that such an exercise contributes to the wholeness and integrity which is essential to the better righteousness.

The intention of the first saying, which contrasts the relative permanence of earthly and heavenly treasures, is to expose the futility of a life style preoccupied with the present and to encourage a life style that looks to the benefits of righteous service before God. The reason for this concern is stated in v. 21: one's heart, that is, the inner reality or the underlying motivation of one's life is inevitably linked to what one treasures.[2] What might constitute treasure in either category is not stated. However, in keeping with the larger Matthaean context it is probably best to interpret 'treasures on earth' as descriptive of those things in life to which a person is naturally directed.[3] The future reward given to the faithful disciple is described by 'treasures in heaven'. It is probably best to regard the heavenly treasure as referring to a share in the future kingdom The comparison with 13.44 may be significant, according to which the kingdom of heaven, likened to a valuable treasure, is to be obtained at all cost.[4] The person whose treasure is located on earth is a person who is interested solely in the present moment and the visible world and who therefore acts as though the immediate and the tangible were all that mattered. As was noted above, that is the error of the hypocrite. The disciple, on the other hand, is to store up treasure in heaven, for when the treasure is located there, invariably the heart is directed to what is

1. Note the imperative θησαυρίζετε in v. 20. It is puzzling indeed that Schweizer (*Matthew*, p. 162) should speak of vv. 19-21 as criticizing the person who 'tries to lay up riches in heaven by acts of devotion'.

2. Hill, *Matthew*, p. 142: 'Each individual sets his heart on what he counts important, and this allegiance determines the direction and content of his life'.

3. Although physical possessions are specifically referred to, Bonnard (*Matthieu*, p. 90) is correct to observe that the term encompasses other 'valuables' such as human appreciation.

4. Cf. K. Koch, 'Der Schatz im Himmel', in B. Lohse and H. P. Schmidt (eds.), *Leben angesichts des Todes* (Tübingen: Mohr, 1968), pp. 47-60 (52). The emphasis inherent in the contrast between earthly treasures and heavenly reward in these verses is similar to that in Heb. 11.26 where it is said of Moses that he rejected the treasures (θησαυρός) of Egypt because he looked ahead to the reward (μισθαποδοσία).

of greatest importance, the doing of the Father's will in the present moment.

The following saying about the eye and the body (vv. 22-23) presumably functions as a reflection on vv. 19-21, yet from a different perspective and employing different terminology. In the language of the saying the 'eye' tells the story of the inner person; that is, a 'sound eye' is the consequence of inner light and an 'evil eye' is the consequence of inner darkness. The saying is very problematic and scholars are far from agreement on how it should be interpreted. Although most commentators work on the assumption that the saying is about light passing into the body through the eye, it is perhaps best to understand the phrase, 'the eye is the lamp of the body', in terms of an extramission theory of vision, that is, the body's own light makes vision possible, and to interpret the genitive τοῦ σώματος as a subjective genitive. Thus the eye is the body's lamp and as such sends out light.[1] In terms of religious expression this means that the person filled with light is employed in the kind of activity, expressed by the 'sound eye', which is commended by God.[2] Conversely, the person filled with darkness is engaged in reprehensible activity, that of the 'evil eye'. The ethical significance of the terms ἁπλοῦς and πονηρός is ambiguous, perhaps intentionally so, since ultimately one need not decide whether by ἁπλοῦς Matthew is referring to single-minded devotion or to generosity, or whether πονηρός refers to evil in general

---

1.   The interpretation presented here is that argued for in the studies of H.D. Betz ('Mt. 6.22-23 and Ancient Greek Theories of Vision', in his *Essays on the Sermon on the Mount* [Philadelphia: Fortress Press, 1985], pp. 71-87) and D.C. Allison, Jr. ('The Eye is the Lamp of the Body [Matthew 6.22-23 = Luke 11.34-36]', *NTS* 33 [1987], pp. 61-83). The allusion to this saying in *Gos. Thom.* 24 lends support to the interpretation that the eye is sending out light: 'There is light within a man of light, and he lights up the whole world. If he does not shine, he is darkness'; cf. *Dial. Sav.* 8 and *P. Oxy.* 655.24. Allison ('Lamp of the Body', pp. 74-76) further argues that the conditional sentences in vv. 22-23 belong to the type in which the causal condition is found in the apodosis rather than in the protasis. Hence the sentence 'if your eye is ἁπλοῦς/πονηρός, your whole body is φωτεινόν/σκοτεινόν' does not mean that a sound/evil eye causes inner light/darkness (which presupposses an intromission theory of vision), but that a sound/evil eye is evidence of inner light/darkness.

2.   Note that in 5.16 the good works of the disciple are likened to light shining out before men.

or to envy and covetousness in particular.[1] The intent of the saying concerns the relationship between inner condition and outward expression.[2] As a reflection on vv. 19-21 the saying would appear to portray the person whose heart is set on heavenly treasure as someone who is full of light, whereas the person committed to earthly treasure is as one full of darkness. The imagery of light and darkness supports this interpretation, in so far as 'light' conveys the presence of God and 'darkness' his absence. Hence the activity of 'treasuring' heavenly treasure testifies to the presence of God in one's life, whereas the 'treasuring' of earthly treasure reveals a detachment from God. The final line of the saying is threatening in tone.[3] The inference is that the person who evinces darkness in the present age, and therein attests to a separation from God, will in the future age experience the profound darkness of total separation from him.

The third saying, about serving two masters (v. 24), provides a fitting conclusion to the section. The implication of the saying for the subject of reward is that it is impossible to lay up treasures both in heaven and on earth since that would involve serving both God and mammon. The term mammon, as it is used here by Matthew, is probably best explained as the conceptual equivalent to treasures on earth,

1. France (*Matthew*, p. 139) is probably correct in assuming that there is a deliberate double entendre here. At the same time, it is noteworthy that the Hebrew תמים may stand behind the Greek ἁπλοῦς, thus suggesting the idea of integrity. Cf. Bonnard, *Matthieu*, p. 91.

2. Allison ('Lamp of the Body', p. 78) correctly observes that the saying of 6.22-23 belongs with those sayings which are concerned with the relation that exists between outward acts and inward states. He includes among these the fruit/tree sayings of 7.16-20 and 12.33-35. It is of interest to note that 12.34-35 combines the concepts of treasure and heart, that is, out of the καρδία/θησαυρός comes forth good or evil.

3. H.B. Green (*The Gospel according to Matthew* [Oxford: Oxford University Press, 1975], p. 92) remarks that the point made in v. 23b is similar to that made in 5.13 about insipid salt. It is interesting that the complement to the 'salt of the earth' saying of 5.13 is the 'light of the world' saying of 5.14. Salt can lose its flavour and light can give way to darkness. When commenting on the paraenetic aim of 6.22-23, Betz ('Mt. 6.22-23', pp. 86-87) states that even though the saying is designed to provoke concern about the state of one's inner light it offers no counsel as to how one might brighten a darkened light. However, since Matthew attaches the saying to the command to store up treasures in heaven, it is possible that he regards this activity as a means by which the inner light can be brightened, that is, this activity, in directing the heart towards God, fills the inner being with light.

that is, it refers to those things in life which are appealing and which can easily distract one from the pursuit of righteousness. Though the word primarily signifies material goods, mammon in one sense stands for anything that prevents complete dependence upon and devotion to God.[1] It is interesting that mammon is referred to as a Lord (κύριος) that one may serve.[2] The temptation for the people of God is no longer foreign gods, such as Baal, but the Lord Mammon. When these sayings are viewed together they add further comment to the previous discussion concerning the need for an uncompromised devotion to God. One must serve him with an inner integrity that is rooted in total dependence on him. Only the meek, who evince such allegiance, will inherit the land God has prepared for them, since only the meek seek it. The proud and arrogant, who delight in earthly fortune, will inherit only darkness.

Matthew 10.40-42
It was noted earlier that frequently in Matthew promises of reward follow statements concerning the cost of discipleship. A case in point is the group of sayings about reward found in 10.40-42. These sayings are immediately preceded by the conditions of discipleship set forth in vv. 37-39. According to these stipulations discipleship means loving Jesus more than all others, taking up one's cross and following him, and, finally, losing one's life for his sake. Nevertheless, the present passage is different from others which link the sacrifices of discipleship with the reward of discipleship, in that the reward in question is promised not to the disciple, although the disciple's reward is always assumed, but rather to the one who receives a disciple.

The promise of vv. 40-42 stands at the conclusion to the discourse section which concerns the mission and fate of the disciples. They are instructed to go only to the 'lost sheep' of Israel taking with them the message of the kingdom of heaven. In the fulfilment of this mission

1.   Minear ('False Prophecy', p. 87) recognizes the relevance of this saying and that of v. 21 to the preceding discussion when he remarks that it is presupposed that 'the hypocrite has vowed to serve one master only. This requires an undivided heart, an uncompromised loyalty, a single treasure.'

2.   H. Riesenfeld ('Vom Schätzesammeln und Sorgen: Ein Thema urchristlicher Paränese. Zu Mt VI 19-34', in W.C. van Unnik (ed.), *Neotestamentica et Patristica* [Leiden: Brill, 1962], pp. 47-58 [48]) is right to state that the gathering of earthly treasures not only proves useless but binds the heart and person to a dominating power.

they will invariably encounter opposition; and in the course of their trials they will have opportunity to bear witness to the Gentiles. Yet not all they meet will be antagonistic to their work. Some will show themselves to be worthy by receiving them and accepting their message (cf. vv. 11-14). It is to these people who receive (δέχομαι) the servants of God that the promise of reward is directed. The reward is granted primarily because these people recognize that the disciples are no ordinary travellers, but are messengers who come in the authority of God. This is the implication of the phrase 'in the name of' (εἰς ὄνομα) which recurs throughout vv. 41-42, that is, the one who receives does so on the grounds that the other is a prophet, righteous one or disciple.[1] Thus, the reward is given not so much in response to a hospitable deed as in response to the spiritual discernment which lies behind the action. Those who receive acknowledge that the disciples are 'worthy' (cf. v. 10), and by that action they show themselves to be 'worthy' (v. 12). Through this act of receiving, solidarity with the disciple is demonstrated, and it is for this reason that the one who receives the disciple receives a corresponding reward.[2] The very thing which the disciples stand to inherit will be

1.   Gundry (Matthew, p. 202) suggests the meaning 'with faith that he is what his title implies'. The designations that appear in these verses, προφήτης, δίκαιος, and ἕνα τῶν μικρῶν τούτων, are best interpreted as different ways of referring to the disciples, the ὑμεῖς of v. 40. It is fitting that such titles as 'prophet' and 'righteous one' appear in a discourse section which in great measure is concerned with the persecution of the disciples, considering that a motif is present throughout Matthew that such ones are rejected, persecuted and even killed (cf. 5.12; 13.57; 23.29-37). This would suggest that the one receiving the disciple accepts the risk that accompanies identification with the persecuted. Elsewhere in Matthew prophets and righteous ones are linked together with reference to important figures of the past (13.17; 23.29). That they are here linked together with reference to figures of the present may indicate Matthew's interest in connecting God's servants of the present time with those of an earlier time (cf. 23.34-35). See Gnilka, Matthäusevangelium, II, p. 402. In v. 42 the phrase 'one of these little ones' stands parallel to the term disciple. The phrase occurs again in ch. 18 in a context dealing with children and serves as an apt description of the disciple who, like a child, is to be totally dependent on the Father. The disciple may stand in succession to the great figures of the past but this involves no repudiation of the title 'little one' and the humility which is essential to it.

2.   There is some debate as to how best to interpret the genitives following μισθός in v. 41. D. Hill ('ΔΙΚΑΙΟΙ as a Quasi-Technical Term', NTS 11 [1965], pp. 296-302 [299]) treats these not as objective genitives but as genitives of origin, that is, the

theirs as well, since they have associated themselves with the work of the disciples.

Up to this point the language of reward has been used to encourage the disciple in the performance of the Father's will. The present text is no exception, even if at first glance it may appear to treat the disciple as incidental while addressing the question of the reward given to the one who receives. An astounding commendation emerges in v. 40: to receive the disciple is to receive Jesus, the one who sent the disciple, and to receive Jesus is to receive God, the one who sent him. Both God and Jesus are inextricably linked with the disciple in the accomplishment of the divine mission. This divine identification with the disciple is assumed in vv. 41-42. The disciple, in effect, becomes the bearer of blessing to those who respond positively to the work and assist in its completion.[1] Just as God had earlier assured Abraham with the promise that he would 'bless those who bless you', the disciple is now assured in a similar fashion.[2] This is as one would expect, since the work that had its beginnings with Abraham and which is to have ramifications for the entire world is now continued by the disciples.

person will receive the reward which the prophet or righteous one gives, which, according to Hill's understanding of the terms, is proclamation and instruction. However, the texts to which Hill refers to support this understanding of the genitives (LXX Isa. 40.10; 62.11; Rev. 22.12) have either Yahweh or Jesus as the subject, that is, they are the ones who bring recompense. In view of the conceptual content of these verses they may be taken to support the position that it is God's recompense that is in view here. Green (*Matthew*, p. 113) similarly understands 'the reward of a prophet' as a reward from the prophet and refers to 1 Kgs 17.8-24 and 2 Kgs 4.8-37 (note v. 13) as examples of what is meant in v. 41. However, considering the theme of persecution which pervades Mt. 10, a more appropriate example from the Old Testament is the promise of reward given to Ebed-melech (Jer. 39.15-18) after he rescues the prophet Jeremiah. It is also noteworthy that according to Ezek. 14.10 the one who inquires of a false prophet receives the same punishment as the false prophet. It is probably best to understand these as objective genitives referring to the reward that the prophet and righteous one will receive from God at the end.

1.   A. Schlatter, *Der Evangelist Matthäus* (Stuttgart: Calwer Verlag, 1957), p. 354: 'Der Junger soll wissen, daß er der Träger des Segens für jeden ist, der ihm die Hand reicht'.

2.   The promise of Gen. 12.3 is also significant to Mt. 25.31-46, a passage which will be discussed in the next chapter.

Matthew 16.24-28

A further example of the linking of reward with the demands of discipleship is found in 16.24-28. Within the context of Matthew this body of teaching is placed after the episode which treats the confession and subsequent rebuke of Peter. Jesus predicts his own fate, from which he is not to be deterred, as one of sacrifice and death. In these verses the way of discipleship is described as one which necessitates the acceptance of a similar fate. In v. 24 discipleship is looked at under a new aspect, the denial of oneself. The idea of self-denial is, of course, implicit in the cross-bearing and following of Jesus that had been demanded earlier in 10.38-39; and indeed in the present text these two terms are used to explain more fully the meaning of self-denial.[1] Nevertheless, the phrase 'to deny oneself' is itself a valuable summation of the nature of discipleship. It has already been noted that the fulfilment of the better righteousness which God demands, in the manner in which he expects, requires sacrifice on the part of the disciple. This sacrifice is possible only when the disciple is fully committed, and such commitment presupposes self-denial.[2] In vv. 25-27 three additional sayings are connected to this affirmation of self-denial by means of the conjunction γάρ, which implies that these successive statements either explain further or tell of the consequences of self-denial. Thus, one is to deny oneself in the first place because only through the loss of one's life for the sake of Jesus is true life to be found. The noun ψυχή in v. 25 is used in two senses: that of the mere physical existence of the person, and that of the everlasting life which the person either gains or loses. For the latter sense compare 10.28. Instead of the save/lose, lose/save pattern of the parallel verses in Mark (8.35) and Luke (9.24), Matthew has save/lose, lose/find (cf. 10.39). Possibly Matthew wishes to associate these texts which treat the sacrifices and final result of committed discipleship with the saying of 7.13-14, that is, the way is difficult that leads to life and only a few, the truly dedicated, find it.[3] In the second place, it is noted that even if

---

1. The use of καί in v. 24 is here understood as explicative and not simply connective. Cf. Bonnard, *Matthieu*, pp. 249-50.

2. Bonnard (*Matthieu*, p. 250) remarks that the one who follows Jesus 'a trouvé un nouveau centre à sa propre vie; il n'est plus à lui-même sa propre raison d'être'.

3. Note also that in 11.29 those who submit to the yoke of Jesus find rest for their souls (ψυχή).

one were able to indulge oneself to the fullest it would be to no avail if true life were lost. Finally, the denial of oneself is worthwhile because in the end it will be rewarded.

An eschatological perspective is presupposed in vv. 25-26, yet especially comes to the foreground in v. 27 with the mention of the Son of man coming in glory with his angels. The reference to angels suggests a separating and gathering (cf. 13.41, 49; 24.31); in this case a separating of the self-denying from the self-indulgent so that each group might receive the appropriate recompense. At that time the Son of man 'will repay (ἀποδίδωμι) each person according to his or her work'. This statement about recompense in v. 27b is unique to Matthew, even though the passage as a whole closely resembles the related passages in Mark (8.34–9.1) and Luke (9.23-27). The declaration could have been modelled after any number of Old Testament texts and appears in various forms elsewhere in the New Testament.[1] The most noticeable feature of the Matthaean formulation is the use of the singular τὴν πρᾶξιν. One inference that can be drawn from this is that according to Matthew the life of the disciple, and that of the non-disciple, is seen as a unity, not divisible into so many individual deeds.[2] One might go a little further and suggest, in keeping with the logic of the passage, that the deed which the Son of man will reward is self-denial, since self-denial epitomizes the life of discipleship. Conversely, it is the lack of commitment, demonstrated in saving one's life and indulging oneself, which is punished. It has already been observed that for Matthew reward is given not merely for what one does, but for what one is.[3] And there is no idea which conveys better the essence of discipleship than self-denial.

The final pronouncement in v. 28 is very problematic.[4] One might

---

1.   Compare, for example, Ps. 61.13 [LXX]: σὺ ἀποδώσεις ἑκάστῳ κατὰ τὰ ἔργα αὐτοῦ; Jer. 17.10; 39.19 [LXX]: δοῦναι ἑκάστῳ κατὰ τὰς ὁδοὺς αὐτοῦ; and Prov. 24.12 [LXX]: ὃς ἀποδίδωσιν ἑκάστῳ κατὰ τὰ ἔργα αὐτοῦ; in the New Testament compare Rom. 2.6; 2 Cor. 5.10; and Rev. 22.12.

2.   Schmid (*Matthäus*, p. 292) remarks that 'belohnt wird der sittliche Wert des Menschen, nicht die Summe seiner einzelnen Taten'. Compare also Schweizer, *Matthew*, p. 347; and Gnilka, *Matthäusevangelium*, II, p. 89.

3.   Mohrlang (*Matthew and Paul*, p. 52) states that in Matthew 'the question of behaviour can never be separated from that of inner character'.

4.   In the parallels of Mark (9.1) and Luke (9.27) it is said that some present will not taste death until they witness the kingdom of God (come with power). Matthew's term 'kingdom of the Son of man' most probably denotes something other than the

suggest, in view of the sequence of events outlined in 13.41-43, according to which the judgment takes place at a time of transition when the 'kingdom of the Son of man' is succeeded by the 'kingdom of the Father', that the Son of man's kingdom culminates with the parousia. One might infer from this that the event which marks the Son of man coming into his kingdom is that described in 28.16-20, when Jesus informs his disciples that 'all authority in heaven and on earth' has been given to him.[1] Hence the 'kingdom of the Son of man' is a *heilsgeschichtlich* concept describing the period of time extending from the resurrection/exaltation of Jesus to the parousia. Many of the disciples present on this occasion will in fact witness the Son of man coming into his kingdom. This gives them the assurance that he will return bringing his recompense with him.

Matthew 19.16–20.16

The last passage in Matthew which employs the vocabulary of reward, and a section which provides a fitting conclusion to the reward texts of the Gospel, is the complex of teaching found in 19.16–20.16. This extended passage includes the encounter with the rich young man (19.16-22), the saying about riches and entrance into the kingdom (19.23-26), the promise of reward to the disciples (19.27-30) and the parable about the wage of the workers (20.1-16).[2] These units of

'kingdom of God'. It is likely that for Matthew the various 'kingdoms' mentioned in the Gospel have different referents.

1. Note the allusion to Dan. 7.13-14 in Mt. 28.18. In the Daniel text the one 'like a son of man' comes to God to receive the authority proper to his kingdom. B. Lindars (*Jesus Son of Man* [London: SPCK, 1983], p. 120) suggests that the idea of 'coming in his kingdom' means the assumption of kingly rule, which for Matthew begins at the resurrection. It is his view that Mt. 16.28 refers to the resurrection as a pledge of the parousia. Note also the discussion in France, *Evangelist and Teacher*, pp. 314-15, where it is argued that the Matthaean references to the 'coming' of the Son of man are not restricted to the parousia.

2. The 'wage of the workers' is perhaps the earliest title given to the parable (cf. *Ap. Jas.* 6.10) and is more to the point than the common title 'the workers in the vineyard'. This parable consistently receives the greatest attention whenever Jesus' teaching on reward is discussed. The parable has, in fact, been the subject of an entire monograph on reward, K. Weiss, *Die Frohbotschaft Jesu über Lohn und Vollkommenheit: Zur evangelischen Parabel von den Arbeitern im Weinberg, Mt 20, 1-16* (Münster: Aschendorff, 1927). It is unfortunate that scholars are so drawn to this parable, treating it as though it were the cornerstone of the gospel teaching on the subject of reward, since the interpretation of the parable is so fraught with difficulty.

teaching are structurally related to each other. The repetition of the saying of 19.30 at the end of the parable links the parable with the teaching of 19.16-30. In addition, the conjunction γάρ in 20.1 connects the parable with the preceding pericope. One might also note that the occurrence of 'eternal life' in 19.16 and 19.29 forms an *inclusio*. In view of these links, it is interesting that Mt. 19.16–20.16 is rarely, if ever, discussed as a unit.

Moreover, certain significant motifs which have appeared already in this discussion recur in these verses; for example, being 'perfect' (19.21), having 'treasure in heaven' (19.21), 'entering into the kingdom of heaven' (19.23), 'inheriting' eternal life (19.29), the 'paying' of a μισθός for service (20.8) and the 'evil eye' (20.15). The echoing of Jesus' assertion that 'One is good' in the response of the vineyard owner that 'I am good' forms an enclosure around the entire section and suggests that the parable is specifically directed at the preceding narrative concerning the rich young man. One might infer from this that the character of the young man who has performed his duty well ('all these things I have kept') but who refuses to walk in the way of perfection which leads to treasure in heaven is mirrored in the character of the first hired who have also worked hard ('we bore the burden and heat of the day') but whose reprehensible conduct prompts the charge that their eye is evil. The initial 'righteousness' of the young man and of the first hired proves, by the end of each story, to be deceptive. They are, in fact, examples of the 'first' who become 'last'. The disciples, on the other hand, have done the will of the Father by giving up everything and following Jesus. In consequence, they will be among the 'first'.

The narrative opens with the question of the young man about the good thing he must do in order to have eternal life. In both Mark (10.17) and Luke (18.18) the man asks about what should be done that he might inherit eternal life (ζωὴν αἰώνιον κληρονομήσω). The wording in Matthew (σχῶ ζωὴν αἰώνιον) may be a deliberate linking of this initial question with the closing remark of v. 22 that the man had (ἔχω) many possessions, that is, in the Matthaean wording lies a hint that the man is treating eternal life merely as one other possession to which he can lay claim.[1] In response to this question Jesus refers

1. Also of interest is the phrase σχῶμεν τὴν κληρονομίαν in the parable of the wicked tenants (21.38). It is perhaps significant that the two times in the Gospel where the aorist subjunctive of ἔχω occurs it is on the lips of 'unworthy'

the man to God, the one who is good, and to the commandments in which his will is revealed. Note that several times in the Old Testament the noun טוב is used of Yahweh in the sense of 'the Good One'. The apparent contrast in vv. 16-17 between the εἷς who seeks to *do* good and the εἷς who *is* good possibly intimates that the young man is one who thinks of goodness as resident in deeds. Ultimately he refuses to be perfect, which, according to 5.48, makes one like God.

The young man has kept all the commandments. Thus it can be said that he possesses a form of righteousness, like that of the scribes and Pharisees (cf. 5.20). Yet, at the same time, the young man falls short of the 'more' that is essential to entrance into the kingdom of heaven. For that reason Jesus issues the challenge to be perfect.[1] For the young man the demand for perfection consists in selling his possessions, giving the proceeds to the poor and following Jesus. This action would express his total devotion to God, which is the essence of perfection.[2] It would also constitute the self-denial which is essential to discipleship. Finally, the action would result in reward for the young man; he would have treasure in heaven. Tragically, the heart of this rich man is too concentrated on earthly treasure to look to a future reward with God. He is unable to bring himself to make the necessary sacrifice, the requisite 'good thing', and thus goes away sorrowful.[3] This young man who had desired 'to have' eternal life forfeits the opportunity 'to have' such treasure in heaven because his real desire is 'to have' treasure on earth.

---

people who want to possess an inheritance.

1. Compare the remarks of Gerhard Barth ('Matthew's Understanding of the Law', in G. Bornkamm, G. Barth and H.J. Held, *Tradition and Interpretation in Matthew* [Philadelphia: Westminster Press, 1963], pp. 58-164 [97 n. 2]): 'It should be noted that τέλειος then means still more than δίκαιος, for it is not denied that the Pharisees are δίκαιοι, but the righteousness of the congregation must exceed that of the Pharisees. . . this lower level of righteousness, which is no τελειότης is not sufficient for entrance into the kingdom'. Note the parallel that exists between εἰ θέλεις εἰς τὴν ζωὴν εἰσελθεῖν and εἰ θέλεις τέλειος εἶναι which suggests that entrance into life and perfection are coincident.

2. The action demanded of the young man is reminiscent of God's call of Abraham. Abraham is instructed to leave behind family and possessions and put his trust in Yahweh.

3. Meier (*Matthew*, p. 220) contrasts the sorrow of the young man with the joy of the man in 13.44 who sells everything to gain the treasure.

Earlier in the Gospel Jesus had emphasized the need to separate one-self from any stumbling block that would prevent one from entering into life (18.8-9). In his comment to the disciples following the young man's refusal to enter, as it were, through the narrow gate, Jesus speaks of riches as one such stumbling block. It is hard for someone who is rich to enter into the kingdom of heaven because many possessions make the required self-denial difficult. The disciples are astounded to hear that it is virtually impossible for a rich person to be saved. Undoubtedly, their upbringing had taught them that goods and property were a gift of God and a sign of his blessing.[1] To their way of thinking this young man who not only kept all the commandments but who also had many possessions is a 'son of the kingdom' *par excellence*. If anyone were to inherit eternal life, surely it would be someone like this man.

The response of Jesus to their surprised outburst implicitly states that it is incorrect to speak of any individual as an excellent candidate for salvation. The verb ἐμβλέπω in v. 26 is perhaps best understood in the sense of a reproachful glance (cf. Lk. 20.17; 22.61). Scholars overlook the significance of this exchange when they are content to understand Jesus' reply simply as an affirmation that salvation is the work of God alone. If that is all that is meant, then this statement seriously weakens the earlier remark about the special disadvantage which comes with riches. In effect Jesus is made to say that it is impossible for the rich to be saved, but, then again, it is impossible for anyone to be saved. Rather, Jesus' response, while affirming the indispensability of God's grace to salvation, is a rebuke of the disciples' endorsement of the rich man. This ideal Israelite, in spite of his righteousness and apparent blessedness, is unable to effect his own salvation. Only God is able to do that. And yet this man has turned away from God's messiah, the very one who came to save the people of Israel (1.21). In his response Jesus is seeking to move his disciples away from such superficial judgments. The outward appearance of

---

1.   Even though the Old Testament teaching on wealth is not unequivocally positive, there are many texts in which riches are depicted as good and as a blessing from God (cf. Gen. 13.2; 2 Chron. 1.12; Prov. 8.21; Eccl. 5.19). At the same time, Jesus' command that the young man sell his possessions and give to the poor presupposes that Israel had not been obedient to the commands of Yahweh, since, according to Deut. 15.4-5, faithful obedience would result in the elimination of poverty from the land (yet note the candour of Deut. 15.11).

righteousness and blessedness is not necessarily a true indication of the inward condition.[1] Entrance into the kingdom, as the disciples should know, is determined not by the station of individuals but only by their response to the call of God. Through Jesus, God is calling all to salvation. Some, like the young man, turn away from that call; others, however, leave all and follow Jesus.

These words of Jesus about riches and salvation prompt Peter to ask about the consequences for the disciples of having left everything to follow him.[2] The answer to this question consists in two promises: the first directed exclusively to the twelve and the second to all disciples. In the first promise the exaltation and vindication of the disciples in the renewed creation is described.[3] When the Son of man sits on his glorious throne they also will sit on twelve thrones judging the twelve tribes of Israel.[4] The meaning of κρίνω in v. 28 is the subject of some disagreement.[5] It is possible to interpret the verb in the sense of

1. Compare Jesus' condemnation of the scribes and Pharisees in 23.28. They appear righteous to others but are actually full of hypocrisy and sin. From the perspective of God, which the disciples are to share, many of those who appear 'first' are in fact 'last', as the judgment will reveal.

2. It is the view of Gnilka (*Matthäusevangelium*, II, pp. 170-71), shared by others, that even though Peter is not rebuked by Jesus, the question is nonetheless a foolish one which is corrected in the following parable. Yet the numerous promises of reward that have appeared already in the Gospel make the question a very natural one. The attitude reflected in the question need not be construed as either foolish or mercenary. The extended narrative makes it clear that the disciples will ultimately be among the 'first', whereas many of their Jewish compatriots, like the young man, will be among the 'last'. This is not to say, however, that a disciple cannot fall into an identical trap of presumption. The theme of false disciples will receive much attention in Chapter 3.

3. The term παλιγγενεσία in v. 28 undoubtedly refers to the renewal of creation at the end of the present age (cf. Isa. 65.17; 66.22).

4. The imagery here is similar to that of other Matthaean judgment scenes (cf. 16.27; 25.31-46). The wording is particularly close to 25.31: ὅταν δὲ ἔλθη ὁ υἱὸς τοῦ ἀνθρώπου . . . τότε καθίσει ἐπὶ θρόνου δόξης αὐτοῦ.

5. This disagreement is due in part to how one understands the phrase 'the twelve tribes of Israel', which can be interpreted as a literal reference to the Jewish nation, or as a metaphorical reference to the church. Considering that elsewhere in Matthew 'Israel' refers to the Jewish people, it would seem best to understand it in that sense here as well. As Grundmann (*Matthäus*, p. 435) notes, Israel is seen in the full number of tribes corresponding to the Jewish hope.

'governing' Israel.[1] However, the absence of lexical support from the New Testament, the reference to the Jewish nation and the verbal links with Mt. 25.31-46 argue against this position.[2] It is best to interpret κρίνω in the more usual sense of administering justice at the last judgment. The people of Israel, like the people of all other nations, will have to give an account at the judgment of the way in which they responded to and treated the Son of man and his agents.[3] The twelve will participate in that judgment because they had participated in the special mission to Israel.[4] The promise concerns a future reversal of position. The disciples who have not only left all but have faced calumny, persecution and condemnation in the fulfilment of their mission to Israel will be elevated to positions of honour and authority at the judgment. On the other hand, their compatriots who would not receive the message of the kingdom will stand condemned. Although the twelve receive special honour at the last judgment corresponding to the special role they played in life, there will be a wonderful return for every person who has made sacrifices to follow Jesus. The 'hundredfold' return they can expect recalls the 'great' reward of 5.12. This return is essentially interpreted by the next phrase which promises that they shall inherit eternal life. The family and property that disciples have left behind will be more than compensated for in the future life in the 'renewed land'. The reference to eternal life brings the passage full circle. The very thing which the young man sought but rejected because of the high cost is gained by the disciples who have sacrificed all in response to the call of God.

The saying of 19.30, which serves both to conclude the preceding pericope and to introduce the following parable, is an affirmation of the future reversal of position. Many that now enjoy the 'first' place will at the judgment be placed among the 'last', just as the 'last' will be elevated to 'first' place. The judgment scene of v. 28 had illustrated

1. Compare Pesch, *Lohngedanke*, pp. 74-75, and Hill, *Matthew*, p. 284.
2. In order to support the opinion that here κρίνω 'could have the broader sense rule', *BAGD* ('κρίνω', 4bβ) is forced back to the Septuagint.
3. Concerning the judgment of Israel, note the threats of 10.15, 11.22-24 and 12.41-42 that the towns and cities of Israel will be judged for not responding to the message of the kingdom nor repenting even though mighty miracles had been done in them.
4. In the words of J. Dupont ('Le logion des douze trônes [Mt. 19, 28; Lc 22, 28-30]', *Bib* 45 [1964], pp. 355-92 [388]), this saying relates to 'un jugement d'Israël, corrélatif à une mission concernant Israël'.

just such a reversal, inasmuch as the twelve, who in their outreach to Israel are very much as 'sheep among wolves' (10.16), will receive positions of power and authority, whereas their Jewish persecutors will face the humiliation of judgment. This saying about reversal also refers back to the narrative of the rich man, since he is the embodiment of what is meant by 'first'. Yet his refusal to answer the call of God leaves no question concerning his final status. The parable of the wage of the workers, which is inserted between 19.30 and its complement of 20.16, is an additional illustration of the reversal of position. The 'last' hired receive a great return from the owner of the vineyard, while the 'first' hired receive his condemnation.

The parable opens with a description of the efforts of a landowner (οἰκοδεσπότης) to find workers for his vineyard. The allusive image of the vineyard associates this parable, and the parables of 21.28-32 and 21.33-44, with the story of God's dealings with his people.[1] It would appear to address the question of why some in Israel inherit eternal life while others do not. Early in the morning the vineyard owner goes out and negotiates a wage of one denarius for the day's work with a group of workers. Then, in the third hour, he approaches a second group and promises to pay them whatever is appropriate.[2] He does the same thing at the sixth and ninth hours. Finally, one hour before the end of the working day, he sends one last group into the vineyard. Up to this point the parable offers a straightforward account of an ordinary working day. When evening comes, however, the story takes an unusual turn. The owner, now described as the 'Lord of the Vineyard', instructs his steward to pay the wages, beginning with the

---

1.   It is improper to argue, as L. Schenke does ('Die Interpretation der Parabel von den 'Arbeiten im Weinberg' [Mt. 20,1-15] durch Matthäus', in L. Schenke [ed.], *Studien zum Matthäusevangelium* [Stuttgart: Katholisches Bibelwerk, 1988], p. 267), that since the other two vineyard parables make it clear that unbelieving Israel is no longer numbered among the vineyard workers, the workers mentioned in this parable must be disciples.

2.   The phrase οἱ δὲ ἀπῆλθον in v. 5 is ambiguous since it can mean either that the men declined the offer of employment and went away, or accepted it and went into the vineyard. According to F.C. Glover ('Workers for the Vineyard', *ExpTim* 86 [1974–75], pp. 310-11 [310]), the presence of the adversative particle δέ makes the first alternative more probable, considering the use of δέ when there is the suggestion of an invitation being refused (cf. 19.22 and 22.5). In any case, for the design of the parable only two groups of workers are essential, the first hired and the last hired, and by the end the focus is strictly on the first hired.

last hired.[1] Yet the payment itself is even more surprising; for not only do the last hired receive a full day's wage, but the first hired, who in witnessing this expect more, receive no more than the agreed wage.[2] The wage paid to each group is identical, yet it could hardly be described as comparable.

The reaction of the first hired to this unexpected outcome and the subsequent reply of the owner constitute the focal point of the parable. The first hired complain to the owner about the incongruity of treating the last hired, whose toil did not compare with their own, as their equals. The grievance of these workers appears to be quite justified. In response to this complaint, the owner reminds them that no wrong has been done since they received the agreed amount. In addition, he affirms his right to give the others more than expected if he so chooses. The words of the owner, while seeming direct and equitable, nonetheless sound a fateful note. The address, 'Friend', in v. 13 expresses reproach with a hint of foreboding, since ἑταῖρε, found only in Matthew, appears elsewhere in contexts of dignified censure (cf. 22.12 and 26.50).[3] Moreover, the accusation that the conduct of these workers evinces the 'evil eye' implies that their inner light is darkened. The depiction of the first workers parallels that of the young man to the extent that one only gradually comes to recognize that their character is essentially false. The veil of righteousness, which conceals an ill-favoured inner condition, impresses at first but by the end is stripped away. It would appear that in both cases the individuals concerned had disregarded the goodness of God, choosing instead to focus on their own accomplishments.[4] Their egotism,

---

1.   It is perhaps significant that in the parable of the wicked tenants when the owner comes in judgment he also is described as the 'Lord of the Vineyard' (21.40).

2.   J.D. Crossan (*In Parables: The Challenge of the Historical Jesus* [San Francisco: Harper & Row, 1973], p. 114) rightly observes that the owner is not portrayed as someone who is particularly generous but as one who violates expectations.

3.   K.H. Rengstorf ('ἑταῖρος', *TDNT*, II, p. 701) remarks that although it would be incorrect to read too much into the term, it can be said that 'in all three cases it is more than a mere form. It always denotes a mutually binding relation between the speaker and the hearer which the latter has disregarded and scorned.' Gnilka (*Matthäusevangelium*, II, p. 179) notes that the address 'läßt nichts Gutes ahnen'.

4.   The question which closes the parable is a forceful reminder to all who are very conscious of their own deeds but prone to forget the goodness of God, on

expressed in the presumption that their outward activity somehow places the 'Lord' under obligation, makes them blind to that goodness which they should embrace so as to be more like the 'Lord' who rewards. It is this condition which will place them among the 'last'. It is, of course, true that the first hired do receive the same wage as the last hired. However, that is not the point of the parable. The μισθός given to the last hired is comparable to a 'hundredfold' return, whereas that given to the first hired is a mere settling of accounts. Their μισθός is not unlike that given to the hypocrites of ch. 6 who similarly 'receive in full' the payment they sought.[1] Elevation to the 'first' place requires a humility which both recognizes and emulates the goodness of God. The honour that is signified by the term 'first' is that which is ultimately bestowed upon the meek whose perfect fulfilment of the will of the Father allows them entrance into the inheritance.

Conclusion

The new covenant which is centred in Jesus and which provides the new basis of membership in the people of God is, like that of Sinai, a covenant of human obligation. Whereas God has made provision for the salvation of both Jews and Gentiles in the life and death of Jesus, the redemption of each is determined by their response to Jesus and their obedience to 'the will of the Father'. Just as in the Old Testament the entrance into and the inheritance of the land of Canaan is conditioned upon the faithfulness of the people in keeping the statutes and commandments of Yahweh, so also in Matthew the entrance into and the inheritance of the spiritualized land of God's future kingdom is conditioned upon the faithfulness of the individual in keeping the commandments of God in accordance with the requirements of Jesus. This inheritance constitutes the reward that is in store for all those whose lives reflect the wholeness and the integrity of the perfect righteousness demanded by Jesus.

The reward promised to the disciples of Jesus is to be viewed

which everything depends. Cf. W. Haubeck, 'Zum Verständnis der Parabel von den Arbeitern im Weinberg (Mt. 20,1-15)', in W. Haubeck and M. Bachmann (eds.), *Wort in der Zeit* (Leiden: Brill, 1980), p. 106.

1. In the words of H.L. Strack and P. Billerbeck (*Kommentar zum Neuen Testament aus Talmud und Midrasch* [Munich: Oskar Beck, 1928], IV.1, p. 487), the first hired are paid 'nach dem kalten Buchstaben des Lohnvertrags'.

against the backdrop of the restoration to land and kingdom which the prophets had foreseen. The land, kingdom, treasure and life which await the disciple are all symbolic of the blessed goal which God has appointed for his own, and the realisation of this goal is, from Matthew's perspective, the return which the prophets had envisaged. Those people who gather around Jesus, confess him as Lord and practice his teaching form the repentant and faithful remnant and thus become the new bearers of the divine promises. These 'few' face hardship and persecution for the sake of Jesus; yet they obediently sacrifice all to follow him. They are the meek and humble whose trust is in God alone. However, as the consequence of this resolute commitment, their 'heavenly Father' will one day reverse their fortunes by exalting them to positions of honour as his 'sons' in the eternal inheritance prepared for them.

Chapter 3

'BUT THOSE HE CURSES SHALL BE CUT OFF'
THE TEACHING ON PUNISHMENT IN THE GOSPEL OF MATTHEW

It is the belief of Matthew that God has prescribed the way of redemption, for both Jew and Gentile, through the new covenant which is concluded in the death of Jesus. Those who avail themselves of this salvation, which is centred in the one who can be designated 'son of God' (3.17; 16.16), are the blessed ones who demonstrate, through their obedience and faithfulness to the will of God, that they too are in fellowship with the 'heavenly Father'. These righteous ones receive the promise of inheritance and one day will be granted entrance into the land and kingdom which God has prepared for all his children. At the same time, however, it is evident from the Gospel that many people are unwilling to follow this way of salvation. There would appear to be a number of reasons why such people refuse the redemption which God has appointed. Some are deluded by a false sense of security based on their ethnic membership in the historic covenant people, others seem content with the level of righteousness they have already attained, and many simply are not willing to make the requisite sacrifice that obedience to God demands. These individuals who spurn the offer of salvation, for whatever reason, are, in the end, punished by God. It has already been noted that the self-assured will be destroyed in the judgment, the self-righteous will be rejected by God, and the self-indulgent will lose everything. Even many who appear to be 'first', in the sense that they seem to be worthy of God's favour, will find themselves numbered among the 'last' because of their failure to do the will of the Father.

Matthew emphasizes reward throughout his Gospel because he wishes to encourage the disciple in what is a difficult vocation. Faithful service to God is both exacting and arduous. Yet the teaching on reward motivates steadfast service by reminding the disciple of the goal of such service. The teaching on punishment serves a corresponding function, inasmuch as the threat of judgment is utilized to prompt movement in the direction of the obedience demanded.[1] Thus, Matthew sees validity in employing both promise and threat to motivate proper behaviour. This two-sided emphasis, which is intrinsic to the paraenesis of the Gospel, is essentially rooted in the nature of the final judgment. It is a judgment which is strictly concerned with the two categories of reward and punishment, and which makes no allowance for a third alternative. For that reason, at the judgment one is placed either among the 'first' or the 'last', either with the 'blessed' or the 'cursed'. Moreover, the two categories of reward and punishment coincide with two very distinct destinations. It has already been shown that reward, according to Matthew, consists in the blissful existence enjoyed in the future kingdom. In a similar way, the punishment envisioned in the Gospel is identified with a place of torment. When the judgment is concluded, the unrighteous are consigned to Gehenna, a place of eternal fire and extreme darkness and characterized by 'weeping and gnashing of teeth'. The summons to walk in the way of righteousness is thus issued against a backdrop of two very disparate landscapes, describing the only two possible ends.

The recurring phrase, 'there will be weeping and gnashing of teeth', which appears like a macabre abstract of the horrors of future punishment, provides a solemn punctuation to a select group of passages in the Gospel. In discussing the subject of punishment in Matthew particular reference will be made to these texts. In addition, attention will be directed to the scene depicting the final judgment of all the nations (25.31-46), a passage to which Matthew has attached special importance by placing it at the conclusion of the final discourse of his Gospel. To begin this discussion of punishment in Matthew, however, the theme of 'fruit' will be examined. On almost every occasion that Matthew employs the imagery of fruit it is within a

---

1.   Mohrlang (*Matthew and Paul*, p. 57) states that 'the threat of eschatological judgement is the strongest and most effective means that the evangelist knows of reinforcing his stringent demands for a life of absolute obedience'. One can appreciate at a glance the extent to which judgment language permeates the Gospel by consulting the table of references which Marguerat (*Jugement*, p. 31) has compiled. The particular stress that Matthew places on the threat of punishment recalls the long list of curses attached to the Sinai covenant which served, in a similar manner, to accentuate the seriousness of disobedience.

context of judgment. Moreover, it is frequently the case that inadequate fruit constitutes the ground for punishment.

Fruitlessness and Judgment

It was observed in Chapter 1 that inherent in the covenant relationship between Yahweh and the people of Israel was the expectation that they would become a fruitful nation. These descendants and heirs of Abraham could be said to have fulfilled this expectation only to the extent that they remained faithful to Yahweh and carried forward the task he had committed to them. Yet the story of the covenant nation is, in many respects, that of the frustration of this hope. The people of Israel strayed from Yahweh and failed miserably in the role assigned to them of becoming a holy and righteous people through whom blessing could be extended to all the other nations of the earth. What fruit the nation did produce was abhorrent to Yahweh. As a result, the people were rejected by the one who had planted and nurtured them and, like a useless vine which is uprooted and discarded, they were cast out of their land into exile. This emphasis on the theme of fruit is carried over into the Gospel of Matthew. Matthew devotes more attention to the subject of bearing fruit than do the other Synoptists. Moreover, one finds in Matthew a particular interest in the contrast between good and bad fruit.[1] There can be little doubt that this accent within the Gospel originates from Matthew's keen interest in the story of God's dealings with his people.

Matthew 3.7-12

The first announcement that appropriate fruit is essential to survive the judgment of God occurs in the preaching of John the Baptist. His statement concerning the need to bear good fruit appears in a context describing a large group of Pharisees and Sadducees who come to his baptism.[2] The association of the Pharisees with the Sadducees in this

---

1. The term καρπός appears 19 times in Matthew, 11 times in Luke, and 5 times in Mark. Concerning the metaphorical expression καρποὺς ποιεῖν, Frankemölle (*Jahwebund*, p. 279) observes that it is one which 'Mt im Vergleich zu seinen Vorlagen erheblich erweitert hat'. The contrast between good and bad fruit is found twice in Matthew, once in Luke, and not at all in Mark.

2. Gundry (*Matthew*, p. 46) is probably correct to understand ἐπὶ τὸ βάπτισμα in the sense of the Pharisees and Sadducees merely coming to the baptism, perhaps

text is unusual, and perhaps results from Matthew's wish to portray
the Jewish leadership as united against the precursor of Jesus.[1] There
is only one other occasion in the Gospels, that described in Mt. 16.1-4,
when these two parties are joined together. In that passage they are
united in the request that Jesus show them a sign from heaven. Jesus
responds to their petition with the indictment that they are 'an evil and
adulterous generation'. Inasmuch as this accusation describes a people
unquestionably ripe for judgment, it is not that far removed from
John's attack on the same group. In condemning these Jewish leaders,
John not only effectively invalidates their claim that physical descent
from Abraham grants them a privileged status, but, in a scathing
denunciation, he describes them as 'children of serpents'.[2] Their only
hope in the face of the coming wrath lies in whole-hearted repentance.[3] Without the presence of fruit consistent with such repentance
they will be destroyed in the inexorable judgment of God.

The judgment that is envisaged in these verses is best described as
single in its application but twofold in its effect. The strong one, who
comes after John, will administer only one baptism in the Holy Spirit
and fire, yet the consequence is different according to the recipient.[4]

---

for the purpose of critical observation, rather than undergoing baptism. In the parallel
passage of Lk. 3.7-9 it is the multitudes, coming to be baptized, who receive John's
rebuke.

1. Meier, *Matthew*, p. 24.

2. The description γεννήματα ἐχιδνῶν may carry the inference that these
leaders have been poisoning the people committed to their charge; cf. Beare,
Matthew, p. 93. To support this one might note that in Mt. 16.11-12 Jesus warns his
disciples against the leaven, or teaching, of the Pharisees and Sadducees. The image
in v. 7 of serpents fleeing calamity, especially when seen in conjunction with the
succeeding picture of the felling of trees, may have been suggested by Jer. 46.22-23,
where Egypt is likened to a serpent fleeing her enemies who come as woodsmen with
axes to cut down her forest.

3. It is noted by Gnilka (*Matthäusevangelium*, I, p. 69) that, in the near
repetition of these words by Jesus in Mt. 23.33, the wrath of God is interpreted as
'the judgment of Gehenna'. The imminence of the coming wrath is emphasized
throughout the passage. The axe is even now laid to the root, and the trees are
represented, in a proleptic manner, as already cut down and thrown into the fire.
Moreover, the coming one is portrayed with the winnowing fork present in his hand.

4. Gundry, *Matthew*, p. 49; cf. Davies and Allison, *Matthew*, I, p. 317 n. 48:
'the Spirit is not the gift for the righteous, the fire a punishment for the wicked.
There is only one "you" in the text.' Considering that the Pharisees and Sadducees
are included in this 'you', it is unacceptable to argue that, whereas v. 12 concerns

Similarly, in v. 12 only one act of winnowing is described, but with opposite results for the wheat and the chaff. That which determines the effect or consequence of the judgment is the condition of the person concerned. The fate of those who are unrepentant will be the same as trees which do not bear good fruit or as the chaff which remains on the threshing floor. Like such useless trees, they will be cut down (ἐκκόπτω) and thrown (βάλλω) into the fire.[1] And, like the chaff, they are of little use except as fuel for the fire.[2] On the other hand, those who demonstrate the sincerity of their repentance by 'bearing fruit' which corresponds to a fundamental change in heart are like trees which bear good fruit.[3] In the language of the complementary simile, they are like the wheat which is gathered into the granary.[4] The burden of John's warning is that good fruit must be produced if one is to stand firm and find acceptance at the judgment.

The bearing of fruit and the quality of fruit are, of course, metaphors for that which reveals the condition of a person's inner being.[5] Fruit does not simply refer to the performance of deeds which can be

---

destruction, v. 11 refers to a redemptive judgment.

1.   The image of God in judgment being as one who fells trees with an axe is found in the Old Testament; cf. Isa. 10.33-34. For the burning of trees as a figure of judgment compare Isa. 10.17-19 (of Assyria) and Jer. 11.16 (of Judah). The passive verbs in v. 10 are best understood as examples of the 'divine passive', that is, the passive voice indicates that the one performing the action is God. See Jeremias, *Theology*, pp. 9-14. The verb βάλλω in the passive appears frequently in Matthew with reference to eschatological judgment; cf. 5.29; 7.19; 18.8-9.

2.   The addition of the word 'inextinguishable' (ἄσβεστος) in v. 12, to an otherwise commonplace description of the winnowing process, introduces the idea of eschatological judgment. This conception of a fire which never goes out recalls Jer. 17.4, which describes the wrath of Yahweh kindling a fire which shall burn for ever. In the Old Testament the wicked are occasionally likened to chaff (cf. Ps. 1.4; Hos. 13.3). The end in view is not burning, however, but scattering by the wind. For the winnowing of Israel by Yahweh, see Jer. 15.7.

3.   The expression καρπὸν ποιεῖν is a Semitism meaning 'to bear fruit' or 'to produce fruit'; see M. Black, *An Aramaic Approach to the Gospels and Acts* (Oxford: Clarendon Press, 1967), pp. 138-39.

4.   According to W.C. Allen (*A Critical and Exegetical Commentary on the Gospel according to S. Matthew* [Edinburgh: T. & T. Clark, 1912], p. 26), the gathering into the granary is a picture of entrance into the kingdom.

5.   The idea behind the metaphor is well expressed in Sir. 27.6: 'The cultivation of a tree is revealed in its fruit; in a similar way, the expression of a thought reveals the heart of a person'.

evaluated as good or bad. Rather, fruit describes that which reflects the basic direction of the heart.[1] The inner reality and the underlying motivation of one's entire life is disclosed in the fruit which one produces. The Jewish leaders, on this occasion, are called upon by John to act in a way that would give evidence of a new orientation of life which would find acceptance with God. Yet within the larger Matthaean context these words serve a much broader purpose than merely recounting John's rebuke of Jewish impenitence. They serve also as a warning to the church, as can be seen in the exact restatement of John's words in 3.10b by Jesus in 7.19.[2] It is clear from Mt. 7.15-23, the next passage to treat the theme of fruit, that presumption and the absence of good fruit are not only a problem within the Jewish community, but are to be found also in the church.

Matthew 7.15-23

It is probably best to treat these verses as an extended unit of teaching which relates to a single theme and which refers to a single group, even though it is comprised of two component parts (vv. 15-20 and vv. 21-23).[3] Verse 19, which, as noted above, reproduces the warning

---

1. Schweizer, *Matthew*, p. 49. In the passage there is no reflection on the power which produces fruit; cf. F. Hauck, 'καρπός', *TDNT*, III, p. 615. It is to go beyond the evidence to assert, as R. Hensel does ('Fruit', *NIDNTT*, I, p. 722), that fruitbearing follows from repentance and is due to the power of the Spirit working within the individual. The initial move in turning back to God expresses a disposition of the heart and is itself a 'good fruit'.

2. Sand (*Matthäus*, p. 68), for example, claims that the warning given to these Jewish leaders 'ist zugleich Mahnrede (und ebenfalls Drohrede) an die Mt-Gemeinde, und auch hier vielleicht schon an solche in der Gemeinde, die besondere Verantwortung tragen'. The author of *2 Clement* (17.7) would appear to have Mt. 3.12 (= Lk. 3.17) in mind when he castigates Christians who have gone astray and denied Jesus in word and deed. Note his use of the phrase πυρὶ ἀσβέστῳ.

3. The thesis of D. Hill ('False Prophets and Charismatics: Structure and Interpretation in Matthew 7,15-23', *Bib* 57 [1976], pp. 335-48) that in the two sections two separate groups are in view, false prophets and charismatics, has not met with wide acceptance. Note the criticism of this position and the arguments in support of considering 7.15-23 as a unit in Guelich, *Sermon*, pp. 397-98 and Davies and Allison, *Matthew*, I, pp. 693, 701-702. There probably exists a logical connection between 7.15-23 and the saying concerning the two ways in 7.13-14, to the extent that the false prophets exemplify a category of people on the way that leads to destruction. France (*Matthew*, p. 147) goes too far, however, when he suggests that the false prophets offer an easier alternative to the narrow way. E. Schweizer

of John the Baptist, helps to connect the two segments by referring back to the imagery of vv. 16-18 while at the same time introducing the theme of judgment which points forward to the judgment scene of vv. 21-23. There is a shift in emphasis as one moves from one part to the other, insofar as the first pericope concerns the identification of false prophets, whereas the second pericope concerns their repudiation at the judgment.[1] Nevertheless, the overarching theme, that appearances can be deceptive, serves to unify the entire passage.

The false prophets of these verses are not described in such precise terms that one can reasonably expect to identify them as a specific group known to Matthew and his church.[2] Presumably, it was Matthew's intention to make the warning of the text indefinite so that it could have wide and continuing application. The primary emphasis is on the false nature of the prophets, that is, on their pretence to be something they are not. There can be little doubt that the prophets in view claim to be Christian.[3] The portrayal of these prophets as

('Observance of the Law and Charismatic Activity in Matthew', *NTS* 16 [1970], pp. 213-30 [226]) notes that the frequent appearance of ποιέω in 7.15-23 leads directly to the parable of the two builders in 7.24-27.

1. P.S. Minear, 'False Prophets and Hypocrisy in the Gospel of Matthew', in J. Gnilka (ed.), *Neues Testament und Kirche* (Freiburg: Herder, 1974), p. 83.

2 In this discussion no attempt will be made to identify the false prophets, except in the general terms permitted by the text. It would seem that Matthew's purpose in transmitting this teaching is not so much to warn against a specific group as to address the perennial problem of spurious Christians, particularly leaders, infiltrating the church.

3. The followers of Jesus are referred to as prophets in 23.34; cf. 5.12 and 10.41. One cannot infer from the use of προσέχω, which is used elsewhere in Matthew with reference to Jewish opponents, that Jewish opposition is in view here. Neither should one attach much importance to the appearance of λύκοι in 10.16, where it describes Jewish adversaries. It is not uncommon for Matthew to use a single metaphor to refer to two very different things. Compare, for example, the use of 'sheep' in 10.6 and 10.16, and 'harvest' in 9.37-38 and 13.39. The suggestion of Hill ('False Prophets', p. 345) that the false prophets are emissaries of the Pharisees sent to convince the Christian congregation of its errors overlooks the statement made by Jesus in 23.2-3. It is unlikely that Matthew would have included this endorsement of what the Pharisees say if his church was threatened by such Pharisaic opposition. Even so, it is illuminating that Matthew's choice of language can be said to point to Jewish opposition, since it informs the reader that dangers from within share common features with dangers from without. The warning (προσέχω) of 6.1, for example, suggests that the Christian can fall into the same trap of hypocrisy as the Jew.

'wolves in sheep's clothing' indicates that they wish to be accepted as genuine disciples and that their outward appearance is such that their true nature is not easily detected.[1] Nonetheless, just as bad trees can be known, so also can these 'wolves' be known.

The repetition of v. 16a in v. 20 forms an *inclusio* and makes the principle expressed in vv. 16-20 applicable to the false prophets of v. 15. The true nature of a person is made evident in the same way that the true nature of a tree is made evident and that is 'by their fruits' (ἀπὸ τῶν καρπῶν αὐτῶν).[2] Thus, the Christian is to observe the fruit that is in evidence so as to know the false prophets when they show themselves. The verb ἐπιγινώσκω signifies discernment (cf. 11.27; 17.12), and implies that only the discerning observer will detect the wolf inside the sheep's clothing.[3] Since words and deeds would be a part of the disguise it is inadequate to speak of fruit strictly in those terms. As was noted earlier, fruit is best defined as

---

1.   The phrase ἐν ἐνδύμασιν προβάτων should be understood as a metaphor for deceptive appearance rather than a literal description of the clothing of the prophets. Strecker (*Sermon*, p. 162) observes that the figure presupposes that the Christian community understood itself as a flock. The depiction of the prophets as wolves recalls the Old Testament passages in which the image is used of bad leaders (cf. Ezek. 22.27; Zeph. 3.3). That these are λύκοι ἅρπαγες may suggest personal greed, although Matthew is silent on this matter. The verb ἔρχομαι in v. 15 need not imply that itinerant prophets are meant.

2.   It is not clear why Matthew should use the plural 'fruits'. Schweizer ('Observance', p. 225) seeks to interpret the plural as a reference to deeds in general and not merely to speech. However, note the objection of Hill ('False Prophets', p. 339 n. 44) that the plural need imply no such thing. It is perhaps best to treat the plural merely as an example of stylistic variation and as such identical in meaning to the singular.

3.   According to Bonnard (*Matthieu*, p. 105), the future tense of the verb has the value of a command or an exhortation. Guelich (*Sermon*, p. 395) misreads the force of the future tense when he interprets it eschatologically in the sense that the community will recognize the fruits only at the last judgment. Compare the assessment of Davies and Allison (*Matthew*, I, p. 706): 'It is far more natural to interpret 7.16-20 as giving guidance to those who are to beware of certain people—even if this does create tension with 7.1-5'. When commenting on this warning against false prophets, Jeremias (*Theology*, pp. 242-43) draws attention to the *agraphon* 'Be approved money changers', which he interprets as an exhortation to learn from the practice of money changers and, like them, acquire a keen eye to spot the counterfeit. This exhortation to evaluate prophets is necessary in view of the deleterious effect that false prophets can have on the community. Compare the warnings against false prophets in Deuteronomy and Jeremiah.

that which discloses the inner reality and underlying motivation of a person's life. Hence an acumen is required that allows one to distinguish between the misleading words and deeds which form the exterior and the revealing words and deeds which lay bare the interior. The text gives no specific indication as to what one should look for in the evaluation of a prophet.[1] Rather, emphasis is placed on the need to discern that which is καλός or πονηρός so that one might thereby determine whether the heart is ἀγαθός or σαπρός.

When one turns to vv. 21-23 the warning against false prophets is replaced by a warning to such 'wolves' that their duplicity will ultimately be judged. It is not sufficient merely to profess Jesus as Lord; one must produce fruit consistent with an affirmation of Jesus' lordship.[2] Just as it is of no value for the Jew to appeal to physical descent from Abraham without showing evidence of true repentance, so also it is of no value for the Christian to appeal to impressive deeds done in the name of the Lord without showing evidence of a genuine relationship with God. In the related passage of Lk. 13.25-27 the warning is directed to Jewish people who have only a superficial association with Jesus. In both texts presumption and the absence of true knowledge are in view. The prophecies, exorcisms and miracles of these individuals were not 'good fruit', but rather a part of their 'sheep's clothing'. It is not necessary to suggest that these were counterfeit works. The passage gives no indication that the claim they were done 'in your name' is a false one. Rather, the point is that just as almsgiving, prayer and fasting can be performed in a manner which God rejects (Mt. 6.1-6, 16-18), so also spiritual gifts can be exercised in a way that brings condemnation. That which determines

1. Minear ('False Prophecy', p. 81) expresses the criticism that because the axioms of vv. 16b-19 do not define what makes fruit good they are so ambiguous as to be virtually useless. One might note that the axiom of 7.12 is similarly ambiguous. When discussing the nature of practicing righteousness and doing the will of God a certain ambiguity and lack of definition is necessary, especially if one is to avoid the casuistry of the scribes and Pharisees.

2. The words κύριε κύριε on the lips of the false workers is a clear indication that they consider themselves to be followers of Jesus. In addition, their deeds are said to have been done τῷ σῷ ὀνόματι, that is, by the authority of Jesus. Gundry (*Matthew*, p. 132) notes that whereas elsewhere in Matthew the expression 'in the name of' takes a preposition, here the simple dative ὀνόματι is used. He suggests that this is due to Matthew conforming Jesus' words to the statements concerning false prophets in Jeremiah; cf. Jer. 34.15 [LXX].

whether or not an action manifests 'good fruit' has less to do with the action itself than with the attitude or motivation which lies behind the action. It is possible, especially in view of the spiritual gifts in question, that these false workers performed their deeds with an eye to the audience.[1] Their testimony of accomplishment does seem to betray an element of self-congratulation. In any case, the fruit they have produced is found to be inadequate.

Jesus, as the eschatological judge, will announce to such fruitless workers that he never knew them.[2] The reason for their rejection is explained by means of two phrases which add substance to what is meant by good or bad fruit. These false disciples who have failed to 'do the will of the Father' are indicted as 'workers of ἀνομία'.[3] It has been observed already that doing the will of the Father is, for Matthew, the equivalent of fulfilling the better righteousness and perfection which is required by God. In the present context the phrase is employed to reveal the important truth that even though prophecy, exorcism and the performance of mighty works are all examples of what the Father wills, they are not necessarily expressions of doing the Father's will. The will of the Father relates to much deeper workings in the heart of the disciple. The precise meaning that should be attached to the term ἀνομία is more difficult to determine. The idea of lawlessness, which is suggested by the word, would indicate that the false prophets are attacked as antinomians.[4] However, it is

---

1. Meier (*Matthew*, p. 74) notes the correspondence between these false Christians and the scribes and Pharisees of 23.5, who perform deeds in order to be seen by others. The discussion of Minear ('False Prophecy', pp. 86-93) concerning the relationship between the present passage and Mt. 23 is instructive.

2. The verb γινώσκω in v. 23 is to be understood in the sense of the Hebrew word ידע, that is, as expressing an intimate relationship (cf. Amos 3.2). With respect to the intimacy connoted by the verb, note the phrase ἐν τῷ κόλπῳ μου in the parallel saying of *2 Clem.* 4.5. Davies and Allison (*Matthew*, I, p. 717) observe that the phrase 'I never knew *you*' stands in contrast with the threefold σῷ of the prophets in v. 22. The passage contains an ironic twist in that while the perceptive disciple will 'know' them by their fruit, the Lord will not 'know' them because of their fruit.

3. Marguerat (*Jugement*, p. 194) correctly remarks that 'le thème des fruits est décodé à l'aide de ποιεῖν τὸ θέλημα τοῦ πατρός (καρποὺς καλούς) et d'ἀνομία (καρποὺς πονηρούς)'.

4. Compare, for example, the discussion of Barth, 'Understanding of the Law', pp. 74-75.

probably best not to press the legal background of the term.[1] With reference to the present passage the word most probably denotes an attitude or action which is at variance with or less than doing the will of the Father.[2] The false prophets have been active in the performance of deeds, and yet they have failed in the performance of the required righteousness. Indeed, their behaviour is so repugnant to the Lord that they are dismissed from his presence. Like the rotten tree of v. 19, they are cut down and cast into the fire.

Matthew 12.33-37

In the teaching of Mt. 12.33-37, which is placed in a context highlighting the verbal criticisms of the Pharisees concerning the miraculous deeds performed by Jesus, the emphasis is placed on that aspect of fruitbearing which is related to speech. The words that a person utters reflect, and often betray, his or her true nature.[3] In his exhortation to the Pharisees in v. 33, Jesus expresses, through the now familiar figure of the tree and its fruit, the principle that the inner reality of a person both determines and is revealed through the words that they speak. For that reason, the Pharisees are enjoined to make the tree good or bad so that it can produce corresponding fruit; that is, they are encouraged to do something about their inner character. The imperative ποιήσατε in v. 33 is probably best understood as a summons to the Pharisees to repent. Their hearts must be changed so that their fruit might be good (compare the notion of fruit consistent

---

1. Following a survey of the Matthaean passages dealing with ἀνομία, Davies (*Sermon*, p. 205) concludes that the term 'may, indeed, be completely devoid of any "legal" connotation and merely signifies sin in a general sense'. See also the discussion in J.E. Davison, '*Anomia* and the Question of an Antinomian Polemic in Matthew', *JBL* 104 (1985), pp. 617-35.

2. Hill, 'False Prophets', p. 337; cf. Gnilka, *Matthäusevangelium*, I, p. 278: 'In diesem Zusammenhang wird die ἀνομία (in diesem Fall der falschen Propheten) als Gegenbegriff zur Gerechtigkeit (die der Schriftgelehrten und Pharisäer reicht nicht aus) erkennbar'. Note that at 23.28 Jesus accuses the scribes and Pharisees of being full of ἀνομία. One might suggest that whereas Matthew employs the adjective ἄκαρπος to refer to the absence of fruit (13.22), he intends the noun ἀνομία to stand for that which is opposite to the good fruit which God demands. Compare the appearance of the term in Isa. 5.7. Yahweh expected his vineyard to produce good fruit, but he found only ἀνομία and κραυγή.

3. Gnilka, *Matthäusevangelium*, I, p. 461: 'Die Rede bringt es an den Tag. Das Herz fließt über im Wort.'

with repentance in 3.8). The second part of the command, about making the tree bad, would then mean that if they will not repent they should at least be consistent and acknowledge the true nature of their hearts which has already been disclosed through their words. If they will not be righteous, they should at least cease to be hypocrites. The suggestion that Jesus' words here amount to a call to repentance is reinforced by the reappearance of the phrase γεννήματα ἐχιδνῶν. When the phrase appears the third and final time in 23.33 there is nothing left to be done but to pronounce woe upon the obdurate Pharisees.

It is imperative that the Pharisees 'make the tree good', since as long as they remain evil they will never be able to speak what is good. If their heart, or treasure, is corrupted, it is inevitable that every expression which stems from it will be tainted by that corruption. The confused and blasphemous allegation of the Pharisees concerning the exorcisms of Jesus is a convincing demonstration of their internal wickedness. They will be judged on the basis of this and other statements, since such remarks represent the fruit of their hidden convictions. If they would escape the harsh judgment of God, they must ensure that the tree, their essential being, is good.

Words reveal the basic orientation of the heart, and for that reason they are important.[1] One will be held accountable at the judgment for even the most useless words, which are consequential because they too are able to divulge the true character of the person.[2] The day of judgment will be a time when such words are weighed and their true significance is established. As part of the assessment of the final judgment words will be evaluated, and on the basis of what has been said one will be either justified (δικαιόω) or condemned (καταδικάζω). The Pharisees are thereby warned to consider carefully their pronouncements against Jesus (v. 24) and his disciples (v. 2). There is a touch of irony in the context, considering that the condemnation of

1.   The notion of words as fruit is brought out by the correspondence between ἐκ γὰρ τῶν λόγων in v. 37 and ἐκ γὰρ τοῦ καρποῦ in v. 33.
2.   A 'useless word' (ῥῆμα ἀργόν) in this context is one that, though 'workless', nonetheless reflects character. It means the kind of word that, far from being neutral, is wicked and godless; cf. Schweizer, *Matthew*, p. 288. This notion of the unproductive, and yet not indifferent, word may have been suggested by the principle stated in v. 30 that there is no neutral ground; people, or their words, are either contributory or detractive.

the disciples by the Pharisees (note the use of καταδικάζω in v. 7) is the kind of 'useless' word that invites condemnation. Judgment, of course, is ultimately concerned with the condition of the heart. Yet to the extent that words form part of the general demeanour which reveals the condition of the heart, they will be crucial witnesses at the judgment.

Matthew 15.13

The question of fruitfulness is not explicitly addressed in Mt. 15.13. Yet, at the same time, this is a saying which is closely related to the theme of fruit in Matthew. These words of Jesus, concerning the uprooting of every plant not planted by the Father, are spoken against a backdrop of Pharisaic hypocrisy. In the preceding passage, which relates the dispute between Jesus and the Pharisees and scribes over the matter of handwashing, Jesus had characterized the hypocritical behaviour of the Pharisees by means of the quotation from Isa. 29.13. They are exposed as religious leaders whose relationship with God is that of the 'lip' and not of the 'heart'; as such, their worship is empty and their teaching consists merely in human precepts. It is this state of separation from God that causes them to subvert the commandments of God for the sake of their own tradition. It is noteworthy that, as distinct from Mark, Matthew at v. 4 has 'God' in place of 'Moses' (cf. Mk 7.10), which heightens the contrast. In effect, Matthew makes the opponents of Jesus issue a decree ('but you say') which runs counter to the divine commandment ('for God commanded').[1] The locus of the Pharisees' hypocrisy would appear to be that, even as they nullify God's word, they still profess to honour him through the observance of such human tradition.

The question of defilement which naturally arises from the issue of handwashing is treated in vv. 10-20. In a categorical statement delivered to the crowd, Jesus incisively observes that it is not what goes into the mouth which defiles but what comes out of the mouth. Jesus' statement is thus a reaffirmation of the importance of words and other means of expression which indicate the true character of the heart. The Pharisees, in keeping with their hypocritical preoccupation with external matters, take offence at this remark, which directs attention towards the internal workings of the heart. When told of

---

1. Cf. Gundry, *Matthew*, p. 304.

their indignation, Jesus compounds the affront by asserting that the Pharisees are not, in fact, the true planting of God, but are, rather, blind guides who should be left alone.[1] This latter designation, which reappears in 23.16, 24, is an attack on the Pharisees in their role as guides who are competent to assist others in the understanding of God's law.[2] It affirms that, far from being capable teachers, their separation from God has effected a condition wherein they themselves fail to understand the essential meaning of the law, as can be seen in the misguided ruling of v. 5. In a sense, the charge of blindness suggests that their inner light has become darkened (cf. 6.23). They are decidedly illsuited for the task of instructing others in the way of God.

The idea that the Pharisees do not represent the true planting of God recalls those Old Testament passages that describe Israel as the choice plant which Yahweh had planted (e.g. Ps. 80.16 [15]; Jer. 2.21), as well as those passages that liken the righteous to planted trees (e.g. Pss. 1.1-3; 92.13-14 [12-13]). Moreover, one is reminded of Isa. 60.21 and 61.3 where the remnant is characterized as the planting of Yahweh. Jesus' statement is thus a very damning reproach.[3] The Pharisees, as well as the blind who follow their lead (cf. v. 14), are denied any standing among the people of God. In many respects this condemnation of the Pharisees echoes the earlier attack by John the

1.   Considering that ἐσκανδαλίσθησαν means 'they were caused to stumble', Green (*Matthew*, p. 145) holds that the verb is used here to furnish a debating point: if the Pharisees had been 'tripped up' by Jesus' remark, that demonstrates their blindness.

2.   The title 'blind guides' is probably an ironic twist on the self-designation 'guides of the blind', which seems to have been appropriated by Jews trained in the law. F. Graber ('Blind', *NIDNTT*, I, p. 220) notes that these Jews 'considered that they were the only authoritative interpreters of the Law, and as such they were the only legitimate leaders and guides of the "blind" heathen'. Trilling (*Israel*, p. 200) is to be followed in his judgment that the two expressions ὑποκριταί and ὁδηγοὶ τυφλοί refer, respectively, to the practice and to the teaching of the Pharisees.

3.   According to *m. Sanh.* 10.1, Isa. 60.21 provides proof that all Israelites have a share in the world to come; cf. *Pss. Sol.* 14.2-3. Gaechter (*Matthäus*, p. 497) is probably correct to regard v. 13 as including in its purview the Jewish contemporaries of Jesus who had been misled by the teaching of the Pharisees. Schweizer (*Matthew*, p. 327) does not overstate the harshness of Jesus' remark when he asserts that 'it would be hard to frame a sharper attack on Israel's faith in its own election: Israel and its ruling class of Pharisees is not the vineyard planted by God but a wild thicket!'

Baptist, for it likewise affirms that any claim by the Pharisees to be members of the covenant community must be a false one. When John denounced the Pharisees he had likened them to fruitless trees which are cut down and thrown into the fire. Here they are compared to unfamiliar plants which will be uprooted. The verb ἐκριζόω recalls Jer. 1.10, the programmatic statement forming part of the call of Jeremiah, in which the tasks of uprooting and destroying are included among the prophet's responsibilities. In the time of Jeremiah, God had uprooted the nation of Israel which by then had become a wild vine. According to this pronouncement by Jesus, the future will witness a comparable uprooting when the wild plants, represented by the scribes, Pharisees and those who follow their lead, will be removed.

Matthew 21.18-22
In ch. 21, which marks the beginning of the final warnings given to obdurate Israel in the Gospel, there are two passages which are crucial to the discussion of fruit in Matthew: the 'acted parable' of the cursing of the fig tree in vv. 18-22, and the parable of the wicked tenants in vv. 33-46. These two passages are not merely the last in Matthew to utilize the image of fruit, but can be said to represent the culmination of the entire Matthaean teaching on fruit. It would appear that Matthew has composed the whole of ch. 21 with great care in order to highlight the subject of fruitfulness, along with other notable themes to which it is closely bound.[1] The theme of Israel's judgment resounds throughout the chapter and its justification is principally rooted in the nation's failure to produce fruit.

The cursing of the fig tree is best interpreted as a prophetic action which prefigures the judgment that is about to befall the nation of Israel.[2] As a symbolic act the cursing stands comparison with the two

1. The assertion of Green (*Matthew*, p. 177), that in Matthew the cursing is simply a miracle story introducing sayings on prayer and faith, fails to do justice to the theme of fruitfulness in the Gospel as a whole and in this chapter in particular. Jesus' action on this occasion is seen by many as out of character and has been frequently misunderstood. The allusion to the cursing of the fig tree in the *Infancy Gospel of Thomas* (3.1-3), when the malicious attack by Jesus on another child is described, indicates that such misunderstandings began early. However, the cursing becomes less problematic and extraordinary once it is interpreted as a symbolic and prophetic action.

2. G. Münderlein, 'Die Verfluchung des Feigenbaumes (Mk xi 12-14)', *NTS* 10 (1963), p. 89-104 (98): 'Mit der Verfluchung handelt Jesus als Prophet.'

other representative actions, the royal entrance into Jerusalem and the cleansing of the temple, which are described earlier in the chapter. Jesus approaches the fig tree in order to satisfy his hunger and fully expects to find fruit on it. When he discovers that the tree has produced nothing but leaves, he announces the curse that it will never again bear fruit, and in an instant the tree withers. The Matthaean account of the cursing differs in many important respects from that of Mark.[1] Matthew does not include the notice that 'it was not the season (καιρός) for figs'. Rather, Jesus is represented as completely justified in expecting to find fruit. In Matthew Jesus acts in a very definite manner; he sees the fig tree, approaches it and finds nothing but leaves. There is nothing in Matthew analogous to the Markan phrase 'if by chance (εἰ ἄρα) he might find anything'. This element of expectation connects the episode with the parable of the wicked tenants, inasmuch as the householder of the parable sends for his produce 'when the season (καιρός) of fruit was near' (v. 34; cf. v. 41). The two passages share a similar purpose of showing that the judgment pronounced on the unfruitful nation is deserved. In Mark the account of the cleansing of the temple is inserted between the cursing of the tree and the report of its destruction. In Matthew's narrative the cleansing of the temple has already taken place. Nothing more remains to be done. Therefore, the symbolic destruction of the nation can take place immediately.

The cursing of the fig tree is reminiscent of a number of Old Testament texts which should be regarded as forming the background against which it can be best interpreted.[2] Two passages that are especially suitable for this purpose are Jer. 8.13 and Hos. 9.10. According to the Jeremiah passage, Yahweh would gather from the nation grapes and figs, but is unable to find any fruit. The leaves are withered; the vine and fig tree have become useless. In Matthew the fig tree remains an image of Israel and it is now Jesus who wishes to gather its fruit. Yet, corresponding to that earlier episode, fruit cannot be found.[3] For

---

1.   The parable of Lk. 13.6-9 is not a real parallel to the present text. As Hill (*Matthew*, p. 294) observes, that story concerns the delay of judgment, whereas this narrative is about immediate judgment. Matthew would have had little interest in relating the Lukan parable, since it is his conviction that the axe, as it were, is already laid to the root.

2.   The most relevant Old Testament texts which help to explain the cursing are listed by Münderlein, 'Verfluchung', pp. 100-101.

3.   H. Giesen ('Der verdorrte Feigenbaum—Eine symbolische Aussage? Zu

Jeremiah the futility of the nation demanded judgment and destruction. The same emphasis is present in Matthew. In Hos. 9.10 Yahweh looks back to the beginning of his relationship with Israel and describes the nation of that time as being to him like 'the first fruit on the fig tree'. Yet, in due course, the people corrupted themselves through idolatry. As a consequence, the nation is depicted in v. 16 as cursed: it is struck down, its root is dried up, and it is unable to bear fruit.[1] A similar scenario, employing similar language, is described in Matthew. It might be noted that the story of Israel, told under the figure of the fig tree, is a narrative of decay. The nation which had begun as a fruitful fig tree has now become a cursed and withered fig tree.

It is noteworthy, in view of what has already been observed concerning the relationship between fruitbearing and repentance, that between the cursing of the fig tree and the parable of the wicked tenants stand two passages which concern John's preaching of repentance. The matter of the origin of John's baptism is raised in vv. 23-27, including the detail that the Jewish leaders had refused to believe his message. Their failure to repent becomes the subject of the subsequent parable about the two sons in vv. 28-32. This will be the last time that John and the theme of repentance are referred to in the Gospel. Considering that ch. 21 also contains the last reference to the theme of fruit, it would seem that Matthew is creating an *inclusio* by means of the double theme of fruit and repentance. John's charge to the nation to repent and produce fruit, which was first heard in ch. 3, is returned to and brought to a crescendo in ch. 21. The case against the nation has been made. It is unrepentant and fruitless. The judgment against it can now be pronounced.

Matthew 21.33-44

The parable of the wicked tenants is found in all three synoptic Gospels, yet it is primarily in Matthew that it becomes a parable about judgment due to the absence of fruit. This Matthaean emphasis can be

Mk 11,12-14.20f', *BZ* 20 [1976], pp. 95-111 [104]) remarks that 'so wie Gott nach Jer. 8,13 nicht die erwünschten Früchte von Israel ernten kann, so ist ebenfalls Jesus Mißerfolg beschieden'.

  1. In view of the close connection between the cleansing of the temple and the cursing of the fig tree, it is interesting to note that Hos. 9.15 speaks of Yahweh driving the people from his house because of their wickedness.

observed in the phrase 'when the season of fruit was near' (v. 34), in the mention of the new tenants who will 'give the fruits in their seasons' (v. 41), and in the concluding statement that the kingdom of God will be given to a nation 'producing its fruits' (v. 43). In Mark and Luke the emphasis is placed primarily on the wickedness of the tenants. It should be noted, however, that the Matthaean version of the parable, in spite of its distinctive angle, does not in any way diminish the wickedness of the tenants.

The parable opens with a description of a vineyard which is clearly intended to recall the 'Song of the Vineyard' in Isaiah 5.[1] As in the Isaiah passage, the owner makes adequate preparations to ensure a good return from his vineyard.[2] The correspondence with the Isaiah passage does not end there, however, but continues even to the unpleasant events which transpire when the owner looks for a yield from his vineyard. When the time for harvest is near, he twice sends his servants for the produce of the vineyard. But on both occasions the servants are beaten, killed and stoned. These servants of the parable are a clear allusion to the prophets which had been sent repeatedly to the nation of Israel.[3] The owner of the vineyard, undeterred by this violent response, finally sends his son, which, in terms of the allegory, is a reference to Jesus, in the belief that the tenants will respect him.

1. Beare (*Matthew*, p. 426) lists the linguistic parallels between the Greek version of Isa. 5.2 and Mt. 21.33. According to J. Jeremias (*The Parables of Jesus* [New York: Charles Scribner's Sons, 1972], p. 74), the question of Mt. 21.40 relates back to the question of Isa. 5.5 [LXX]. The reference to a vineyard (ἀμπελών) links the parable with the preceding parable of the two sons. That parable had emphasized the doing of the Father's will; this parable emphasizes its theological complement, bearing fruit.

2. The ἄνθρωπος of Mark and Luke is described in Matthew as an οἰκοδεσπότης, which emphasizes ownership and a claim to the produce; cf. Meier, *Matthew*, p. 243. In v. 34 Matthew speaks of the householder sending for 'his fruit' (in Mark and Luke he sends for 'some of the fruit'). C.E. Carlston (*The Parables of the Triple Tradition* [Philadelphia: Fortress Press, 1975], p. 41) suggests that this is an indication that Matthew understands fruit allegorically.

3. Note in particular Jer. 7.25-27, where Yahweh complains that the people have refused to listen even though he has continuously sent his servants the prophets to them (cf. 2 Chron. 24.19). The only other appearance of λιθοβολέω in Matthew (23.37) specifically refers to the prophets; note the stoning of Zechariah in 2 Chron. 24.21. On the relationship between the violent treatment of the prophets and the judgment of Israel, see O.H. Steck, *Israel und das gewaltsame Geschick der Propheten* (Neukirchen–Vluyn: Neukirchener Verlag, 1967), pp. 298-302.

The tenants, however, treat the coming of the heir as an opportunity to gain possession of the inheritance. Therefore they cast him out of the vineyard and kill him. Nonetheless, their conspiracy is ineffectual. Coinciding with the counsel of Jesus' opponents, the 'Lord of the Vineyard' will come and destroy the wicked tenants.[1] What is more, he will let out the vineyard to new tenants who will give back to him the fruits in their seasons.

The emphasis of the parable, as the additional statement found in v. 43 makes clear, is on this transfer of the vineyard from one group of tenants to another group. Speaking directly to the Jewish leadership, which represent the unfaithful nation, Jesus declares that the kingdom of God will be taken from them and given to a nation (ἔθνος) which produces its fruits. The phrase 'kingdom of God' most probably refers to the privileges entrusted to and enjoyed by the Jewish nation on account of its special relationship with God.[2] These privileges will be taken away and given to a people who will accept the responsibilities that necessarily accompany such privileges.[3] The 'nation' which receives the kingdom is supra-national, in that it is comprised of both Jews and Gentiles. What distinguishes this nation from the rejected nation is its fruitfulness, that is, its willingness to do the will of God and to become that righteous and just nation which God had hoped for when he first chose Israel.[4] Israel's unique status is

---

1. In Isa. 5.5 it is the vineyard that is destroyed, here it is the tenants. Nonetheless, in both texts hardened Israel is in view, considering that the vineyard of Isa. 5.1-7 is described as the 'house of Israel'.

2. Allen, *Matthew*, pp. 232-33.

3. According to Frankemölle (*Jahwebund*, pp. 253-54), v. 43 expresses the idea 'daß Jahwe einst Israel unter sein Königtum stellte (Bundestheologie und Königs-Vorstellung sind miteinander verschmolzen), wobei er aber die Freiheit hat, aufgrund der Untreue seines Volkes sich zurückzuziehen und ein anderes Volk zu erwählen'. Concerning the unfaithful Jews to whom the parable is directed, Pesch (*Lohngedanke*, p. 47) remarks that 'sie haben gleichsam ihre Plätze beim Gastmahl, ihre Sohnesrechte, ihren Weinberg verscherzt'. The words spoken by Samuel to the disobedient Saul in 1 Sam. 15.28 provide a noteworthy parallel to this verse: the kingdom is to be taken away and given to a more deserving neighbour.

4. Marguerat (*Jugement*, p. 311) defines the 'fruits' of the kingdom as 'l'impératif inhérent à l'élection'. He relates this image to 6.33, which refers to the 'righteousness' of the kingdom, and observes (p. 318) that ' "fruits" et justice désignent la même réalité, l'obéissance à la Loi réinterprétée par le Christ de Mt'. Gnilka (*Matthäusevangelium*, II, p. 232) is correct to stress that v. 43 is conditional: only to the extent that individual Christians bear fruit can they be said to be members of the new nation.

revoked because of its failure to produce fruit.[1] Its inheritance is now transferred to another nation which, by contrast, bears fruit and, as v. 42 implies, recognizes and accepts the heir of the parable.

Matthew has inserted the quotation from Ps. 118.22-23, concerning the validation of the rejected stone, between vv. 41b and 43 which describe this transfer of privileges. Within the conceptual framework introduced by the parable the quotation serves as a reminder that the story does not end with the destruction of the wicked tenants and the establishment of new tenants. The rejected son is himself restored and vindicated.[2] He becomes the cornerstone of a new building, the restored people of God.[3] This building, which is constructed around him, is essentially a metaphor for the new nation. The quotation is thus utilized to emphasize that membership in the new people of God is based not only on fruitfulness but also on a relationship with the son of God. The rejected son is, in fact, the basis of the new nation which receives the inheritance.

The stone metaphor is continued in the warning of v. 44 which concludes the parable. The saying of v. 44 is regarded by many scholars as an interpolation from Lk. 20.18.[4] The external evidence in support of its authenticity is, however, very strong.[5] With respect to internal evidence, the divergence in wording between Matthew and Luke is noteworthy, since one might expect that interpolation would

1. It is to demand too much precision of parabolic discourse to speak, as Gundry does (*Matthew*, p. 430), of the 'discrepancy' that in the parable fruits were produced but not handed over, whereas in v. 43 they are not even produced.

2. In view of how Ps. 118.22 is interpreted elsewhere in the New Testament (cf. Acts 4.11; 1 Pet. 2.7), it is likely that here also it refers to the resurrection and exaltation of Jesus. It is frequently noted, albeit at the level of the presumed Semitic background to the tradition, that the quotation and the parable coalesce through a play on the Hebrew words 'son' (בן) and 'stone' (אבן).

3. Cf. Meier, *Matthew*, p. 244. Note that at 16.18 the church is represented as a building.

4. In the Nestle-Aland 26th edition the verse is enclosed within single brackets indicating that the verse is of doubtful authenticity. In the UBS 3rd edition the verse is enclosed within double square brackets since in the opinion of the editors the verse is 'an accretion to the text'; see B.M. Metzger, *A Textual Commentary on the Greek New Testament* (n.p.: United Bible Societies, 1971), p. 58.

5. It is acknowledged by Kurt and Barbara Aland (*The Text of the New Testament* [Grand Rapids: Eerdmans, 1987], p. 232), for example, that the external evidence 'would be conclusive if it were supported by one of the great early papyri'.

have resulted in identical texts. Furthermore, if v. 44 were a later interpolation it would have made better sense to place it immediately after the Psalm quotation, as is the case in the Lukan parallel. This delay is the probable cause of the omission of the verse from some witnesses.[1] One might also observe that, although v. 43 completes the parable, it is not uncommon for Matthew to attach menacing statements to parables in order to underscore their meaning. This can be illustrated with reference to the parable of the unforgiving servant in 18.23-35. The parable proper is complete at v. 34, at which point is attached the warning of v. 35.

Presumably, this cryptic remark of v. 44, which alludes to both the stone of offence of Isa. 8.14-15 and the stone of Dan. 2.34-35, 44-45, was added to the parable of the wicked tenants to inform those who would consider themselves members of the new nation that failure to produce fruit leads to judgment. If they are not obedient, the cornerstone which now supports them will become a stone which breaks and crushes them. The appearance of the verb λικμάω in this verse may be significant, in view of its basic meaning 'to winnow'.[2] The theme of fruit which had been introduced by the words of John the Baptist, concerning the coming one who stands with the winnowing fork in his hand ready to separate the wheat from the chaff, is now concluded with this related image of the coming one who, like a stone, pulverizes and destroys what is useless.

The prophets had explained the rejection and destruction of Israel as the consequence of the nation's failure to produce fruit befitting its chosen status. The nation was to be fruitful, so that it might bring glory to Yahweh and blessing to the nations, but in the end it was made desolate. In a similar way, Matthew employs the image of fruit in order to explain why the Jewish nation of his day, exemplified in its leaders, was rejected by God. In the time of their visitation the people

---

1. It is ironic that some of the scholars who dismiss the verse as non-Matthaean do so, in part, because of this awkward delay. Note the defence of the authenticity of v. 44 in Gundry, *Matthew*, pp.430-31 and Gnilka, *Matthäusevangelium*, II, pp. 224-25.

2. See the discussion of the term in G. Bornkamm, 'λικμάω', *TDNT*, IV, pp. 280-81. The word appears frequently in prophetic judgment oracles; note especially its use in Jer. 38.10 [LXX] and Ezek. 36.19 in reference to the 'scattering' of Israel among the nations. In the Daniel passage (2.34-35) alluded to in v. 44 the stone breaks the great image which becomes as chaff blown away in the wind.

of Israel were found to be without fruit, or at least, without good
fruit. As a result, the nation has lost its chosen status; the kingdom,
and with it the promised inheritance, is awarded to a new nation.
Matthew's purpose does not end there, however. It is evident from the
way in which he recounts this judgment on Israel that the followers of
Jesus are never far from his mind. The individual Christian, like the
individual Jew, can become a fruitless tree and as such deserving of
God's judgment. To a notable degree, self-confidence and presumption
prove to be the downfall of both the smug Jew and the deceitful
disciple. The true planting of God are those who are repentant, who
do the will of the Father, whose words reflect an undefiled heart, and
who, like the blessed man of Psalm 1, may be compared to a tree
which 'bears its fruit in season'. The unrepentant, deceitful, and
corrupt, however, are repudiated by God and like false shoots are
rooted up or like worthless chaff are thrown into the fire.

'There will be Weeping and Gnashing of Teeth'

The fearful announcement that 'there will be weeping and gnashing of
teeth' (ἐκεῖ ἔσται ὁ κλαυθμὸς καὶ ὁ βρυγμὸς τῶν ὀδόντων)
appears once in Luke (13.28) but is found six times in Matthew (8.12;
13.42, 50; 22.13; 24.51; 25.30). Whatever the origin or tradition
history of the declaration, it is quite clear that in Matthew's Gospel it
fulfils an important function as a solemn refrain underscoring the
distress experienced by the cursed in the place of future punishment.[1]
The noun 'weeping' in the expression is generally understood in the
sense of the sorrow experienced by those who, following the judgment, realize what they have lost. A most terrifying sentence has been
pronounced against them. They have been rejected by God and, in
consequence, have lost irretrievably the wonderful blessings which he
has prepared for his servants. They are now consigned to a place far
from the presence of God and far from his kingdom. Through
perversity and neglect they have forfeited their share in the inheritance. It is perhaps significant that the only other appearance of the
noun κλαυθμός in the Gospel is at 2.18, in the Jeremiah quotation
describing the sorrow that attended the exile of the Jewish people

1. Compare the comment of Schlatter (*Matthäus*, p. 280) that 'das Ziel Jesu
ist erreicht, wenn der Hörer ermißt, was er, wenn er der ἀπώλεια verfällt,
verloren hat'.

from the land of Israel, since the eschatological expulsion which befalls those who are condemned is tantamount to a perpetual exile from the land of God. In association with 'weeping', the phrase 'gnashing of teeth' most probably denotes a desperate remorse and self-reproach which causes the whole body to tremour.[1] The unrighteous will at last comprehend the folly of the way they had chosen, but by then it will be too late. It is this recognition, that they will never experience the joy and festivity of eternal life but only the torments of eternal punishment, which pitches them into a frenzy of misery.

The usual term in Matthew for the place of torment to which the unrighteous are sentenced is Gehenna (cf. 23.33).[2] The word is derived from the valley of the son of Hinnom, to the west and south of Jerusalem, which achieved notoriety in the pre-exilic period as the scene of child sacrifice. The image of fire which is intrinsic to the concept of Gehenna ($\gamma\acute{\epsilon}\epsilon\nu\nu\alpha$ $\tauο\hat{υ}$ $\pi\upsilon\rhoός$, 5.22; 18.9) is presumably related to this idolatrous practice of burning children to foreign deities.[3] It is in Jeremiah (7.30-34; 19.6-9) that the valley is first designated a place of punishment. The prophet enunciates Yahweh's disgust at the behaviour of the people and proclaims that because of the evil committed there it will become known as the valley of Slaughter. In that dishonoured place the people of Judah will be slain by their enemies and their unburied corpses will become food for the birds and beasts. These horrific associations ultimately resulted in the appropriation of the valley to signify the place of eschatological punishment.[4] In addition, Matthew twice employs the term Hades (11.23; 16.18), which in the Septuagint regularly translates the Hebrew Sheol.[5] Yet it would appear that in the Gospel the two terms,

1. K.H. Rengstorf, '$\beta\rho\upsilon\gamma\muός$', *TDNT*, I, p. 642. Note also the discussion of the phrase in B. Schwank, 'Dort wird Heulen und Zähneknirschen sein', *BZ* 16 (1972), pp. 121-22.

2. Gehenna is mentioned seven times in Matthew, three times (all in one passage) in Mark, and once in Luke.

3. C. Milikowsky, 'Which Gehenna? Retribution and Eschatology in the Synoptic Gospels and in Early Jewish Texts', *NTS* 34 (1988), pp. 238-49 (239).

4. M. Himmelfarb (*Tours of Hell* [Philadelphia: Fortress Press, 1983], p. 110) opines that the 'cast into' language present in many punishment texts requires, or at least suggests, a valley or pit.

5. Note, however, that in Matthew the term Hades is used particularly in a metaphorical and figurative way; cf. W.J.P. Boyd, 'Gehenna—According to J. Jeremias', in E.A. Livingstone (ed.), *Studia Biblica 1978*. II. *Papers on the*

Gehenna and Hades, bear the same, or at least a similar, meaning.[1] As the realm of despair and disgrace, Gehenna is to be avoided at all costs. Whatever might cause one to stumble towards it must be sacrificed, regardless of its value (5.29-30; 18.8-9). People are not to be feared but God, who alone has the power to destroy both soul and body in Gehenna (10.28), is to be feared. Most important of all, however, in view of the centrality of Jesus to salvation, is obedience to his commands. Only those who confess him before others will receive a favourable verdict at the last judgment and thus escape sentence to Gehenna.

Matthew 8.11-12

The first passage in Matthew to employ the expression 'there will be weeping and gnashing of teeth' is 8.11-12 which was treated in the previous chapter. It was noted there that the absence of faith among so many in Israel would result in the exclusion of these 'sons of the kingdom' from the eschatological meal prepared for the patriarchs and their heirs. The haughty and complacent within Israel will witness the blessings and the inheritance which they had taken for granted enjoyed by others. They will be divested of those privileges that should have been theirs as descendants of the patriarchs. The kingdom, to which they had a natural birthright, will be taken from them and given to others (cf. 21.43), the 'many from east and west'. Ultimately, they will be cast into 'the outer darkness', where they will experience bitter remorse and convulsive anguish over the good fortune that they have thrown away and lost for ever.

The phrase 'the outer darkness' (τὸ σκότος τὸ ἐξώτερον), which occurs only in Matthew, appears three times (8.12; 22.13; 25.30) and always in association with the expression about weeping and gnashing

---

Gospels (Sheffield: JSOT Press, 1980), pp. 9-12 (10).

1. In 11.23 Hades appears in a judgment context with reference to the adverse fate of the unrighteous. The use of Hades in 16.18 is exceptional, yet even there it identifies a place which stands in opposition to the purpose of God. The assertion of Jeremias ('γέεννα', *TDNT*, I, pp. 657-58 [658]), that ᾅδης refers to a place of provisional judgment between death and resurrection, whereas γέεννα denotes the place of eternal punishment, cannot be supported from Matthew. With respect to the synonymous nature of the two terms, compare the remark of F. Lang ('πῦρ', *TDNT*, VI, pp. 928-52 [945 n. 89]) that 'the combination of πῦρ and σκότος for the place of perdition reflects the fact that dark sheol and fiery Gehinnom had now merged into a single concept'.

of teeth. Inasmuch as light suggests the glory and radiance of God, this phrase describes a place which is far removed from his presence.[1] Furthermore, light is symbolic of the redemption which is introduced with the coming of Jesus (4.16). Thus, to be cast into outer darkness is to be removed as far as possible from the sphere of salvation.[2] It has been observed in this study that darkness also conveys the idea of exile. When Yahweh had resolved to chastise the rebellious people who had rejected his word, he had them thrust into the 'thick darkness' of captivity (Isa. 8.22). For as long as they suffered the curse of Yahweh, the people of Israel sat 'in absolute darkness' and lived 'in a land of utter darkness' (Ps. 107.10-11; Isa. 9.1).[3] The 'sons of the kingdom', who through disbelief have rejected the call of God given through Jesus, stand again under his curse. Many of these 'sons of the kingdom' are later designated 'sons of Gehenna' (cf. 23.15). Due to their lack of faith, they are, in a sense, banished from one realm and consigned to another. Once more they will be cast into the darkness of exile. This time, however, there is no promise of return from captivity.[4] The redemption that had been offered in the coming of Jesus was spurned. There can be no hope, only the prospect of eternal exile from the inheritance that has been forfeited.

Matthew 13.24-30, 36-43, 47-50

The parabolic discourse of ch. 13 opens with Jesus speaking publicly to the crowds and concludes with his private instruction to his disciples. Throughout the chapter the accent is placed upon the necessity of an understanding of and a commitment to the demands of the kingdom. Two parables, that concerning the weeds, which binds together the public and private portions of the discourse, and that of

1. Marguerat (*Jugement*, p. 252) avers that darkness signifies existence without God.

2. According to Gnilka (*Matthäusevangelium*, I, p. 304), outer darkness describes the place 'der am weitesten vom Heil entfernt ist'.

3. The Greek τὸ σκότος τὸ ἐξώτερον corresponds to the Hebrew צלמות, which denotes darkness in a superlative degree.

4. The idea of eschatological imprisonment is hinted at in Mt. 5.25-26 and 18.30, 34; compare, for example, G. Bertram, 'φυλακή', *TDNT*, IX, pp. 241-44 (244). The prison into which the judge or master confines the wrongdoer is no doubt an allusion to Gehenna, yet at the same time the image recalls those passages which describe exile as imprisonment (cf. Ps. 107.10; Isa. 42.7; Zech. 9.11). Gehenna represents not only the place of torment but also the place of everlasting exile.

the net, warn of the judgment which is to befall those who fail to take these demands seriously. The two parables may be examined together, since they describe analogous situations and share a common paraenetic purpose. The call of Jesus to righteous obedience is reinforced in both parables by the threat that a separation of the evil from the righteous will be carried out in the future. Matthew's main interest would seem to lie with the weeds, as can be seen in the title which is given to the first parable in v. 36, and with the bad fish or evil ones, seeing that in the second parable their fate alone is described. In this respect, the emphasis is similar to that which obtains in the preaching of John the Baptist. John's concern is not to portray the fate of those trees which bear good fruit, but rather the fate of those which do not bear good fruit. Although he remarks that the wheat is gathered into the granary, to which there is corresponding statement in 13.30, his primary interest lies in the chaff which is burned. The words of John are a threat, warning complacent Jews to consider their position. These parables fulfil a similar admonitory function, except that now the warning is addressed chiefly to those within the Christian community.

The parable of the weeds does, however, incorporate a supplementary caution, directed not to the 'weeds' which infiltrate the community but to the community itself, regarding the appropriate response to such false members. The faithful are to be patient. They are not to initiate an operation of separating the false from the true; for it is probable that such an undertaking would be rather imperfect, eradicating the good along with the bad.[1] They are to wait instead for the definitive separation which will take place at the harvest time which coincides with the end of the age.[2] Even so, the present is a time to be

---

1. It is implicit in the parable that part of the intention of the enemy is to provoke premature uprooting. It is noted by C.W.F. Smith ('The Mixed State of the Church in Matthew's Gospel', *JBL* 82 [1963], pp. 149-68 [153]) that 'the work of the enemy will not succeed unless precipitate interference, intended to cure the situation, is permitted to do the very opposite and bring the opposing purpose to fruition'.

2. It is often assumed that the interpretation of the parable in vv. 36-43 misses the real point of the parable which lies in this admonition to patience. Yet such a judgment, as J.R. Michaels (*Servant and Son* [Atlanta: John Knox, 1981], p.120) observes, 'assumes that the interpretation intends to reveal what the story is about in such a way that nothing is left to the reader or hearer'. It is better to assume that the interpretation is in harmony with the parable and serves merely to clarify certain details. Concerning the emphasis of the interpretation on the final separation, France

mindful of such interlopers whose effect on the church may be detrimental. This demand for patience does not obviate the necessity of discerning the 'wolves' in their midst (7.15-20), nor of implementing a programme of discipline within the community (18.15-20). The caution is given primarily to protect the righteous who might suffer in an indiscriminate purge, and yet implicit in the injunction is the idea that before the harvest there is always time for weeds to be changed into wheat. Hence, the proper involvement of faithful disciples in the interim is in the mission of gathering the lost. The task of separation, which must await the end, will be carried out by others, the angels of the Son of man.

In the interpretation of the parable of the weeds the world (κόσμος) in which the disciples carry out their mission is designated the kingdom of the Son of man.[1] As the gospel is proclaimed throughout the world and that kingdom is increased, people of diverse quality will join the ranks of the disciples. In the figurative language of the parable some of these adherents will be good seed sown by the Son of man, but others will be weeds sown by the devil. The church is

---

(*Matthew*, p. 224) correctly notes that 'it is precisely in the expectation of this ultimate division that the call for patience is grounded'.

1. It seems best to accept the opinion of those, like Gundry (*Matthew*, p. 275), who regard the world as the sphere into which the Son of man extends his kingdom through the proclamation of the gospel. It is noteworthy that at the temptation the devil can speak of all the kingdoms of the world (πάσας τὰς βασιλείας τοῦ κόσμου) as though they are in his gift. Yet Jesus, the stronger one who overpowers this 'strong man' (cf. 12.29), by the end of the Gospel can claim to have been given all authority in heaven and on earth. J.D. Kingsbury (*The Parables of Jesus in Matthew 13* [London: SPCK, 1969], p. 98) is correct to remark that 'the "Kingdom of the Son of Man" embodies the idea that in the "present age" (between Easter and the Parousia) Jesus Son of Man is Lord of the world'. In the judgment of Gnilka (*Matthäusevangelium*, I, p. 502), the naming of the kingdom after the Son of man expresses his unique and lasting significance in the process of salvation history, since salvation, judgment and fulfilment are all bound up in him. According to Frankemölle (*Jahwebund*, p. 271 n. 31), the relationship of the kingdom of the Son of man (v. 41) to the kingdom of the Father (v. 43) is to be regarded 'als funktionales, nicht aber als sukzessives', yet it is hard to avoid the conclusion that the 'kingdom of the Son of man' is a *heilsgeschichtlich* concept describing a period of time which culminates at the end of the age and which is succeeded by the 'kingdom of the Father'. Green (*Matthew*, p. 136) contrasts the kingdom of Christ which is progressively realized, and the kingdom of the Father which the righteous enter as their reward.

therefore a mixed community in which the righteous and unrighteous live side by side.[1] The first group receive the title 'sons of the king-dom' since they belong to that new nation which has become the beneficiary of the privileges that had been lost by the nation of Israel, the former 'sons of the kingdom'. The second group, however, are termed 'sons of the evil one'.[2] The phrase, which is reminiscent of 'children of serpents', indicates that these are people who are of a kind with the one who planted them. They, like the false prophets mentioned earlier in the Gospel, are an impediment to the work of the church, inasmuch as they wrong others within the community and are engaged in activity which is antagonistic to its goals.[3] In the future the Son of man will send his harvesting angels who will gather these evil-doers out of his kingdom and cast them into the furnace of fire (ἡ κάμινος τοῦ πυρός), where they will weep and gnash their teeth.

The fiery furnace, which is here a picture of Gehenna, appears in the Old Testament as an image of captivity and exile. In Deut 4.20 and Jer. 11.4 (cf. 1 Kgs 8.51) Egypt is portrayed as the 'iron furnace' (כור הברזל; ἡ κάμινος τῆς σιδηρᾶς) from which Yahweh delivered his people. Similarly, in Isa. 48.10 the exile is described as 'the furnace (כור; κάμινος) of affliction' (cf. Ezek. 22.17-22). However, whereas in those contexts the furnace is a metaphor for an ordeal which tests and purifies the people, here it has become a metaphor for the final destruction of the wicked. The righteous, on the other hand,

---

1.   In the view of G. Bornkamm ('End-Expectation and Church in Matthew', in *Tradition and Interpretation in Matthew*, p. 19), the characteristic thought for Matthew regarding the church is that it 'is not a collection of the elect and eternally secure, but a mixed body which has to face the separation between the good and evil at the final judgment'. Note that in both parables the evil are represented as being 'in the midst of' the righteous (vv. 25, 49).

2.   In view of the statement in v. 41, that these people are doers of ἀνομία, it is intriguing to compare the description of sinful Israel in Isa. 1.4 [LXX]: σπέρμα πονηρόν, υἱοὶ ἄνομοι.

3.   In 18.7 a woe is pronounced against such people who cause others to sin (δι' οὗ τὸ σκάνδαλον ἔρχεται). This parable may be seen as the fulfilment of that woe. With respect to the peculiar mention of 'stumbling blocks' in 13.41, reference is sometimes made to the Hebrew text of Zeph. 1.3 which depicts Yahweh sweeping away 'the stumbling blocks and the wicked'. The false prophets of 7.23 are con-demned as οἱ ἐργαζόμενοι τὴν ἀνομίαν; in similar language these false disciples are referred to as οἱ ποιοῦντες τὴν ἀνομίαν.

will shine as the sun in the kingdom of their Father.[1] The radiance which they display, as they dwell in the presence of God, stands in marked contrast to the extreme darkness which surrounds those in Gehenna.

Inserted between the parable of the weeds and the parable of the net are the matching parables of the treasure and the pearl. It is likely that Matthew has introduced these parables at this point in order to illustrate the behaviour that is essential if one is to be numbered among the righteous and thus avoid the punishment of Gehenna.[2] According to these succinct and forceful parables, the message of the kingdom is one which calls for absolute sacrifice and obedience. By implication the false disciples are characterized as people who have failed to give up everything in the face of the exclusive claim present in Jesus' teaching. In the parable of the net these false disciples are presented under the figure of bad (σαπρός) fish. The use of this distinctive adjective relates the fish of the parable to the bad trees and the inedible fruit of 7.17-18 and 12.33. These evil ones will be separated from the righteous and, like those worthless trees, will be cast into the fire.[3] In the furnace of fire they will weep and gnash their teeth.

Matthew has placed the parable of the net at the end of the series of parables which form the third discourse of his Gospel. It is noteworthy that the crowds, who at the beginning of the chapter are gathered about Jesus on the shore, find a counterpart in the fish of the parable which are also gathered on the shore. The crowds are, in a sense, symbolic of the world in which the kingdom of the Son of man extends and from which the good and bad enter into the church. In this position the parable furnishes a grim punctuation to the teaching of the entire chapter by concentrating attention firmly on the fate of those who neglect the urgent call to live according to the requirements of the kingdom.

1. Similar language appears in Mt. 17.2 in the description of the transfigured Jesus. One might infer from this that the disciples will share Jesus' glory; cf. Gundry, *Matthew*, p. 274. According to Dan. 12.3, following the resurrection the wise and instructors in righteousness will shine brightly like the stars.

2. Cf. Bornkamm, 'End-Expectation', p. 19 n. 6.

3. The verb ἀφορίζω relates this passage to 25.31-46 (cf. v. 32). In that scene of judgment the 'goats' are likewise sent off to eternal fire.

Matthew 22.1-14

Many of the prominent themes which have been surveyed already in this chapter are brought together in the parable of the wedding feast. The parable provides a concise lesson in the story of God's dealings with his people, by rehearsing once again the explanation for the rejection of the Jewish nation, while at the same time reminding members of the church that they are not immune from punishment but must seek to justify the calling they have received if they are to avoid a judgment similar to that which has befallen the disobedient and unfruitful within Israel.[1] The first part of the parable of the wedding feast is closely connected to the parable of the wicked tenants which it succeeds. The two share many common features: the device of a father and son, the sending of servant envoys, the mistreatment and killing of those servants, the punishment of the murderers, and the transfer of privilege from an unworthy group to a new group. Within the context of the Gospel, the opening verses of the parable reiterate the proposition of the previous parable that the repudiation of the people of Israel is no arbitrary action by God, but the consequence of their own indifference and antipathy to his will.[2] Repeatedly the Jewish people received the call of God communicated through his servants.[3] Yet they excluded themselves from the banquet through negligence and defiance, and thus revealed themselves to be unworthy of the divine invitation.[4] The denouement of their wilful action is catastrophic

1. The parable is described by Meier (*Matthew*, p. 249) as 'an allegory of the whole of salvation history, from the initial invitation to the Jews to the final judgment of Christians'.

2. Hill (*Matthew*, p. 302) comments that, like the earlier parable, 'it reveals to the Jews the gravity of their refusal of Jesus'.

3. Whereas the servants of the parable of the tenants clearly refer to the Old Testament prophets, the servants of this parable would seem to include Christian missionaries. In 23.34-36 Jesus announces to the Jewish leadership, the descendants of those who murdered the prophets, that he is sending to them emissaries whom they will similarly abuse. The tragic fate of the Christian missionaries sent to Israel is also reflected in 10.17, 23. It is notable that the command given the servants in 22.9 that they should 'go' (πορεύεσθε) is paralleled in the commissioning texts of 10.6-7 and 28.19.

4. It is correctly observed by Bonnard (*Matthieu*, p. 320) that the unworthiness of those invited 'ne consistait pas en divers défauts ou ignorances naturels; leur indignité, c'est leur refus'. The appearance of ἄξιος in v. 8 clearly echoes 10.11-13, 37-38. The wedding feast, like the banquet of 8.11, is a figure of the meal

destruction for themselves and their city and the forfeiture of their specially invited status.

At the same time that the invitation to the first group is rescinded, the circle of the call is extended to include as many as possible. As a result, both evil and good are gathered into the wedding hall. This image of a hall filled with people of varied character, which corresponds to that of a field containing weeds and wheat, is a further representation of the Matthaean conviction that the church is a mixed community. The call of God now embraces all, yet, as the second part of the parable makes clear, the invitation is not given without condition. The effect of the missionary endeavours of the church is that many are gathered into it, but not all will be able to stand the scrutiny of the last judgment. This judgment is depicted in vv. 11-13 under the figure of the king coming to inspect his guests.[1] When the king discovers a man in the hall who is not wearing the suitable wedding garment, he turns to his attendants and orders that the man be bound, like the weeds of the earlier parable, and cast into the outer darkness, the place of weeping and gnashing of teeth.[2] The wedding garment, which the man did not possess, is evidently a symbol of the better righteousness and perfection which is demanded of all those who receive the call of God. The parallel with Isa. 61.10 is often noted. In that text the restored remnant is clothed with the wedding apparel of salvation and righteousness.[3] The ejected guest exemplifies those in the church who in the end are renounced and excluded from the restored community. The reason for their repudiation is that their response to the invitation had been illusory to the extent that they failed to

enjoyed by those who are included in the eschatological restoration.

1.   The coming of the king serves the same purpose as the harvest in the parable of the weeds; cf. Smith, 'Mixed State', p. 157.

2.   This unworthy Christian is subject to a punishment identical to that announced to unworthy Jews in 8.12. The διάκονοι of 22.13 are distinct from the δοῦλοι of vv. 3-10 in the same way that the harvesters of the parable of the weeds are distinct from the servants. The term διάκονοι, which is the common designation for those servants charged with table service, is appropriate to this part of the parable, yet, as Marguerat (Jugement, p. 341) comments, 'elle satisfait également aux exigences du scénario apocalyptique, dans la mesure où les διάκονοι endossent la fonction traditionnelle des exécutants du verdict eschatologique'.

3.   Jeremias (Parables, p. 189) remarks that 'to be clothed with this garment is a symbol of membership of the redeemed community'.

respond to the demands inherent in the invitation.[1] They had neglected to produce the fruit appropriate to their calling and thus have no part in that nation which produces fruit in season.

The concluding statement of v. 14 acts a summary of what has transpired in the parable. At various times throughout the story many receive the call to the wedding feast, yet only a part of that number participate in the banquet. The unworthiness of the many excludes them from the wedding feast; the faithfulness and fruitfulness of the few places them among the chosen.[2] The contrast between πολλοί and ὀλίγοι is reminiscent of 7.13-14, where the terms designate, respectively, those who choose the easy way leading to destruction and those who find the difficult way leading to life. It was observed that the idea suggested by 'few' complements the prophetic emphasis that the redeemed community, which is here termed the chosen, represents merely a remnant.[3] The burden of the parable is that members of the Christian community must not commit the error, which distinguished so many in the Jewish community, of presuming upon the call of God. It is possible that Matthew placed this parable immediately after that of the tenants so that any triumphalist doctrine of election, which the statement in 21.43 may have generated, would be overcome at the outset.[4] If members of the Christian community are to stand at the last

---

1. When commenting on the necessity of a manner of life consistent with God's gracious call, D.O.Via, Jr (*The Parables* [Philadelphia: Fortress Press, 1967], p. 132) states that 'the attempt to live within the gift of God while rejecting the inseparable demand to respond appropriately to grace is a misguided effort which splits one's existence and issues in the loss of the situation where grace is present'.

2. Gnilka, *Matthäusevangelium*, II, p. 243: 'Zwischen Ruf und Erwählung liegt die Zeit der Bewährung'.

3. It is affirmed by Jeremias (*Theology*, p. 131) that ἐκλεκτοί is a fixed technical term for 'the messianic community of salvation'. B.F. Meyer ('Many [= All] are Called, but Few [= Not All] are Chosen', *NTS* 36 [1990], pp. 89-97) is correct to understand πολλοί and ὀλίγοι as correlative comparatives; yet this should not obscure the fact that 'few' is a *heilsgeschichtlich* category. Israel is warned in Deut. 4.27 (cf. Deut. 28.62; Lev. 26.22) that only a few (מְתֵי מִסְפָּר; ὀλίγος) will survive the judgment of Yahweh. In Jer. 44.28 it is observed that those who return to the land of Judah are few (מְתֵי מִסְפָּר; ὀλίγος) in number. Note that at Jer. 42.2 the remnant is defined by the phrase 'we are left but a few from many' (the Septuagint [49.2] reads κατελείφθημεν ὀλίγοι ἀπὸ πολλῶν).

4. Cf. E.E. Lemcio, 'The Parables of the Great Supper and the Wedding Feast: History, Redaction and Canon', *HBT* 8 (1986), pp. 1-26 (18). Marguerat (*Jugement*, p. 343) comments that 'la dignité de l'Eglise est une question ouverte, qui ne sera

judgment, they must demonstrate by their character and conduct that they are worthy to be among the chosen and thus capable of the place prepared for them to which they were called.

Matthew 24.45-51

This theme of the worthiness of the disciple is also treated in the parable of the faithful and wicked servant. The parable, which appears in a section of the Gospel dominated by the motif of watchfulness, explains, at least in part, what it means to watch for the coming of the Son of man (cf. 24.42-44; 25.13). The interval between the call to discipleship and the judgment which takes place when the Son of man returns is to be used as an opportunity for service and for the accomplishment of those obligations which adhere to the profession of Christian faith.[1] In the parable two possible courses of action are contrasted which can be pursued by a servant left in charge of the household during his master's absence. It is clear that the parable is not describing two servants, but rather two possible, though completely disparate, responses open to the one servant. The warning is directed to all disciples; yet it is those entrusted with responsibilities of leadership who are especially in view. The servant, if 'faithful and wise', will carry out his responsibilities conscientiously and will be duly rewarded when the master returns. However, if the servant chooses to be 'bad' and treats the master's absence as an opportunity to be exploited for selfish ends, then he can expect to be severely punished when the master returns.

The punishment meted out to the servant is unusual. He is to be cut in two and sent to the same fate as the hypocrites, that is, to Gehenna. In the parable neither the wicked servant nor his actions are said to be hypocritical. Nonetheless, this statement suggests that he is characterized by hypocrisy. His hypocrisy undoubtedly consists in the fact that, even though 'in his heart' he has determined to follow a wicked and self-seeking course which runs counter to the demands of the master, he persists in referring to him as 'my master'. His conduct is not unlike that of the hypocritical Pharisees and scribes in 15.7-8 who pay

tranchée qu'au jugement dernier'.

1. Though his primary interest lies with the Q parable, the conclusion of H. Fleddermann ('The Householder and the Servant Left in Charge', *SBLSP* 25 [1986], pp. 17-26 [26]) also holds true for Matthew that the wise servant recognises the master's delay as 'an opportunity to demonstrate his fidelity'.

deference to God even while their hearts are far removed from him. Yet the fruit which this servant yields during the absence of the master establishes that he is, in fact, a wolf in sheep's clothing. In ch. 23 Jesus had delivered a series of woes to the hypocritical scribes and Pharisees informing them that their punishment was inevitable. These woes culminate in the rhetorical question of v. 33 where it is affirmed that these hypocrites, whose deeds had not been consistent with their profession, will not escape being sentenced to Gehenna. The consignment of this wicked servant to the same fate is a forceful reminder that the unfaithful disciple is treated no differently from the unfaithful Jew.[1] Both are relegated to the place of weeping and gnashing of teeth. It is a reminder also that the wrath of God is especially directed against those who abuse a position of responsibility.

The 'cutting in two' ($\delta\iota\chi o\tau o\mu\acute{e}\omega$) of the servant is a particularly brutal depiction of God's wrathful judgment and can be compared to the punishment suffered by the unforgiving servant who is handed over to the torturers (18.34).[2] It does, however, seem a fitting punishment for this hypocritical and contemptuous servant. Inasmuch as hypocrisy, at least to a certain extent, consists in leading a dichotomized life, it is appropriate that the hypocrite in the end is split in two. It might also be observed that the punishment recalls the fate suffered by those who transgress such covenants as are established by means of the ceremony described in Gen. 15.9-17 and Jer. 34.18-20.[3] The wicked servant had indeed betrayed the understanding that

1.   Grundmann (*Matthäus*, p. 514) has rightly observed that 'die großen Wehe von Kap. 23 zugleich paränetische Bedeutung für die in ähnlicher Gefahr stehende Gemeinde besitzen'. Note that the blessing ($\mu\alpha\kappa\acute{\alpha}\rho\iota o\varsigma$) conferred on the good servant in v. 46 implies that a woe is pronounced on the wicked servant.

2.   In an intriguing article on the punishment of the servant, O. Betz ('The Dichotomized Servant and the End of Judas Iscariot', *RevQ* 5 [1964], pp. 43-58) argues that the parable is an eschatological version of Ps. 37 and that the punishment apportioned to the servant was originally understood as the eschatological act of 'cutting off' or expelling the wicked. He contends that in the present form of the parable this one eschatological act has been divided into two stages: the killing of the body in this age and the giving up of the person to eternal torment. Yet it is unlikely that Matthew regarded the cutting in two as a non-eschatological event. It is, in a sense, a graphic metaphor of the eternal 'cutting off' which confinement to Gehenna signifies.

3.   Note that the noun $\delta\iota\chi o\tau\acute{o}\mu\eta\mu\alpha$ appears in the Septuagint at Gen. 15.11, 17 (as well as in Aquila at Jer. 34.18, 19).

obtained between himself and the master. The false disciple, who stands behind this representation, is guilty in a similar way of violating the covenant relationship centred in the Lord whom he or she is committed to obey. The period of delay which occurs before the coming of the Son of man is intended to be a time when faithfulness to that covenant relationship is demonstrated. This parable warns that transgressors of that covenant are visited by curses similar to those attached to former covenants.

Matthew 25.14-30
The parable of the talents addresses this same issue of the conduct of the disciple during the period of delay. The conjunction γάρ in v. 14 connects the parable with the immediately preceding exhortation to vigilance. This suggests that the parable, like that of 24.45-51, serves to illustrate what it means to be watchful. As with the earlier parable, however, more attention is given to a negative example. Although the parable relates the reactions of three servants in a situation where they are entrusted with the master's property, it is evident that the main concern lies with the third servant, whose failure to produce a return during the interval results in his punishment.[1] When the responses of this servant and the wicked servant of the earlier parable are viewed together, it becomes apparent that a position of trust can be abused as easily through inaction as through wrongful action. Whereas the wicked servant had taken the unwise risk that the master would not return so quickly, this servant is loath to take any risk. As a consequence, he loses everything.[2] The proverbial statement in v. 29, which appeared in a slightly different form in 13.12, emphasizes the necessity of making the best use of the opportunities available. Those who respond diligently to the pressing demands of the kingdom will gain everything when they enter into 'the joy of the master'.[3] On the

1. In terms of the larger Matthaean context, the increase of talents may be representative of the fruit which each disciple is expected to produce; cf. Gnilka, *Matthäusevangelium*, II, p. 362.

2. In his assessment of the failing of this servant, D.O. Via Jr ('Ethical Responsibility and Human Wholeness in Matthew 25:31-46', *HTR* 80 [1987], pp. 79-100 [88]) concludes that 'risk is the possibility which must be actualized if one is to have the something which leads to something more and not to outer darkness'. The perspective of the servant would seem to correspond to that of the person who seeks to save his or her life but in the end loses it (16.25).

3. The statements in this parable and in the earlier parable concerning the

other hand, those who neglect to make the requisite sacrifices that faithful discipleship demands lose all as they are cast into 'the outer darkness', where they will weep and gnash their teeth.[1] The knowledge that the Son of man will return extends hope to the disciple whose task is often difficult. Yet in these parables that awareness is used as a prod to stimulate faithful and obedient activity in the interim.

An alarm is sounded in these and other menacing passages which appear throughout the Gospel. Presumption in the face of God's goodness, indifference to his call and unfaithfulness in his service place one in a position of danger. A terrible judgment had come upon Israel because of its failure to conform to the will of God. The pride of many in Israel had prevented them from following the path of obedience and had caused them even to spurn God's offer of redemption. As a consequence, the covenant relationship had been revoked and they had been cut off from the blessing of God. The church is warned that it too is not exempt from judgment, but must face a day of reckoning when it will be called upon to present fruit befitting the call and advantages it has received.

The prospect of a harrowing judgment is especially intended for those within the church, which is made up of the good and the bad, who do not take seriously the demands that accompany the call to discipleship. They are reminded that their true nature will at last be exposed at the dramatic separation when the weeds are gathered up and the unseemly are thrown out. At that time a terrible sentence will be pronounced on them. Like the false in Israel before them, these false members of the church will be rejected by God. Their unworthiness will bar them from entrance into the inheritance they could have enjoyed. Moreover, because they have violated that covenant established through Jesus, they stand under the curse of God. The curses that befall them are not unlike those which came upon the transgressors of the Sinai covenant. They too will enter the furnace and be cast

---

rewards of the faithful servants, that they will be 'set over the master's possessions' (24.47) and 'set over much' (25.21, 23), form part of the narrative background and hence do not offer a sound basis for reflections concerning the nature of the eschatological reward.

  1. The 'harshness' of the master does point to a reality outside of the parable, insofar as Jesus prescribes a difficult and demanding course for those who choose to follow him; cf. Gundry, *Matthew*, pp. 507-508.

into the darkness. In their case, however, a tone of finality distinguishes the punishment meted out. Never again will these false disciples return from the exile to which their own perversity has consigned them, for they have spurned the all important invitation to restoration. For that reason, their future existence will be characterized by a most frenzied remorse. In that place of banishment there will be weeping and gnashing of teeth.

A Picture of the Last Judgment

The last two parables that were examined are representative of the teaching which pervades chs. 24–25. In this 'apocalyptic discourse' the church receives instruction, albeit principally through negative examples, concerning the course it should follow prior to the final coming of the Son of man. This teaching is concluded with the remarkable scene of judgment described in 25.31-46. It must be noted, however, that this depiction of the last judgment does much more than complete the final discourse section of the Gospel. In a sense, the passage provides the climax to the entire teaching of Jesus, especially his teaching on recompense.[1] Though it follows a series of judgment parables, the passage is not strictly speaking a parable, despite the presence of figurative language especially in its introductory verses.[2] The passage would be best described as a highly artificial, yet otherwise straightforward, portrayal of the final judgment in which the criterion of assessment is explained. The centrality of Jesus to salvation and the coincident requirement that he be acknowledged in the present age has been stressed already in the Gospel. The startling emphasis communicated in this passage is that the confession or denial of Jesus is, to a large measure, linked to the treatment his followers receive in the present as they fulfil the task

1. It is noted by L. Cope ('Matthew xxv: 31-46 "The Sheep and the Goats" Reinterpreted', *NovT* 11 [1969], pp. 32-44 [33-34]) that Matthew employs the technique of referring to the future judgment in the concluding section of each discourse. The dramatic scene of judgment in the present passage may be regarded as the crown of all these previous references.

2. The opening simile, in which the Son of man is compared to a shepherd, was probably suggested by the judgment scene of Ezek. 34.17-24. In that passage Yahweh judges between the good and bad in his flock, removing and punishing the oppressors while setting his servant David as shepherd over the oppressed.

committed to them of taking the gospel to all peoples.

When the Son of man comes with his angels to sit upon the throne of judgment, all the nations will be gathered before him. The scene described is not dissimilar to that found in certain Old Testament texts, especially Joel 4.2-3 [3.2-3], which recount Yahweh's gathering of the nations so that he might enter into judgment against them for the way they have treated his people. The term 'all the nations', particularly in view of these Old Testament associations, might suggest that it is Gentiles who are being judged. Yet it seems best to interpret the phrase in the sense that all humanity will be gathered for judgment. Gentiles, Jews and even the church, composed as it is of the righteous and iniquitous, are encompassed by this phrase.[1] It might be observed that, as a consequence of the judgment pronounced against the Jewish nation in 21.43, Israel is now regarded as merely one among the other nations which need to be evangelized (cf. 28.19) and which will be judged on the basis of their response to disciples. The church is included in the judgment, since every Christian is charged with the care of other Christians and must answer for any mistreatment or neglect (18.5-6, 10-14). It cannot be presumed, of course, that all its members will be included among the sheep.[2] Individuals from these gathered nations will be separated into two groups, the sheep and goats, and placed, respectively, at the right hand and at the left hand of the judge.[3] Those on the right, the 'righteous' sheep, are

---

1. D. Catchpole ('The Poor on Earth and the Son of Man in Heaven: A Re-Appraisal of Matthew xxv.31-46', *BJRL* 61 [1979], pp. 355-97 [387-89]) argues from Matthaean usage that, whereas τὰ ἔθνη refers to non-Jews, 'the stronger term πάντα τὰ ἔθνη includes all without distinction'. Concerning the inclusion of Jews in the term, compare the comment of Gnilka, *Matthäusevangelium*, II, p. 371: 'Für Mt aber ist der Begriff durch die Mission geprägt, die auch die Juden nicht ausschließt'.

2. The 'least of these my brothers' do not constitute a third group which witness the proceedings. The judgment of H.E.W. Turner ('Expounding the Parables. VI. The Parable of the Sheep and the Goats (Matthew 25.31-46)', *ExpTim* 77 [1966], pp. 243-46 [245]) should be followed that τούτων is 'probably a redundant demonstrative and the brethren can be absorbed into the company of those who come to judgment'.

3. This act of separating brings to mind the separation of the weeds from the wheat and the rotten fish from the good fish. Gundry (*Matthew*, p. 512) notes that the shift from the neuter πάντα τὰ ἔθνη to the masculine αὐτούς in v. 32 implies individual rather than national judgment.

pronounced blessed and are granted entrance into the inheritance prepared for them. The goats, however, are pronounced cursed and are sent into the eternal fire. The standard of evaluation, according to which their disparate destinies are decided, is their response to those people in whom the Son of man had been concealed, that is to say, 'the least of these my brothers'.

There can be little doubt that this phrase refers to disciples. The related expression 'one of these little ones' is employed in 18.6-14 to describe members of the Christian community.[1] Moreover, in 10.40-42, which presents the closest parallel in the Gospel to 25.31-46, the 'one of these little ones' to whom a cup of cold water is given and with whom Jesus identifies himself is clearly a disciple.[2] Concerning the term ἀδελφός, Matthaean usage suggests once again that disciples are in view. In 12.48-50 the designation is used of all those who 'do the will of the Father', which, according to Matthew, is a definition of discipleship. Furthermore, in 28.10 the risen Jesus speaks of his disciples as 'my brothers'.[3] Thus, 'the least of of these my brothers' are those disciples who, like the 'little one' of 10.42, are dedicated to the task which the risen Jesus has delegated to his 'brothers'.[4] When

1.   Note that ἐλάχιστος is the superlative of the adjective μικρός.

2.   In the opinion of Green (*Matthew*, p. 206), the judgment scene of 25.31-46 amounts to an 'extended dramatization' of 10.42.

3.   Those scholars who wish to interpret 'the least of these my brothers' in terms of the needy in general must often resort to special pleading, as when Marguerat (*Jugement*, p. 511) attaches to ἀδελφός an epithetic value, or when Gnilka (*Matthäusevangelium*, II, p. 375) speaks of 'diese einmalige Ausweitung des Brudernamens'. The correct emphasis of the text is well expressed by J.R. Michaels ('Apostolic Hardships and Righteous Gentiles: A Study of Matthew 25.31-46', *JBL* 84 [1965], pp. 27-37 [37]): 'Jesus' disciples are not so much called upon to "help" the poor as they are to *become* the poor and outcast themselves in the completion of their world mission' (his italics).

4.   It is sometimes argued that the surprise motif which is crucial to the judgment scene disallows the identification of 'the least' with disciples. Via ('Ethical Responsibility', p. 92), for example, contends that 'since the sheep do not know that they had met Jesus prior to judgment, they apparently had not met disciples either'; cf. Catchpole, 'Re-Appraisal', p. 394. Yet what is surprising to both the sheep and goats is that this exalted and omnipotent Son of man was that humble Jesus represented by the humble disciple whom they had accepted or rejected. They had shown themselves to be either worthy or unworthy of acknowledgment by the glorified Jesus (10.32-33) when they received or refused his unpretentious representatives (10.11-15). Note the comment of J.M. Court ('Right and Left: The Implications for

Jesus commissioned his disciples, he promised that he would be 'with them' in their missionary endeavours (28.20). This scene of judgment gives insight into the nature of this bond between the risen Lord and his followers.[1] Jesus goes with his own as they face deprivation and persecution in the performance of their task, and inasmuch as others receive or reject them, they receive or reject the one who is 'with them'.

When commenting, in the previous chapter, on the divine identification with the disciple in 10.40-42, the parallel with Gen. 12.3 was noted. The disciple of Jesus receives an assurance similar to the pledge given to Abraham that God would 'bless those who bless you'. It would appear that the same promise is central to the present passage. The disciples of Jesus are charged with the task of taking the message of God's salvation to 'all the nations'. As such they are involved in the fulfilment of that other key promise made to Abraham that through him all nations would be blessed. The declaration that Yahweh would treat others in accordance with the way they treat Abraham is intimately connected to this promise. The vow demonstrates that the task assigned to Abraham is of such significance that salvation and condemnation are determined by the response of others to him. Those who bless him will be blessed and those who curse him will be cursed. The judgment scene of 25.31-46 illustrates the realization of this pledge. Those who respond positively to the disciple are pronounced 'blessed', whereas those who respond negatively are pronounced 'cursed'.[2] It is noteworthy that the terms εὐλογέω and καταράομαι appear both in the Septuagint at Gen. 12.3 and in Mt. 25.34, 41. The work that had begun with Abraham continues until the coming of the Son of man and is reinforced by this singular pronouncement of blessing and curse.

Matthew 25.31-46', *NTS* 31 [1985], pp. 223-33 [231]) that, in a context of various and conflicting religious claims, people may be so bewildered 'as to fail to recognise any ultimate authority'.

1.   Cf. J.R. Donahue, 'The 'Parable' of the Sheep and the Goats: A Challenge to Christian Ethics', *TS* 47 (1986), pp. 3-31 (18, 20).

2.   The goats do not actively oppose the work of the disciple. However, in view of the principle stated in 12.30 that whoever is not for Jesus is against him, the indifference of the goats is tantamount to opposition. It was noted above that the judgment scene can be compared to certain Old Testament texts where the nations are judged according to their treatment of Israel. The scene is identical but the roles have been changed. Israel is now numbered among the other nations while it is the 'nation producing the fruits of the kingdom' which is vindicated.

The blessed enter into the eternal life of the kingdom prepared for them from the foundation of the world. The inheritance they receive has been in existence from the beginning since it always formed part of God's intention for his people.[1] The cursed, on the other hand, depart towards a fate that was never intended for them. They are relegated to the eternal fire prepared for the devil and his angels.[2] While the righteous enjoy eternal life, these damned will endure eternal punishment (κόλασις).[3] In that final separation the story of salvation will have come to a close. For Matthew the present responsibility of the church is to extend to all the nations the offer of redemption centred in Jesus. He discloses in this passage that at the final judgment individual members of these nations will be held accountable for their response to this message of salvation, as shown in their attitude towards the messengers and ultimately towards the one standing behind the message. Those who accept the offer of salvation experience the blessing which God designed for the nations when he first called Abraham. But those who decline the offer are the truly cursed who have defeated their proper destiny by cutting themselves off for ever from the inheritance first promised to Abraham.

Conclusion

The punishment texts in Matthew provide a lesson in the reversals that mark the story of redemption. In the beginning the nation of Israel is called to serve God in holiness and righteousness to the end that other nations might share in the blessing God has purposed for all peoples. Yet the objective of God is hindered when Israel disappoints in the assigned role. Far from becoming the fruitful instrument of God's design, the nation had disregarded its task and closed its ear to the

---

1. Furthermore, as Schweizer (*Matthew*, p. 477) observes, the statement that the kingdom has been prepared from the creation of the world 'underlines the certainty of the promise'.

2. Gnilka, *Matthäusevangelium*, II, p. 376: 'Wenn im zweiten Fall der Rückgriff auf die Schöpfung fehlt, ist der Primat des Heiles herausgestellt'.

3. Etymology, of course, provides a precarious guide to meaning. Yet it is worth noting that the noun κόλασις seems to have been derived from the verb κολάζω which means 'to prune off' or 'to cut off'. As it happens, in this case the etymology of the word offers a precise insight into the nature of the punishment suffered by the cursed. They are, without remedy, cut off from the eternal life for which they were created.

appeals and warnings of the one whom it claimed to serve. In the end, God turns from the nation and its unique status is annulled. The call is now extended to all and a new nation is formed comprising those who do the will of God and who assume the responsibilities first given to Israel. This new nation may approximate, but it is far from identical with, the church. In a sense, the church grows out of Israel and, like its predecessor, is a mixed community. For that reason, its members will also be assessed as to their response to the call of God. At the final judgment, the unfaithful in the church will fare no better than the unfaithful in Israel.

The threats of judgment which appear frequently in Matthew are designed to provoke faithful and obedient service among members of the church, so that they might avoid the reversal which had overtaken so many in Israel. They too have entered into a covenant relationship and must take seriously its demands and obligations. The past history of God's dealings with his people demonstrates the importance he attaches to the obligations which are a part of this covenant relationship. Moreover, it reveals that he will not allow violations of trust to go unanswered. Yet, whereas in the past, under the old covenant, the punishment of disobedient Israel took place within history, now, under the new covenant, the punishment is meted out at the end of the present age. Accordingly, the final judgment is given a transcendent character which makes it even more terrible. Israel's history of disobedience, which had now culminated in the rejection of the son whom God had sent to redeem the nation, reaches a conclusion which marks a dramatic change in the fortunes of the people. This nation which had once enjoyed divine favour and a special station above other nations is now considered by God as merely one nation among other nations. The church has, in many respects, take over the role once filled by Israel, but under identical terms. The same prospect of divine disapproval and repudiation stands before the church if it fails in the responsibilities assigned to it. For that reason, the church must never simply equate itself with the new nation which receives the inheritance. The members of that nation are not revealed until the final judgment.

There are those in the church who will betray their position of trust and assume that being among the called automatically places them among the chosen. Such a superficial response to the call of God is inadequate and ultimately dangerous. God still expects fruit from those he calls, and he still visits his curse upon those who transgress his covenants. The fate of the false within the church is identical to the fate of the disobedient within Israel. Such unworthy ones will face the wrath of God. They will be uprooted and burned in eternal fire like unwanted weeds. They will be cast into a prison of outer darkness befitting those who reject the light of God. They will be cut off for ever from the reward and blessing of God with no hope of return.

Chapter 4

CONCLUSION

The entire sweep of salvation history from the call of Abraham to the close of the age is sketched in the Gospel of Matthew. The purpose of God that would eventually encompass all the families of the earth is founded on the covenant established with Abraham and on the mission entrusted to his family. In accordance with this covenant, the land of Canaan is given to Abraham, an inheritance which is to be the locus of reward for his descendants. Yet, inasmuch as the promised blessing is not restricted to this one family, it was the desire of God that the descendants of Abraham fulfil the task committed to them. This required that they be a fruitful people, that is, a righteous and faithful people, influenced by the nature of the one who called them and qualified to accomplish his objective. In consequence, the Sinai covenant is established, according to which a new significance is attached to the inheritance. Israel's possession of the land now assumes a conditional dimension. Attending the gracious call and gift of God are obligations and demands which must be met. The land retains its significance as reward, yet at the same time it becomes the sphere in which the nation's loyalty to God is tested. Ultimately, true possession of the land is dependent upon the fruitfulness of the nation.

The story of Israel and its inheritance is marked by two catastrophic reversals. Early in the story, the people on entry into the land are presented with two ways leading to life or death. In choosing the latter, this people, which had been so favoured, is made to experience the full force of God's curse. The blessings they had received are taken away, and they themselves are forcibly removed from the land which constituted the greatest of these blessings. Later in the story Israel is once again presented with a choice. A new covenant, centred in the son of God, is concluded which makes provision for the restoration of the nation to its inheritance. If the people of Israel respond in repentance and faith to the message of Jesus, the one born to save them from their sins and to become their king, they will share in that blessing prepared for all genuine children of Abraham. But if they refuse, they forfeit the advantage accruing from their status as the nation specially called by God. Moreover, they will experience absolute banishment from the inheritance of God. For a second time, the nation, characterized by obstinacy, favours a wayward course. In consequence, the 'kingdom of God' is taken from Israel. These 'sons of the kingdom' are cut off from the blessing of God. The call of God is now extended to others and a new nation is formed to take the place of Israel as the fruitful steward of God's purpose.

The paraenetical emphasis present in the Gospel of Matthew has been formulated in the light of this story of reversal and tragedy. The promises and warnings contained in the Gospel are directed primarily to those who regard themselves as members of that new nation which has obtained the call and gift of God. These followers of Jesus are reminded that it is not sufficient merely to receive the call of God. An appropriate response is essential. In the end, only those who have fulfilled the responsibilities inhering in the call will be among the chosen. Not all who receive the invitation will take their place alongside the patriarchs at the eschatological banquet. Only those who acknowledge the 'heir' and who demonstrate their worthiness, by conducting themselves in accordance with his commandments, will be designated righteous and granted entrance into the inheritance. These faithful ones comprise the 'few', the righteous remnant that is restored to the land and kingdom of God. The others who reject God's offer or who presume upon his grace are the 'many', the cursed who are cut off for ever from the blessing of God. Thus the lamentable story of Israel is made to serve the didactic purpose of warning those within the church that the same reversal which had befallen so many in Israel may also befall them. At the same time, however, the story of Israel, as it might have been, provides insight into the goal God intends for his people. Insofar as the righteous inherit a kingdom characterized by joy and festivity, their reward replicates in many important aspects the reward of the land God had prepared for Israel. To an extent, the eternal kingdom is a resumption of the life, joy and rest which, although begun in this age, could not be experienced fully until the renewal of creation at the end of the present age. God's purpose is not realized until the descendants of Abraham, now comprised of the faithful from every nation, are planted securely in the inheritance he has prepared for them.

It is a credit to Matthew's artistry that the recompense schema connected with the story of Israel in the Old Testament is presented as a paradigm for the recompense schema developed in his Gospel. In this way, the continuity in God's dealings with his people is underscored. Coincident with God's offer of grace is human accountability to his law, that is, to those demands which are the expression of his will. And presumed in the law of God is the possibility of blessing and curse. Consequently, the interplay between obedience and reward or disobedience and punishment is as much a feature of the new covenant as it was of the old covenant. Adhering to both covenants are stipulations which can be either observed or ignored and rewards which can be either attained or lost. It was undoubtedly this recognition, that at the level of grace and demand God's dealings with his people remained unchanged, which caused Matthew to accentuate the theme of recompense. He desired his readers to be in no doubt as to the gravity of their present situation. Whether they wish it or not, they are now characters in this universal story which is moving to an inexorable denouement. It is their relation to Jesus that determines the outcome of their own personal story. The lot apportioned to them when the larger story is concluded depends entirely on how in this life they play the role of accepting and furthering the message of Jesus and of practicing the righteousness and perfection he demands. Their performance in that role becomes the basis of the final judgment when it will be decided whether they are to be placed with the blessed or the cursed.

The composition critical method adopted in this inquiry has proved its effectiveness in carrying through the argument of the thesis, inasmuch as it has facilitated the delineation of the recompense schema developed in Matthew and, especially, has enabled the establishment of those links with the Old Testament recompense schema which have granted insight into the function of the reward and punishment statements within the conceptual framework of the Gospel. The examination of the relationship between the themes of reward and punishment and other significant Matthaean themes, such as the restoring/rejecting of Israel, entrance into and inheritance of the kingdom, fruit and judgment, and obedience and discipleship, has proved beneficial to a satisfactory completion of the study. Attention to the conceptual and terminological connections within the Gospel has revealed certain details and accents which are necessary to a complete undertanding of Matthew's thought on the subject of recompense. Moreover, by encouraging one to look at the larger picture, the method of composition criticism prompted the examination of those ideas and terms within the Old Testament which have considerable bearing on the recompense pattern discernible in Matthew. The verbal associations between Matthew and the Old Testament that have proved significant for the demonstration of the thesis are beyond mere coincidence. Yet it is unlikely that these connections would have been detected without the implementation of the composition critical method. The kind of analysis required by this study demanded a method which requires one to concentrate on Matthew as a finished whole.

This study serves to enhance the contribution made by earlier investigations which demonstrated that the elements of demand and threat are particularly accentuated in the teaching of Matthew.[1] Although the issue of grace and demand has not been the focus of exegetical attention, certain observations could be made based on the conclusions reached by this inquiry. It is correct to say that grace is always assumed by Matthew: the call of God, extended to the good and bad alike, is completely unearned. Yet Matthew's main interest lies with the responsibilities now borne by those who have received this call. The grace of God is basic and essential to salvation; yet in itself it does not effect salvation. That requires an additional ingredient, the appropriate human response of faith and obedience. The difference between the called and the chosen is that the latter have shown themselves to be worthy of the call they received. That is not to say the obedient disciple merits the blessing and reward of God. The disciple is in no position to make demands of God. Even so, the disciple can be said to have earned the blessing and reward to the extent that he or she has obediently followed Jesus in the way of righteousness.

It is against this context of accountability to the law of God expressed in the demands of Jesus that the problem of Matthew's perspective on the law might be viewed. In the Gospel the authority of the Mosaic law is not opposed or rejected, yet neither is it regarded as final. With the establishment of a new covenant relationship between God and his people centred in Jesus, redemption is now located in one's acknowledgement of Jesus and obedience to the way prescribed

1. Note, in particular, the studies of Mohrlang (*Matthew and Paul*) and Marguerat (*Jugement*).

by him. This emphasis on the centrality of Jesus to salvation, while placing Matthew in harmony with the general witness of the New Testament, would have put the Gospel in a position at variance with the prevailing Jewish view regarding the relationship of covenant, law and redemption. According to the conventional Jewish view of the period, which in recent discussion is described by the term 'covenantal nomism',[1] it was sufficient for salvation to be born into the covenant community and observe the Mosaic law. Yet Matthew is careful to note that this position is called into question by the preaching of both John the Baptist and Jesus. It is not enough that one is born a Jew. The covenant established with Abraham is maintained, but it must not be assumed that physical descent from Abraham automatically confers immunity from judgment or entitlement to the promises. Even many conscientious Jews, typified by the rich young man, fail to meet the condition of redemption. In the new order that has been introduced with the coming of Jesus salvation is dependent upon repentance and obedience, but especially upon one's response to this one who was born to redeem his people. As a consequence of this new centre to salvation, Jew and Gentile are placed on an equal footing. A decision is required of all, and it is on the basis of this decision that one is either incorporated into or excluded from the covenant community of the redeemed.

At the same time, however, it should be noted that Matthew is in agreement with the view, also inherent in 'covenantal nomism', that the means by which one stays within the covenant relationship is faithful obedience to the law of God, which is now, of course, understood with reference to the fulfilment introduced by the coming of Jesus. The new covenant, which God in his grace established to renew hope following the failure of the Sinai covenant, operates on a different level from the old to the extent that it no longer has an ethnic basis. It is not concerned exclusively with one nation, but rather with a new nation which embraces people from every nation. Yet this new covenant operates on the same level as the old in respect of the requirement of obedience for the continuing maintenance of the covenant relationship. Matthew would agree with his Jewish contemporaries regarding the interface between law and covenant. He would disagree with them regarding which covenant is now in effect.

1. The term is taken from the very influential book by E.P. Sanders, *Paul and Palestinian Judaism* (Philadelphia: Fortress Press, 1977).

In view of this emphasis on the central place ascribed to Jesus and the importance attached to his teaching on recompense, one might draw certain conclusions regarding the community which stands behind the Gospel and to which it was addressed. It would seem to be a community, comprised of both Jews and Gentiles, which regards itself as standing in continuity with God's people of the Old Testament and yet, at the same time, enjoying an advantage over these forebears inasmuch as the time of fulfilment has arrived. The conviction of the community, that the hopes of Israel have been realized in Jesus and that in him a new covenant has been concluded, results in missionary outreach to the Jewish community. Yet it is clear from the Gospel that such endeavours meet with Jewish hostility. The rejection of Jesus and his followers by so many in Israel is regarded as the most recent manifestation of a national obduracy which has had a long and tragic history. At the same time, however, this Jewish antipathy marks the transfer of privilege away from the nation of Israel to a new nation.

The community addressed by the Gospel, though identifying itself with this new nation, is very much a mixed group. Like the people of God in earlier times it is comprised of the good and the bad, the faithful and the unfaithful. Some attached to the community, apparently even in positions of leadership, do not pay due attention to the demands of discipleship. The history of Israel provides a lesson for the church as to the dire consequences if the influence of deceitful members is allowed to go unchecked. The bad are not to be rooted out, but the church must exercise discernment and implement a programme of discipline. It would appear, then, that the Gospel was written in a context where true discipleship is forced to defend itself on two fronts.[1] In this setting Matthew places emphasis on punishment to warn both Jewish opponents and false Christians of the consequences should they not turn to God in obedience. The emphasis on reward is designed in part to encourage the faithful caught up in the midst of this struggle.

It was noted in the introduction that the present study would not attempt to determine the extent to which the Gospel of Matthew accurately reflects the teaching of the 'historical Jesus' on the subject of

---

1. Compare, for example, the thesis of Barth ('Understanding of the Law') that, on the one hand, Matthew is opposing Pharisaic interpretations of the law and, on the other hand, battling against those within the church who do not give due consideration to the law.

recompense. It is possible that the teaching presented in the Gospel bears, to a remarkable degree, the stamp of the Evangelist himself. Yet, inasmuch as Matthew purports to be giving an account of the teaching of Jesus and since most of what can be known about Jesus' teaching on recompense is contained in his Gospel, it is imperative that future attempts to delineate the teaching of Jesus treat seriously the representation that obtains in Matthew. In this area of inquiry dogma has exerted an unreasonable influence. A responsible description of Jesus' teaching on this subject requires the equitable evaluation of all the relevant evidence.

The main contribution of this study consists in its assessment of Matthew's use and understanding of the Old Testament. One could be excused, amidst the flurry of new methods and directions in Gospel studies, for gaining the impression that the subject of Matthew's interest in the Old Testament is seen by many interpreters as passé. There seems to be a tacit assumption that the relationship between Matthew and the Old Testament has been sufficiently explored and that as an area of research it holds little promise of granting fresh insight into the Gospel. The present study, it is hoped, has demonstrated that a careful reading of Matthew against the backdrop of the Old Testament yields a valuable return. It is very probable that sufficient investigation has been made into the formula quotations and into many of the prominent allusions found throughout the Gospel. If that investigation may be likened to the study of individual trees, then what is now needed is an examination of the entire wood. Presumably, the perspective gained as the result of viewing Matthew as a whole against the Old Testament as a whole would reveal new features of the Gospel which may have considerable bearing on its interpretation. The story related in Matthew is a resumption of the story recounted in the Old Testament. Yet, to an extent, Matthew has juxtaposed the two stories. In a manner recalling the scribe of 13.52, he has produced a rich narrative by correlating new and old. It would not be imprudent to suggest that the degree to which Matthew's new story is understood depends on how well Matthew's reading of the old story is understood.

Bibliography

Aland, K., and B. Aland, *The Text of the New Testament*. Grand Rapids: Eerdmans, 1987.

Allen, W.C., *A Critical and Exegetical Commentary on the Gospel according to S. Matthew*. Edinburgh: T. & T. Clark, 1912.

Allison, D.C., Jr., 'Jesus and the Covenant: A Response to E.P. Sanders', *JSNT* 29 (1987), pp. 57-78.

—'The Eye Is the Lamp of the Body (Matthew 6.22-23 = Luke 11.34-36)', *NTS* 33 (1987), pp. 61-83.

—'Who Will Come from East and West? Observations on Matt. 8.11-12–Luke 13.28-29', *IBS* 11 (1989), pp. 158-70.

Anderson, A.A., *The Book of Psalms*. 2 vols. Grand Rapids: Eerdmans, 1972.

Bach, R., 'Bauen und Pflanzen', in R. Rendtorff and K. Koch (eds.), *Studien zur Theologie der alttestamentlichen Überlieferungen*. Neukirchen–Vluyn: Neukirchener Verlag, 1961, pp. 7-32.

Baltzer, K., *The Covenant Formulary*. Oxford: Basil Blackwell, 1971.

Barth, G., 'Matthew's Understanding of the Law', in G. Bornkamm, G. Barth and H.J. Held, *Tradition and Interpretation in Matthew*. Philadelphia: Westminster Press, 1963, pp. 58-164.

Beare, F.W., *The Gospel according to Matthew*. San Francisco: Harper & Row, 1981.

Beasley-Murray, G.R., *Jesus and the Kingdom of God*. Grand Rapids: Eerdmans, 1986.

Bertram, G., 'φυλακή', *TDNT*, IX, pp. 241-44.

Betz, H.D., 'An Episode in the Last Judgment (Matt. 7.21-23)', in his *Essays on the Sermon on the Mount*. Philadelphia: Fortress Press, 1985, pp. 125-57.

—'Matt. 6.22-23 and Ancient Greek Theories of Vision', in *Sermon on the Mount*, pp. 71-87.

Betz, O., 'The Dichotomized Servant and the End of Judas Iscariot', *RevQ* 5 (1964), pp. 43-58.

Black, M., *An Aramaic Approach to the Gospels and Acts*. Oxford: Clarendon Press, 1967.

Bonnard, P., *L'Evangile selon saint Matthieu*. Neuchatel: Delachaux & Niestlé, 1970.

Bornkamm, G., 'Der Lohngedanke im Neuen Testament', in his *Studien zu Antike und Urchristentum: Gesammelte Aufsätze*. Munich: Kaiser Verlag, 1963, II, pp. 69-92.

—'End-Expectation and Church in Matthew', in Bornkamm *et al.*, *Tradition and Interpretation*, pp. 15-51.

—'λικμάω', *TDNT*, IV, pp. 280-81.

Böttger, P.C., B. Siede and O. Becker, 'Recompense', *NIDNTT*, III, pp. 134-45.

Boyd, W.J.P., 'Gehenna—According to J. Jeremias', in E.A. Livingstone (ed.), *Studia Biblica 1978*. II. *Papers on the Gospels*. Sheffield: JSOT Press, 1980, pp. 9-12.

Bracke, J.M., 'shûb shᵉbût: A Reappraisal', *ZAW* 97 (1985), pp. 233-44.

170   *The Theme of Recompense in Matthew's Gospel*

Braun, H., *Spätjudisch-häretischer und frühchristlicher Radikalismus*. Tübingen: Mohr, 1969.

Brayley, I.F.M., ' "Yahweh is the Guardian of His Plantation" A Note on Is 60,21', *Bib* 41 (1960), pp. 275-86.

Brueggemann, W., *Genesis*. Atlanta: John Knox, 1982.

—'Israel's Sense of Place in Jeremiah', in J.J. Jackson and M. Kessler (eds.), *Rhetorical Criticism*. Pittsburgh: Pickwick Press, 1974, pp. 149-65.

—*The Land*. Philadelphia: Fortress Press, 1977.

Buchanan, G.W., 'Matthean Beatitudes and Traditional Promises', in W.R. Farmer (ed.), *New Synoptic Studies*. Macon, GA: Mercer University Press, 1983, pp. 161-84.

Carlston, C.E., *The Parables of the Triple Tradition*. Philadelphia: Fortress Press, 1975.

Carroll, R.P., *Jeremiah*. London: SCM Press, 1986.

Cassuto, U., *A Commentary on the Book of Genesis: Part 2*. Jerusalem: Magnes Press, 1964.

Catchpole, D., 'The Poor on Earth and the Son of Man in Heaven: A Re-Appraisal of Matthew xxv.31-46', *BJRL* 61 (1979), pp. 355-97.

Charette, B., ' "To Proclaim Liberty to the Captives": Matthew 11.28-30 in the Light of OT Prophetic Expectation', *NTS* 38 (1992), pp. 290-97.

Clements, R.E., *Abraham and David*. London: SCM Press, 1967.

—*God's Chosen People*. London: SCM Press, 1968.

—*Prophecy and Covenant*. London: SCM Press, 1965.

Coats, G.W., 'The Curse in God's Blessing', in J. Jeremias and L. Perlitt (eds.), *Die Botschaft und die Boten*. Neukirchen–Vluyn: Neukirchener Verlag, 1981, pp. 31-41.

Cope, L., 'Matthew xxv: 31-46: "The Sheep and the Goats" Reinterpreted', *NovT* 11 (1969), pp. 32-44.

Court, J.M., 'Right and Left: The Implications for Matthew 25.31-46', *NTS* 31 (1985), pp. 223-33.

Craigie, P.C., *The Book of Deuteronomy*. Grand Rapids: Eerdmans, 1976.

—*Psalms 1–50*. Waco, TX: Word Books, 1983.

Crossan, J.D., *In Parables: The Challenge of the Historical Jesus*. San Francisco: Harper & Row, 1973.

Davies, W.D., *The Gospel and the Land*. Berkeley: University of California Press, 1974.

—*The Setting of the Sermon on the Mount*. Cambridge: Cambridge University Press, 1964.

Davies, W.D., and D.C. Allison, Jr., *The Gospel according to Saint Matthew*. Edinburgh: T. & T. Clark, 1988, I.

Davison, J.E., '*Anomia* and the Question of an Antinomian Polemic in Matthew', *JBL* 104 (1985), pp. 617-35.

DeRoche, M., 'Contra Creation, Covenant and Conquest (Jer 8.13)', *VT* 30 (1980), pp. 280-90.

Derrett, J.D.M., 'Palingenesia (Matthew 19.28)', *JSNT* 20 (1984), pp. 51-58.

Diepold, P., *Israels Land*. Stuttgart: Kohlhammer, 1972.

Dietrich, E.L., שוב שבות: *Die endzeitliche Wiederherstellung bei den Propheten*. Giessen: Töpelmann, 1925.

Donahue, J.R., 'The "Parable" of the Sheep and the Goats: A Challenge to Christian Ethics', *TS* 47 (1986), pp. 3-31.

Dreyfus, F., 'Le thème de l'héritage dans l'Ancien Testament', *RSPT* 42 (1958), pp. 3-49.

Driver, S.R., *A Critical and Exegetical Commentary on Deuteronomy*. Edinburgh: T. & T. Clark, 1902.

Dupont, J., 'Le logion des douze trônes (Mt 19,28; Lc 22,28-30)', *Bib* 45 (1964), pp. 355-92.

—*Les Béatitudes*. 3 vols. Paris: Gabalda, 1969–73.

Edgar, S.L., 'Respect for Context in Quotations from the Old Testament', *NTS* 9 (1962), pp. 55-62.

Eichler, J., 'Inheritance', *NIDNTT*, II, pp. 295-303.

Fensham, F.C., 'Covenant, Promise and Expectation in the Bible', *TZ* 23 (1967), pp. 305-22.

—'Malediction and Benediction in Ancient Near Eastern Vassal-Treaties and the Old Testament', *ZAW* 74 (1962), pp. 1-9.

—'The Good and Evil Eye in the Sermon on the Mount', *Neot* 1 (1967), pp. 51-58.

Fitzmyer, J.A., *The Gospel according to Luke (I–IX)*. Garden City, NY: Doubleday, 1981.

Fleddermann, H., 'The Householder and the Servant Left in Charge', *SBLSP* 25 (1986), pp. 17-26.

France, R.T., 'Exegesis in Practice: Two Examples', in I.H. Marshall (ed.), *New Testament Interpretation*. Grand Rapids: Eerdmans, 1977, pp. 252-81.

—*Matthew*. Grand Rapids: Eerdmans, 1985.

—*Matthew: Evangelist and Teacher*. Exeter: Paternoster Press, 1989.

—'The Formula-Quotations of Matthew 2 and the Problem of Communication', *NTS* 27 (1981), pp. 233-51.

Frankemölle, H., *Jahwebund und Kirche Christi*. Münster: Aschendorff, 1974.

Freedman, D.N., 'Divine Commitment and Human Obligation', *Int* 18 (1964), pp. 419-31.

Gaechter, P., *Das Matthäus Evangelium*. Innsbruck: Tyrolia, 1963.

Gammie, J.G., 'The Theology of Retribution in the Book of Deuteronomy', *CBQ* 32 (1970), pp. 1-12.

George, A., 'La justice à faire dans le secret (Matthieu 6,1-6 et 16-18)', *Bib* 40 (1959), pp. 590-98.

Geyser, A.S., 'Some Salient New Testament Passages on the Restoration of the Twelve Tribes of Israel', in J. Lambrecht (ed.), *L'Apocalypse johannique et l'apocalyptique dans le Nouveau Testament*. Leuven: Leuven University Press, 1980, pp. 305-10.

Giesen, H., *Christliches Handeln*. Frankfurt: Peter Lang, 1982.

—'Der verdorrte Feigenbaum—Eine symbolische Aussage? Zu Mk 11,12-14.20f', *BZ* 20 (1976), pp. 95-111.

Glover, F.C., 'Workers for the Vineyard', *ExpTim* 86 (1974–75), pp. 310-11.

Gnilka, J., *Das Matthäusevangelium*. 2 vols. Freiburg: Herder, 1988.

Gowan, D.E., *Eschatology in the Old Testament*. Edinburgh: T. & T. Clark, 1986.

Graber, F., 'Blind', *NIDNTT*, I, pp. 218-20.

Green, H.B., *The Gospel according to Matthew*. Oxford: Oxford University Press, 1975.

Gross, H., 'Remnant', *EBT*, II, pp. 741-43.

Grundmann, W., *Das Evangelium nach Matthäus*. Berlin: Evangelische Verlagsanstalt, 1968.

Guelich, R.A., *The Sermon on the Mount*. Waco, TX: Word Books, 1982.

Gundry, R.H., *Matthew: A Commentary on his Literary and Theological Art*. Grand Rapids: Eerdmans, 1982.

Ha, J., *Genesis 15*. Berlin: de Gruyter, 1989.

Hamilton, V.P., *The Book of Genesis: Chapters 1–17*. Grand Rapids: Eerdmans, 1990.

Haubeck, W., 'Zum Verständnis der Parabel von den Arbeitern im Weinberg (Mt 20,1-15)', in W. Haubeck and M. Bachmann (eds.), *Wort in der Zeit*. Leiden: Brill, 1980, pp. 95-107.

Hauck, F., 'καρπός', *TDNT*, III, pp. 614-16.

Hausmann, J., 'עִנָי', *ThWAT*, V, cols. 727-30.

Hensel, R., 'Fruit', *NIDNTT*, I, pp. 721-23.

Hester, J.D., *Paul's Concept of Inheritance*. Edinburgh: Oliver & Boyd, 1968.

Hill, D., 'False Prophets and Charismatics: Structure and Interpretation in Matthew 7,15-23', *Bib* 57 (1976), pp. 327-48.

—*The Gospel of Matthew*. Grand Rapids: Eerdmans, 1972.

—'ΔΙΚΑΙΟΙ as a Quasi-Technical Term', *NTS* 11 (1965), pp. 296-302.

Hillers, D.R., *Treaty-Curses and the Old Testament Prophets*. Rome: Pontifical Biblical Institute, 1964.

Himmelfarb, M., *Tours of Hell*. Philadelphia: Fortress Press, 1983.

Holladay, W.L., *Jeremiah 1*. Philadelphia: Fortress Press, 1986.

—'The Covenant with the Patriarchs Overturned: Jeremiah's Intention in "Terror on Every Side" (Jer 20.1-6)', *JBL* 91 (1972), pp. 305-20.

—'The New Covenant', *IDBSup*, pp. 623-25.

Hood, R.T., 'The Genealogies of Jesus', in A. Wikgren (ed.), *Early Christian Origins*. Chicago: Quadrangle Books, 1961, pp. 1-15.

Jeremias, J., *Jesus' Promise to the Nations*. Philadelphia: Fortress Press, 1982.

—*New Testament Theology*. New York: Charles Scribner's Sons, 1971.

—*The Parables of Jesus*. New York: Charles Scribner's Sons, 1972.

—'γέεννα', *TDNT*, I, pp. 657-58.

—'λίθος', *TDNT*, IV, pp. 268-80.

—'ποιμήν', *TDNT*, VI, pp. 485-502.

Johnson, M.D., *The Purpose of the Biblical Genealogies*. Cambridge: Cambridge University Press, 1969.

Joüon, P., ''ΥΠΟΚΡΙΤΗΣ dans l'évangile et hébreu ḤANEF,' *RSR* 20 (1930), pp. 312-16.

Kapelrud, A.S., *The Message of the Prophet Zephaniah*. Oslo: Universitetsforlaget, 1975.

Kertelge, K., ''Selig, die verfolgt werden um der Gerechtigkeit willen" (Mt 5,10)', *IKZ* 16 (1987), pp. 97-106.

Kingsbury, J.D., *Matthew as Story*. Philadelphia: Fortress Press, 1986.

—*The Parables of Jesus in Matthew 13*. London: SPCK, 1969.

Koch, K., 'Der Schatz im Himmel', in B. Lohse and H.P. Schmidt (eds.), *Leben angesichts des Todes*. Tübingen: Mohr, 1968, pp. 47-60.

Lach, J., 'Die Pflicht zur Versöhnung und Liebe (Mt 5,43-48)', *CollTh* 57 (1987), pp. 57-69.

Lambrecht, J., 'The Parousia Discourse: Composition and Content in Mt., XXIV-XXV', in M. Didier (ed.), *L'évangile selon Matthieu*. Gembloux: Duculot, 1972, pp. 309-42.

Lang, F., 'πῦρ', *TDNT*, VI, pp. 928-52.

Lemcio, E.E., 'The Parables of the Great Supper and the Wedding Feast: History, Redaction and Canon', *HBT* 8 (1986), pp. 1-26.

Lindars, B., *Jesus Son of Man*. London: SPCK, 1983.

Lipiński, E., 'נָחַל', *ThWAT*, V, cols. 342-60.

Lohfink, N., 'יָרַשׁ', *TDOT*, VI, pp. 368-96.

Lust, J., ''Gathering and Return" in Jeremiah and Ezekiel', in P.-M. Bogaert (ed.), *Le livre de Jérémie*. Leuven: Leuven University Press, 1981, pp. 119-42.

Luz, U., *Matthew 1–7*. Minneapolis: Augsburg, 1989.

McCarthy, D.J., 'Covenant in the Old Testament: The Present State of Inquiry', *CBQ* 27 (1965), pp. 217-40.

—*Treaty and Covenant*. Rome: Pontifical Biblical Institute, 1963.

McDonald, J.I.H., 'The Concept of Reward in the Teaching of Jesus', *ExpTim* 89 (1978), pp. 269-73.

Manson, T.W., *The Sayings of Jesus*. Grand Rapids: Eerdmans, 1957.

Marguerat, D., *Le jugement dans l'évangile de Matthieu*. Geneva: Labor et Fides, 1981.

Marshall, I.H., 'Uncomfortable Words. VI. "Fear him who Can Destroy both Soul and Body in Hell" (Mt 10.28 R.S.V.)', *ExpTim* 81 (1970), pp. 276-80.

Mattill, A.J., Jr., ' "The Way of Tribulation" ', *JBL* 98 (1979), pp. 531-46.

Meier, J.P., *Matthew*. Wilmington, DE: Michael Glazier, 1980.

Metzger, B.M., *A Textual Commentary on the Greek New Testament*. N.p. United Bible Societies, 1971.

Meyer, B.F., 'Jesus and the Remnant of Israel', *JBL* 84 (1965), pp. 123-30.

—'Many (= All) are Called, but Few (= Not All) are Chosen', *NTS* 36 (1990), pp. 89-97.

—*The Aims of Jesus*. London: SCM Press, 1979.

Michaels, J.R., 'Apostolic Hardships and Righteous Gentiles: A Study of Matthew 25.31-46', *JBL* 84 (1965), pp. 27-37.

—*Servant and Son*. Atlanta: John Knox, 1981.

Michel, O., 'Der Lohngedanke in der Verkündigung Jesu', *ZST* 9 (1931), pp. 47-54.

—'ὁμολογέω', *TDNT*, V, pp. 199-220.

Milikowsky, C., 'Which Gehenna? Retribution and Eschatology in the Synoptic Gospels and in Early Jewish Texts', *NTS* 34 (1988), pp. 238-49.

Miller, P.D., Jr., 'The Gift of God: The Deuteronomic Theology of the Land', *Int* 23 (1969), pp. 451-65.

Minear, P.S., *And Great Shall Be Your Reward*. New Haven: Yale University Press, 1941.

—*Commands of Christ*. Nashville: Abingdon Press, 1972.

—'False Prophecy and Hypocrisy in the Gospel of Matthew', in J. Gnilka (ed.), *Neues Testament und Kirche*. Freiburg: Herder, 1974, pp. 76-93.

Mohrlang, R., *Matthew and Paul*. Cambridge: Cambridge University Press, 1984.

Montgomery, J.A., 'The Holy City and Gehenna', *JBL* 27 (1908), pp. 24-47.

Moore, S.D., *Literary Criticism and the Gospels*. New Haven: Yale University Press, 1989.

Münderlein, G., 'Die Verfluchung des Feigenbaumes (Mk xi 12-14)', *NTS* 10 (1963), pp. 89-104.

North, C.R., *The Second Isaiah*. Oxford: Oxford University Press, 1964.

Ottosson, M., 'יָרַץ', *TDOT*, I, pp. 393-405.

Pamment, M., 'The Kingdom of Heaven according to the First Gospel', *NTS* 27 (1981), pp. 211-32.

Pesch, W., *Der Lohngedanke in der Lehre Jesu verglichen mit der religiösen Lohnlehre des Spätjudentums*. Munich: Karl Zink, 1955.

Piper, J., *'Love Your Enemies'*. Cambridge: Cambridge University Press, 1979.

Plöger, J.G., *Literarkritische, formgeschichtliche und stilkritische Untersuchungen zum Deuteronomium*. Bonn: Peter Hanstein, 1967.

Preisker, H., and E. Würthwein, 'μισθός', *TDNT*, IV, pp. 695-728.

Rad, G. von, *Genesis*. Philadelphia: Westminster Press, 1972.

—'The Promised Land and Yahweh's Land in the Hexateuch', in his *The Problem of the Hexateuch and Other Essays*. Edinburgh: Oliver & Boyd, 1966, pp. 79-93.

174   *The Theme of Recompense in Matthew's Gospel*

—'There Remains still a Rest for the People of God: An Investigation of a Biblical Concept', in *The Problem of the Hexateuch*, pp. 94-102.

Reicke, B., 'The New Testament Conception of Reward', in *Aux sources de la tradition chrétienne*. Paris: n.p., 1950, pp. 195-206.

Reindl, J., 'נָטַע', *ThWAT*, V, cols. 415-24.

Rengstorf, K.H., 'Die Frage des gerechten Lohnes in der Verkündigung Jesu', in *Festschrift Karl Arnold*. Cologne: Westdeutscher Verlag, 1955, pp. 141-55.

—'βρυγμός', *TDNT*, I, pp. 641-42.

—'ἑταῖρος', *TDNT*, II, pp. 699-701.

Riesenfeld, H., 'Vom Schätzesammeln und Sorgen: Ein Thema urchristlicher Paränese. Zu Mt VI 19-34', in W.C. van Unnik (ed.), *Neotestamentica et Patristica*. Leiden: Brill, 1962, pp. 47-58.

Ringgren, H., 'הָיָה', *TDOT*, IV, pp. 324-44.

—'חָשַׁךְ', *ThWAT*, III, cols. 265-76.

Ru, G. de, 'The Conception of Reward in the Teaching of Jesus', *NovT* 8 (1966), pp. 202-22.

Sand, A., *Das Evangelium nach Matthäus*. Regensburg: Pustet, 1986.

—*Das Gesetz und die Propheten*. Regensburg: Pustet, 1974.

Sanders, E. P., *Jesus and Judaism*. Philadelphia: Fortress Press, 1985.

—*Paul and Palestinian Judaism*. Philadelphia: Fortress Press, 1977.

Sarna, N., *Understanding Genesis*. New York: Schocken Books, 1966.

Schenke, L., 'Die Interpretation der Parabel von den "Arbeiten im Weinberg" (Mt 20,1-15) durch Matthäus', in L. Schenke (ed.), *Studien zum Matthäusevangelium*. Stuttgart: Katholisches Bibelwerk, 1988, pp. 247-68.

Schlatter, A., *Der Evangelist Matthäus*. Stuttgart: Calwer Verlag, 1957.

Schmid, J., *Das Evangelium nach Matthäus*. Regensburg: Pustet, 1959.

Schwank, B., 'Dort wird Heulen und Zähneknirschen sein', *BZ* 16 (1972), pp. 121-22.

Schwarz, G., 'Matthäus vii 13a: Ein Alarmruf angesichts höchster Gefahr', *NovT* 12 (1970), pp. 229-32.

Schweizer, E., 'Observance of the Law and Charismatic Activity in Matthew', *NTS* 16 (1970), pp. 213-30.

—*The Good News according to Matthew*. Atlanta: John Knox, 1975.

Seitz, O.J.F., 'Love Your Enemies', *NTS* 16 (1970), pp. 39-54.

Sidebottom, E.M., '"Reward" in Matthew v. 46, etc.', *ExpTim* 67 (1955–56), pp. 219-20.

Smith, C.W.F., 'The Mixed State of the Church in Matthew's Gospel', *JBL* 82 (1963), pp. 149-68.

Smith, M., *Tannaitic Parallels to the Gospels*. Philadelphia: SBL, 1961.

Steck, O.H., *Israel und das gewaltsame Geschick der Propheten*. Neukirchen–Vluyn: Neukirchener Verlag, 1967.

Stewart, G.W., 'The Place of Rewards in the Teaching of Christ', *Expositor* 10 (1910), pp. 97-111, 224-41.

Strack, H.L., and P. Billerbeck, *Kommentar zum Neuen Testament aus Talmud und Midrasch*. Munich: Oskar Beck, 1928, IV.1.

Strecker, G., *Der Weg der Gerechtigkeit*. Göttingen: Vandenhoeck & Ruprecht, 1966.

—*The Sermon of the Mount*. Edinburgh: T. & T. Clark, 1988.

Thomas, D.W., 'צְלָמָוֶת in the Old Testament', *JSS* 7 (1962), pp. 191-200.

Thompson, J.A., *Deuteronomy*. London: Inter-Varsity Press, 1974.

Thompson, W.G., 'An Historical Perspective in the Gospel of Matthew', *JBL* 93 (1974), pp. 243-62.

Travis, S., 'Reward in the Teaching of Jesus', The Drew Lecture on Immortality, 1983: unpublished lecture.

Trilling, W., *Das wahre Israel*. Munich: Kösel, 1964.

Tuckett, C.M., 'Redaction Criticism', in R.J. Coggins and J.L. Houlden (eds.), *A Dictionary of Biblical Interpretation*. London: SCM Press, 1990, pp. 580-82.

Turner, H.E.W., 'Expounding the Parables. VI. The Parable of the Sheep and the Goats (Matthew 25.31-46)', *ExpTim* 77 (1966), pp. 243-46.

Van Seters, J., *Abraham in History and Tradition*. New Haven: Yale University Press, 1975.

Van Tilborg, S., *The Jewish Leaders in Matthew*. Leiden: Brill, 1972.

Via, D.O., Jr, 'Ethical Responsibility and Human Wholeness in Matthew 25:31-46', *HTR* 80 (1987), pp. 79-100.

—*Self-Deception and Wholeness in Paul and Matthew*. Philadelphia: Fortress Press, 1990.

—*The Parables*. Philadelphia: Fortress Press, 1967.

Waetjen, H.C., 'The Genealogy as the Key to the Gospel according to Matthew', *JBL* 95 (1976), pp. 205-30.

Wagner, M., 'Der Lohngedanke im Evangelium', *NKZ* 43 (1932), pp. 106-39.

Weinfeld, M., 'Davidic Covenant', *IDBSup*, pp. 188-92.

—*Deuteronomy and the Deuteronomic School*. Oxford: Clarendon Press, 1972.

—'בְּרִית', *TDOT*, II, pp. 253-79.

Weiser, A., *The Psalms*. Philadelphia: Westminster Press, 1962.

Weiss, K., *Die Frohbotschaft Jesu über Lohn und Vollkommenheit: Zur evangelischen Parabel von den Arbeitern im Weinberg, Mt 20,1-16*. Münster: Aschendorff, 1927.

Wenham, G.J., *Genesis 1-15*. Waco, TX: Word Books, 1987.

Westermann, C., *Genesis 12-36*. Minneapolis: Augsburg, 1985.

—*Isaiah 40-66*. London: SCM Press, 1969.

—*The Promises to the Fathers*. Philadelphia: Fortress Press, 1980.

Wilckens, U., 'ὑποκρίνομαι', *TDNT*, VIII, pp. 559-71.

Zerwick, M., *Biblical Greek Illustrated by Examples*. Rome: Biblical Institute Press, 1963.

Zimmerli, W., 'Die Seligpreisungen der Bergpredigt und das Alte Testament', in E. Bammel, C.K. Barrett and W.D. Davies (eds.), *Donum Gentilicium*. Oxford: Clarendon Press, 1978, pp. 8-26.

INDEXES

INDEX OF REFERENCES

OLD TESTAMENT

Genesis

12.2-3	60
12.2	23, 27, 52, 60
12.3	27, 60, 106, 158
12.7	23
13.2	112
13.14-15	24
13.15	23
13.17	23
15	24, 27
15.1-6	24
15.1	26, 90
15.6	25
15.7	23, 24
15.9-17	25, 152
15.17	32
15.18-21	24
15.18	23
17	25
17.1	25, 95
17.6	27, 28, 60
17.7	26
17.8	23, 26
17.9	25
17.10	25
17.13	26
17.19	26
18.18	27
18.19	26
22.17	43
22.18	27, 60
24.7	23
26.35	26
26.3	23
26.4	27
28.22	28
28.13	23
28.14	27
32.12	43
35.11	26
35.12	23
48.4	23, 28
50.24	23, 69

Exodus

1.7	29
3.7-8	24
3.8	2
3.16-17	28
4.5	69
4.22	94
6.2-8	29
15.17	44
24.6	77
32.13-14	29
33.1	69

Leviticus

18.24-25	32
25.23	31
25.88	24
26	34
26.22	150
26.42	69

Numbers

27.17	72

Deuteronomy

1.8	30
1.21	30
1.35	30
1.39	30
3.20	33
4	36
4.1	33
4.20	31, 146
4.25-31	53
4.26	36
4.27	150
4.37-40	30
5.33	33
6.3	32
6.10	30
6.18	30
6.23	30
7.6	34
7.12	52
7.13	30
8.1	30, 33
8.7-10	32
8.11-20	36
9.3	32
9.4-5	32
9.5	30
10.1	30

10.16	57	28.31	35	18.36	69
11.9-12	32	28.33	35	22.17	72
11.9	32	28.36	35		
11.17	36	28.37	36	*2 Kings*	
11.9	30	28.38-42	35	4.8-37	106
11.21	30	28.45	36	4.13	106
11.26	33	28.48	35	13.23	69
11.28	33	28.60-61	35		
12.7	33	28.62	35, 150	*1 Chronicles*	
12.9-10	33	28.63	36, 47,	29.18	69
13.1-5	37		53		
13.5	33	28.64	35	*2 Chronicles*	
13.6-11	37	28.68	35	1.12	112
15.4-5	112	29	36	7.19-20	47
15.11	112	29.18-21	37	24.19	136
16.15	33, 80	29.18	37	24.21	136
16.20	32	29.28	37		
17.2-7	37	30.1-10	53	*Psalms*	
17.19	40	30.2	69	1	140
18.13	94, 95	30.3	53	1.1-3	132
19.8	30	30.4	70	1.4	128
21.22-23	32	30.6	57	36	59, 95,
24.1-4	32	30.15-20	33		152
25.19	33	30.15	33, 79,	36.2	59
26.1-11	31		81	36.9	59
26.3	30	30.19	33	36.11	59, 86,
26.11	33, 80	30.20	30		87
26.15	30, 32	31.7	30	36.18	59
26.19	34, 60	31.29	32	36.20	59
27.3	32	32.4	95	36.22	59, 61
28	34, 36	32.33	36, 42	36.28	59
28.3-5	34	34.4	30, 69	36.29	59
28.4	34			36.34	59, 86
28.7	34	*1 Samuel*		39.38	59
28.8	34	15.28	137	44.3	44
28.9	34			61.13	108
28.10	34	*2 Samuel*		72.12	52
28.11	30, 34	7	52	80	45
28.12	34	7.9-11	58	80.9-10	45
28.20	35, 36	7.9	52	80.16	132
28.21	36	7.10-11	58	92.13-14	132
28.23-24	35	14.16	27	101.6	95
28.25	35, 36			105.8-11	69
28.26	35	*1 Kings*		107.10-11	50, 143
28.27	35	8.51	146	107.10	143
28.28	49	9.6-7	47	118.22-23	138
28.29	35, 49	14.15	47		
28.30-32	35	17.8-24	106		

Proverbs
2.20-21   95
8.21   112
24.12   108
28.10   95

Ecclesiastes
5.19   112

Isaiah
1.4   146
2.2-4   70
5   46, 48, 136
5.1-7   137
5.2   46, 136
5.5   136, 137
5.6   45
8.14-15   139
8.22   50, 143
8.23–9.1   73
9.1-6   53
9.1   50, 143
10.17-19   123
10.33-34   123
11.1   53
11.15-16   55
14.1   55
14.32   56
16.5   53
24.5-6   41
25–27   69, 71
27.2-6   45
27.13   70
29.13   98, 131
29.19   56
29.22   52
35.1-10   55
40.3   67
40.10   100
40.11-12   76
40.11   55, 76
41.8-10   52
42   78
42.7   50, 143
43.5   70
43.16   55
43.19   55

47.5   50
48.10   146
49.8   78
49.9   50, 55
49.13   56
51.1-2   52, 68
53   78
53.12   77
55.6-7   69
57.13   59
57.14   55
59.9-10   49
60–66   87
60.19-22   58
60.21   59, 60, 132
60.22   60
61.1-3   56
61.3   58, 132
61.7   86
61.10   149
62.10-12   76
62.10   55
62.11   76, 106
65.17   113
66.22   113

Jeremiah
1.10   46, 133
2.2-3   39
2.3   48
2.7   27, 39, 41
2.8   40
2.12   55
2.20   43
2.21   40, 45, 46, 132
3.1   40
3.2   41
3.3   42
3.19   94
3.21   39
4.4   57
4.6-7   42
5.2-4   55
5.10   48
5.24-25   42

5.31   41
6.13   41
6.16   43, 81
6.19   48
6.22   42
6.30   42
7.13   39
7.15   42
7.20   42
7.24   40
7.25-27   136
7.25-26   40
7.30-34   141
7.30   41
7.31   41
7.34   43
8.10   41
8.13   43, 46, 134
9.13-15   40
9.13   89
10.16   27
10.18   42
10.21   55
11.3   41
11.4   39, 146
11.5   39
11.8   41
11.16   123
11.17   48
12.2   47
12.4   42
12.7   42, 48
12.14-17   60
12.14   48
12.15   48
13.13-14   41
13.16   42
13.24   42
14.1   42
14.14   40
14.18   41
15.1   42
15.4   42
15.7   123
15.8   43
16.4   42
16.9   43

16.13	42	30.11	54	18.31	57
16.14-15	54	30.16	50, 54	19.10-14	47
17.4	42, 43,	30.20	54	20.34-42	55
	123	31.7-8	54	22.17-22	146
17.7-8	46	31.8-9	56, 71	22.27	126
17.10	47, 108	31.9	94	33.24	43
17.23	39	31.10	55	34	55
18.7	48	31.11	54	34.5	72
18.9-10	46	31.15-17	54	34.16	56
18.12	39	31.15	75	34.17-24	155
19.4-5	41	31.18-20	56, 69	34.23-24	53
19.6-9	141	31.20	94	36.19	139
19.7	42	31.25	58	36.26-27	57
20.1-6	43	31.28	48, 58	37.24-26	53
21.5	42	31.31-34	57, 78	37.24	56
21.8	42, 79,	31.40	48		
	81	32.19	47	*Daniel*	
22.3	40	32.21	42	2.34-35	139
22.9	41	32.22	39	2.44-45	139
22.13	40	32.34	41	7.13-14	109
22.15	40	32.35	41	12.3	147
22.17	40	32.37	58		
22.19	40	32.40	57	*Hosea*	
22.28-30	52	32.41	58	2.17	56
22.28	40	33.10-11	58, 80	3.5	53
23.1-2	72	33.14-26	52	5.15–6.3	69
23.1	41, 55	33.26	54	9.10	46, 134,
23.4	56	34.15	127		135
23.5	52	34.18-20	25, 152	9.15	135
23.7-8	54	35.15	40	9.16	135
23.11	41	36.30	40	10.1	40
23.15	40	38.10	139	11	67, 94
23.26	40	39.15-18	106	11.1	67, 94
23.33	41	39.19	108	11.5	55
24.6-7	58	42.2	150	11.11	55, 70
24.6	48	42.10	48	13.3	123
25.5	40	44.28	150	14.2-4	69
25.9	42	45.4	48		
25.10	43	46.22-23	122	*Joel*	
27.15	40	50.6	55, 72	2.12-14	128
28.14	43	52.3	42	4.2-3	156
29.13	56, 69				
29.28	47	*Lamentations*		*Amos*	
30–33	54	3.2	50	3.2	128
30.3	54	4.14	49	9.11	53
30.8-9	52			9.14-15	58
30.8	54	*Ezekiel*			
30.10	54	11.19-20	57		

Micah		3.3	126	9.11	77, 143
2.12-13	82	3.11-13	56, 72	10.2	55, 72
4.6-7	56, 71	3.12	80	10.10	70
5.1-3	72	3.13	57		
5.1	53	3.20	60	Malachi	
7.18-20	51	7.14	42	3.7	89
		6.7	70		
Zephaniah				Sirach	
1.3	146	Zechariah		27.6	123
1.17	50	9.9	76, 85	49.7	48

NEW TESTAMENT

Matthew			98, 102	8–9	69
1.1	66	5.17-19	83	8.8	85
1.21	78, 88, 112	5.20	80, 81, 83	8.10-12	69
				8.10	69
1.23	20	5.22	141	8.11-12	70, 142, 143
2.6	72	5.25-26	143		
2.15	67	5.29-30	142	8.11	148
2.16-18	75	5.43-48	91-95	8.12	140, 149
2.18	140	5.48	111	9.2	71
3.3	67	6	117	9.9	15
3.7-12	121-24	6.1-18	100	9.22	71
3.7-10	67	6.1-6	95-100, 127	9.29	71
3.8	130			9.36	72
3.10	124	6.1	79, 125	9.37-38	125
3.12	124	6.16-18	95-100, 127	10	106
3.17	87, 119			10.6-7	148
4.8	98	6.19-24	100-104	10.6	72, 125
4.12-17	73	6.22-23	103	10.10	90
4.16	143	6.23	132	10.11-15	157
5–7	69	6.25-34	100	10.11-14	105
5.3-10	85, 91	6.33	137	10.11-13	148
5.3	88	7.12	127	10.12	105
5.5	16, 80, 84-91	7.13-14	79, 80, 107, 124, 150	10.15	114
				10.16	115, 125
5.10-12	88, 91			10.17-20	79
5.10	89, 91	7.15-23	124-29	10.17	148
5.11-12	88	7.15-20	145	10.23	88, 148
5.11	89	7.16-20	145	10.24-25	88
5.12	26, 80, 84-91, 105, 114, 125	7.17-18	147	10.27	79
		7.19	123, 124	10.28	79, 107, 142
		7.21-23	79, 81		
		7.21	80, 84	10.29-31	79
5.13	103	7.23	79, 146	10.32-33	78, 157
5.14	104	7.24-27	125	10.32	79, 89
5.16	79, 93,	7.26	81	10.33	79

10.37-39	104	15.4	131	21.23-27	135
10.37-38	148	15.5	132	21.28-32	115, 135
10.38-39	107	15.6	97	21.31-32	69
10.39	81, 89,	15.7-8	151	21.31	84
	107	15.10-20	131	21.33-46	133
10.40-42	104-106,	15.13-14	72	21.33-44	115,
	157, 158	15.13	131-33		135-40
10.41	125	15.14	132	21.34	134
10.42	157	15.24	72	21.38	109
11.5	78	15.28	71	21.41	134
11.22-24	114	16.1-4	122	21.43	142,
11.23	141, 142	16.11-12	122		150, 156
11.25	85	16.16	87, 119	22.1-14	148-51
11.27	126	16.18	138,	22.3-10	149
11.28-30	74		141, 142	22.5	115
11.29	81, 85,	16.24-28	107-109	22.9	148
	86, 107	16.25	81, 89,	22.12	80, 116
12.2	130		153	22.13	140, 142
12.17-21	78	16.27	12, 113	22.15-22	96
12.24	130	16.28	109	22.32	67, 69
12.29	145	17.2	147	23	72, 128,
12.30	73, 130,	17.12	126		152
	158	18	105	23.1-33	96
12.33-37	129-31	18.3	80, 84	23.2-3	125
12.33-35	103	18.5-6	156	23.5	96
12.33	147	18.6-14	157	23.12	86
12.34-35	103	18.7	146	23.13	80
12.41-42	114	18.8-9	80, 112,	23.15	143
12.48-50	157		123, 142	23.16	132
12.50	84	18.9	141	23.23	69
13	143	18.10-14	156	23.24	132
13.12	153	18.15-20	145	23.28	96, 113
13.17	105	18.20	20	23.29-37	105
13.22	129	18.23-25	139	23.29	105
13.24-30	143-47	18.34	152	23.33	122,
13.36-43	143-47	19.16–20.16	109-17		130, 141
13.38	70	19.17	80, 84	23.34-36	148
13.39	125	19.22	115	23.34-35	105
13.41-43	109	19.23	80	23.34	88, 89,
13.41	108	19.26	87		125
13.42	140	19.29	15, 89,	23.37	137
13.44	101, 111		90	24–25	155
13.47-50	143-47	19.30	14	24.3	108
13.49	108	20.1-15	13, 14	24.42-44	151
13.50	140	20.16	14	24.45-51	151-53
13.52	168	21	133, 135	24.47	154
13.57	105	21.5	76, 85	24.51	140
15.1-9	96	21.18-22	133-35	25.10	80

25.13	151	8.35	107	18.30	90
25.14-30	153-55	9.1	108	20.17	112
25.21	80	10.17	109	20.18	138
25.23	80	10.30	90	22.20	77
25.30	140, 142	14.24	77	22.61	112
25.31-46	113, 114, 120, 147, 155-59	*Luke*		*Acts*	
		3.3	70	4.11	138
		3.7-9	122		
25.31	113	3.17	124	*Romans*	
25.32	156	6.23	90	2.6	108
25.34	18, 91, 158	6.35	90, 91		
		6.36	94	*1 Corinthians*	
25.41	158	7.9	69	11.25	77
26.28	77	9.23-27	108		
26.50	116	9.24	107	*2 Corinthians*	
28.10	157	9.27	108	5.10	108
28.16-20	109	10.7	90		
28.18	109	11.34-36	100	*Hebrews*	
28.19	148, 156	12.8-9	78	11.26	101
28.20	20, 158	12.33-34	100		
		12.35-38	14	*1 Peter*	
Mark		13.6-9	134	2.7	138
1.4	78	13.25-27	127		
6.6	69	13.28	140	*Revelation*	
7.10	131	16.13	100	22.12	106, 108
8.34–9.1	108	17.7-10	13, 14		
		18.18	109		

OTHER ANCIENT SOURCES

2 Clement		*Pss. Sol.*		*Inf. Gos. Thom.*	
3.2-3	79	14.2-3	132	3.1-3	133
3.4	79				
4.5	128	*m. Sanh*		*P. Oxy.*	
17.7	124	10.1	132	655.24	102
Gos. Thom.		*Dial. Sav.*			
24	102	8	102		

INDEX OF AUTHORS

Aland, B. 130
Aland, K. 130
Allen, W.C. 123, 137
Allison, D.C., Jr. 65, 66, 68, 70-72, 74, 78, 81, 85, 92, 98, 102, 103, 122, 124, 126, 128
Anderson, A.A. 45

Bach, R. 44, 48
Baltzer, K. 35
Barth, G. 111, 124, 167
Beare, F.W. 74, 100, 122, 136
Beasley-Murray, G.R. 70, 89
Bertram, G. 143
Betz, H.D. 78, 102, 103
Betz, O. 152
Billerbeck, P. 117
Black, M. 123
Bonnard, P. 93, 99, 101, 107, 126, 148
Bornkamm, G. 13, 139, 146, 147
Boyd, W.J.P. 141
Bracke, J.M. 53, 54
Braun, H. 99
Brayley, I.F.M. 45
Brueggemann, W. 23, 24, 27, 39, 43, 88
Buchanan, G.W. 85, 88

Carlston, C.E. 136
Carroll, R.P. 44, 46
Cassuto, U. 28
Catchpole, D. 156, 157
Charette, B. 74
Clements, R.E. 23, 24, 30, 37, 53
Coats, G.W. 28
Cope, L. 155
Court, J.M. 157
Craigie, P. 35, 59
Crossan, J.D. 116

Davies, W.D. 24, 43, 51, 65, 66, 68, 74, 81, 85, 87, 92, 98, 122, 124, 126, 128, 129

Davison, J.E. 129
DeRoche, M. 43
Diepold, P. 33, 41, 56
Dietrich, E.L. 53
Donahue, J.R. 158
Dreyfus, F. 24, 27, 86
Dupont, J. 67, 6, 114

Edgar, S.L. 75
Eichler, J. 31

Fensham, F.C. 30, 34
Fitzmyer, J.A. 92
Fleddermann, H. 151
France, R.T. 13, 71, 75, 94, 103, 109, 124, 144
Frankemölle, H. 20, 121, 137, 145
Freedman, D.N. 25, 31

Gaechter, P. 68, 90, 100, 132
Geyser, A.S. 72, 74
Giesen, H. 90, 97, 134
Glover, F.C. 115
Gnilka, J. 65, 66, 73, 81, 86, 93, 105, 108, 113, 116, 122, 129, 137, 139, 143, 145, 150, 153, 156, 157, 159
Gowan, D.E. 55
Graber, F. 132
Green, H.B. 103, 106, 132, 133, 145, 157
Gross, H. 71
Grundmann, W. 80, 89, 99, 113, 152
Guelich, R.A. 80, 91, 124, 126
Gundry, R.H. 78, 79, 92, 96, 105, 121, 122, 127, 131, 138, 139, 145, 147, 154, 156

Ha, J. 26
Hamilton, V.P. 27
Haubeck, W. 117
Hauck, F. 124
Hausmann, J. 48

Hensel, R. 124
Hester, J.D. 27
Hill, D. 78, 88, 101, 105, 114, 124-26, 129, 134, 148
Hillers, D.R. 34, 38
Himmelfarb, M. 141
Holladay, W.L. 42, 43, 48, 55, 57
Hood, R.T. 64

Jeremias, J. 68, 70, 73, 99, 123, 126, 136, 142, 149, 150
Johnson, M.D. 66
Joüon, P. 97

Kapelrud, A.S. 56
Kertelge, K. 88
Kingsbury, J.D. 17, 145
Koch, K. 101

Lach, J. 94
Lang, F. 142
Lemcio, E.E. 150
Lindars, B. 109
Lust, J. 50
Luz, U. 66, 89, 92, 93, 95

McCarthy, D.J. 84, 89
McDonald, J.I.H. 11, 14
Manson, T.W. 93
Marguerat, D. 15, 70, 81, 120, 128, 137, 143, 149, 150, 157, 165
Meier, J.P. 77, 111, 122, 126, 136, 138, 148
Metzger, B.M. 138
Meyer, B.F. 71, 73, 84, 150
Michaels, J.R. 144, 157
Michel, O. 11, 79
Milikowsky, C. 141
Miller, P.D., Jr. 30, 31
Minear, P.S. 14, 89, 97, 104, 125, 127, 128
Mohrlang, R. 13, 15, 108, 120, 165
Moore, S.D. 17, 19
Münderlein, G. 133, 134

Noth, C.R. 50

Ottosson, M. 24, 30

Pamment, M. 90

Pesch, W. 11, 78, 114, 137
Piper, J. 93
Plöger, J.G. 33, 34, 36

Rad, G. von 28, 29, 30
Reindl, J. 45, 46
Rengstorf, K.H. 116, 141
Riesenfeld, H. 104
Ringgren, H. 33, 50
Ru, M. de 11

Sand, A. 82, 89, 124
Sanders, E.P. 72, 166
Sarna, N. 25
Schenke, L. 115
Schlatter, A. 106, 140
Schmid, J. 11, 13, 108
Schwank, B. 141
Schwarz, G. 80
Schweizer, E. 66, 85, 90, 96, 101, 108, 124, 126, 130, 132, 159
Smith, C.W.F. 144, 149
Smith, M. 89, 92
Steck, O.H. 136
Stewart, G.W. 11
Strack, H.L. 117
Strecker, G. 79, 86, 89, 99, 126

Thomas, D.W. 50
Thompson, J.A. 36
Thompson, W.G. 17
Travis, S. 11, 14
Trilling, W. 94, 132
Tuckett, C.M. 17
Turner, H.E.W. 156

Van Seters, J. 26, 52
Van Tilborg, S. 97
Via, D.O., Jr. 97, 150, 153, 157

Waetjen, H.C. 64, 66
Weinfeld, M. 25, 32, 52
Weiser, A. 59
Weiss, K. 109
Wenham, G.J. 25, 28
Westermann, C. 23, 24, 26, 76
Wilckens, U. 97

Zerwick, M. 92
Zimmerli, W. 85

JOURNAL FOR THE STUDY OF THE NEW TESTAMENT

Supplement Series

1 THE BARREN TEMPLE AND THE WITHERED TREE
William R. Telford
2 STUDIA BIBLICA 1978
II. PAPERS ON THE GOSPELS
Edited by E.A. Livingstone
3 STUDIA BIBLICA 1978
III. PAPERS ON PAUL AND OTHER NEW TESTAMENT AUTHORS
Edited by E.A. Livingstone
4 FOLLOWING JESUS:
DISCIPLESHIP IN THE GOSPEL OF MARK
Ernest Best
5 THE PEOPLE OF GOD
Markus Barth
6 PERSECUTION AND MARTYRDOM IN THE THEOLOGY OF PAUL
John S. Pobee
7 SYNOPTIC STUDIES:
THE AMPLEFORTH CONFERENCES OF
1982 AND 1983
Edited by C.M. Tuckett
8 JESUS ON THE MOUNTAIN:
A STUDY IN MATTHEAN THEOLOGY
Terence L. Donaldson
9 THE HYMNS OF LUKE'S INFANCY NARRATIVES
THEIR ORIGIN, MEANING AND SIGNIFICANCE
Stephen Farris
10 CHRIST THE END OF THE LAW:
ROMANS 10.4 IN PAULINE PERSPECTIVE
Robert Badenas
11 THE LETTERS TO THE SEVEN CHURCHES OF ASIA
IN THEIR LOCAL SETTING
Colin J. Hemer
12 PROCLAMATION FROM PROPHECY AND PATTERN:
LUCAN OLD TESTAMENT CHRISTOLOGY
Darrell L. Bock
13 JESUS AND THE LAWS OF PURITY:
TRADITION HISTORY AND LEGAL HISTORY IN MARK 7
Roger P. Booth
14 THE PASSION ACCORDING TO LUKE:
THE SPECIAL MATERIAL OF LUKE 22
Marion L. Soards

15   HOSTILITY TO WEALTH IN THE SYNOPTIC GOSPELS
     Thomas E. Schmidt
16   MATTHEW'S COMMUNITY:
     THE EVIDENCE OF HIS SPECIAL SAYINGS MATERIAL
     Stephenson H. Brooks
17   THE PARADOX OF THE CROSS IN THE THOUGHT OF ST PAUL
     Anthony Tyrrell Hanson
18   HIDDEN WISDOM AND THE EASY YOKE:
     WISDOM, TORAH AND DISCIPLESHIP IN MATTHEW 11.25-30
     Celia Deutsch
19   JESUS AND GOD IN PAUL'S ESCHATOLOGY
     L. Joseph Kreitzer
20   LUKE:
     A NEW PARADIGM (2 Volumes)
     Michael D. Goulder
21   THE DEPARTURE OF JESUS IN LUKE–ACTS:
     THE ASCENSION NARRATIVES IN CONTEXT
     Mikeal C. Parsons
22   THE DEFEAT OF DEATH:
     APOCALYPTIC ESCHATOLOGY IN 1 CORINTHIANS 15 AND ROMANS 5
     Martinus C. de Boer
23   PAUL THE LETTER-WRITER
     AND THE SECOND LETTER TO TIMOTHY
     Michael Prior
24   APOCALYPTIC AND THE NEW TESTAMENT:
     ESSAYS IN HONOR OF J. LOUIS MARTYN
     Edited by Joel Marcus & Marion L. Soards
25   THE UNDERSTANDING SCRIBE:
     MATTHEW AND THE APOCALYPTIC IDEAL
     David E. Orton
26   WATCHWORDS:
     MARK 13 IN MARKAN ESCHATOLOGY
     Timothy J. Geddert
27   THE DISCIPLES ACCORDING TO MARK:
     MARKAN REDACTION IN CURRENT DEBATE
     C. Clifton Black
28   THE NOBLE DEATH:
     GRAECO-ROMAN MARTYROLOGY
     AND PAUL'S CONCEPT OF SALVATION
     David Seeley
29   ABRAHAM IN GALATIANS:
     EPISTOLARY AND RHETORICAL CONTEXTS
     G. Walter Hansen
30   EARLY CHRISTIAN RHETORIC AND 2 THESSALONIANS
     Frank Witt Hughes

31 THE STRUCTURE OF MATTHEW'S GOSPEL:
    A STUDY IN LITERARY DESIGN
    David R. Bauer

32 PETER AND THE BELOVED DISCIPLE:
    FIGURES FOR A COMMUNITY IN CRISIS
    Kevin Quast

33 MARK'S AUDIENCE:
    THE LITERARY AND SOCIAL SETTING OF MARK 4.11-12
    Mary Ann Beavis

34 THE GOAL OF OUR INSTRUCTION:
    THE STRUCTURE OF THEOLOGY AND ETHICS
    IN THE PASTORAL EPISTLES
    Philip H. Towner

35 THE PROVERBS OF JESUS:
    ISSUES OF HISTORY AND RHETORIC
    Alan P. Winton

36 THE STORY OF CHRIST IN THE ETHICS OF PAUL:
    AN ANALYSIS OF THE FUNCTION OF THE HYMNIC MATERIAL
    IN THE PAULINE CORPUS
    Stephen E. Fowl

37 PAUL AND JESUS:
    COLLECTED ESSAYS
    Edited by A.J.M. Wedderburn

38 MATTHEW'S MISSIONARY DISCOURSE:
    A LITERARY CRITICAL ANALYSIS
    Dorothy Jean Weaver

39 FAITH AND OBEDIENCE IN ROMANS:
    A STUDY IN ROMANS 1-4
    Glenn N. Davies

40 IDENTIFYING PAUL'S OPPONENTS:
    THE QUESTION OF METHOD IN 2 CORINTHIANS
    Jerry L. Sumney

41 HUMAN AGENTS OF COSMIC POWER
    IN HELLENISTIC JUDAISM AND THE SYNOPTIC TRADITION
    Mary E. Mills

42 MATTHEW'S INCLUSIVE STORY:
    A STUDY IN THE NARRATIVE RHETORIC OF THE FIRST GOSPEL
    David B. Howell

43 JESUS, PAUL AND TORAH:
    COLLECTED ESSAYS
    Heikki Räisänen

44 THE NEW COVENANT IN HEBREWS
    Susanne Lehne

45 THE RHETORIC OF ROMANS:
ARGUMENTATIVE CONSTRAINT AND STRATEGY AND PAUL'S
DIALOGUE WITH JUDAISM
Neil Elliott

46 THE LAST SHALL BE FIRST:
THE RHETORIC OF REVERSAL IN LUKE
John O. York

47 JAMES AND THE Q SAYINGS OF JESUS
Patrick J. Hartin

48 TEMPLUM AMICITIAE:
ESSAYS ON THE SECOND TEMPLE PRESENTED TO ERNST BAMMEL
Edited by William Horbury

49 PROLEPTIC PRIESTS:
PRIESTHOOD IN THE EPISTLE TO THE HEBREWS
John M. Scholer

50 PERSUASIVE ARTISTRY:
STUDIES IN NEW TESTAMENT RHETORIC
IN HONOR OF GEORGE A. KENNEDY
Edited by Duane F. Watson

51 THE AGENCY OF THE APOSTLE:
A DRAMATISTIC ANALYSIS OF PAUL'S RESPONSES
TO CONFLICT IN 2 CORINTHIANS
Jeffrey A. Crafton

52 REFLECTIONS OF GLORY:
PAUL'S POLEMICAL USE OF THE MOSES–DOXA TRADITION IN
2 CORINTHIANS 3.12-18
Linda L. Belleville

53 REVELATION AND REDEMPTION AT COLOSSAE
Thomas J. Sappington

54 THE DEVELOPMENT OF EARLY CHRISTIAN PNEUMATOLOGY
WITH SPECIAL REFERENCE TO LUKE–ACTS
Robert P. Menzies

55 THE PURPOSE OF ROMANS:
A COMPARATIVE LETTER STRUCTURE INVESTIGATION
L. Ann Jervis

56 THE SON OF THE MAN IN THE GOSPEL OF JOHN
Delbert Burkett

57 ESCHATOLOGY AND THE COVENANT:
A COMPARISON OF 4 EZRA AND ROMANS 1–11
Bruce W. Longenecker

58 NONE BUT THE SINNERS:
RELIGIOUS CATEGORIES IN THE GOSPEL OF LUKE
David A. Neale

59 CLOTHED WITH CHRIST:
    THE EXAMPLE AND TEACHING OF JESUS IN ROMANS 12.1–15.13
    Michael Thompson
60 THE LANGUAGE OF THE NEW TESTAMENT
    CLASSIC ESSAYS
    Edited by Stanley E. Porter
61 FOOTWASHING IN JOHN 13 AND THE JOHANNINE COMMUNITY
    John Christopher Thomas
62 JOHN THE BAPTIZER AND PROPHET:
    A SOCIO-HISTORICAL STUDY
    Robert L. Webb
63 POWER AND POLITICS IN PALESTINE:
    THE JEWS AND THE GOVERNING OF THEIR LAND 100 BC–AD 70
    James S. McLaren
64 JESUS AND THE ORAL GOSPEL TRADITION
    Edited by Henry Wansbrough
65 THE RHETORIC OF RIGHTEOUSNESS IN ROMANS 3.21-26
    Douglas A. Campbell
66 PAUL, ANTIOCH AND JERUSALEM:
    A STUDY IN RELATIONSHIPS AND AUTHORITY IN EARLIEST CHRISTIANITY
    Nicholas Taylor
67 THE PORTRAIT OF PHILIP IN ACTS:
    A STUDY OF ROLES AND RELATIONS
    F. Scott Spencer
68 JEREMIAH IN MATTHEW'S GOSPEL:
    THE REJECTED PROPHET MOTIF IN MATTHAEAN REDACTION
    Michael P. Knowles
69 RHETORIC AND REFERENCE IN THE FOURTH GOSPEL
    Margaret Davies
70 AFTER THE THOUSAND YEARS:
    RESURRECTION AND JUDGMENT IN REVELATION 20
    J. Webb Mealy
71 SOPHIA AND THE JOHANNINE JESUS
    Martin Scott
72 NARRATIVE ASIDES IN LUKE–ACTS
    Steven M. Sheeley
73 SACRED SPACE:
    AN APPROACH TO THE THEOLOGY OF THE EPISTLE TO THE HEBREWS
    Marie E. Isaacs
74 TEACHING WITH AUTHORITY:
    MIRACLES AND CHRISTOLOGY IN THE GOSPEL OF MARK
    Edwin K. Broadhead
75 PATRONAGE AND POWER:
    STUDIES ON SOCIAL NETWORKS IN CORINTH
    John Kin-Man Chow

76   THE NEW TESTAMENT AS CANON:
      A READER IN CANONICAL CRITICISM
      Robert Wall and Eugene Lemcio
79   THE THEME OF RECOMPENSE IN MATTHEW'S GOSPEL
      Blaine Charette